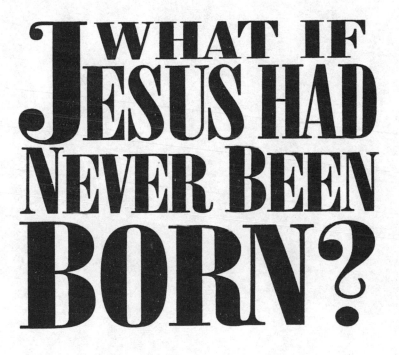

# WHAT IF JESUS HAD NEVER BEEN BORN?

## THE POSITIVE IMPACT OF CHRISTIANITY IN HISTORY

## D. JAMES KENNEDY
### AND JERRY NEWCOMBE

THOMAS NELSON PUBLISHERS
Nashville • Atlanta • London • Vancouver

Copyright © 1994 by D. James Kennedy and Jerry Newcombe.

Published in Nashville, Tennessee, by Thomas Nelson, Inc., Publishers, and distributed in Canada by Word Communications, Ltd., Richmond, British Columbia, and in the United Kingdom by Word (UK), Ltd., Milton Keynes, England.

Scripture quotations are from the NEW KING JAMES VERSION of the Bible. Copyright © 1979, 1980, 1982, Thomas Nelson, Inc., Publishers.

Library of Congress Cataloging-in-Publication Data

Kennedy, D. James (Dennis James), 1930–
     What if Jesus had never been born? / D. James Kennedy and Jerry
Newcombe.
          p.  cm.
     Includes bibliographical references.
     ISBN 0-7852-8261-0 (hc)
     ISBN 0-7852-7178-3 (pb)
     1. Jesus Christ—Influence.   2. Church history—Miscellanea.
I. Newcombe, Jerry.   II. Title.
BT304.3.K46   1993
232.9′04—dc20                                                          93-42372
                                                                          CIP

Printed in the United States of America
8 9 10 11 12 13 – 00 99 98 97

*Dedicated to Jesus Christ*
*King of kings and*
*Lord of lords*

# TABLE OF CONTENTS

# ACKNOWLEDGMENTS

There are numerous people to thank for their contributions to this book. We are grateful for our loving wives and families who patiently endured the tedious process of writing and rewriting. Special thanks go to Kirsti Newcombe for her invaluable help with this project. Also to be thanked are my secretaries, Mary Anne Bunker and Ruth Rohm. Additionally, thanks are due to Robert Folsom, who edited an earlier version of the manuscript, and Dr. Charles Wolfe, who has helped answer many specific questions of content. Thanks for computer help go out to Robert Newcombe and Alan Harrison. We are also grateful to all those on the Thomas Nelson team (past and present) who have made this book possible—including Dan Benson, whose faith in the project helped convert it from an idea to reality, Larry Hampton, and the editorial staff at Thomas Nelson Publishers.

# INTRODUCTION

**W**e live in an age in which only one prejudice is tolerated—anti-Christian bigotry. Michael Novak, the eminent columnist, once said that today you can no longer hold up to public pillorying and ridicule groups such as African-Americans or Native Americans or women or homosexuals or Poles, and so on. Today, the only group you can hold up to public mockery is Christians. Attacks on the Church and Christianity are common. As Pat Buchanan once put it, "Christian-bashing is a popular indoor sport."

But the truth is this: Had Jesus never been born, this world would be far more miserable than it is. In fact, many of man's noblest and kindest deeds find their motivation in love for Jesus Christ; and some of our greatest accomplishments also have their origin in service rendered to the humble Carpenter of Nazareth. To prove that truth is the purpose of this book.

# CHAPTER 1

# CHRIST AND CIVILIZATION

## A Quick Overview of Christ's Impact on World History

*"The kingdom of heaven is like a mustard seed, which a man took and sowed in his field, which indeed is the least of all the seeds; but when it is grown it is greater than the herbs and becomes a tree, so that the birds of the air come and nest in its branches."*

Jesus Christ (Matt. 13:31–32)

Some people have made transformational changes in one department of human learning or in one aspect of human life, and their names are forever enshrined in the annals of human history. But Jesus Christ, the greatest man who ever lived, has changed virtually every aspect of human life—and most people don't know it. The greatest tragedy of the Christmas holiday each year is not so much its commercialization (gross as that is), but its trivialization. How tragic it is that people have forgotten Him to whom they owe so very much.

Jesus says in Revelation 21:5, "Behold, I make all things new." (Behold! [*idou* in Greek]: "Note well," "look closely," "examine carefully.") Everything that Jesus Christ touched, He utterly transformed. He touched time when He was born into this world; He had a birthday and that birthday utterly altered the way we measure time.[1]

Someone has said He has turned aside the river of ages out of its course and lifted the centuries off their hinges. Now, the whole world counts time as Before Christ (B.C.) and A.D. Unfortunately, in most cases, our illiterate generation today doesn't even know that A.D. means *Anno Domini,* "In the year of the Lord."

It's ironic that the most vitriolic atheist writing a propagandistic letter to a friend must acknowledge Christ when he dates that letter. The atheistic Soviet Union was forced in its constitution to acknowledge that it came into existence in 1917, in the "year of our Lord." When you see row after row of books at the library, every one of them—even if it contains anti-Christian diatribes—has a reference to Jesus Christ because of the date.

# THE GROWTH OF THE MUSTARD SEED

Jesus said that the kingdom of heaven is like a mustard seed, which is tiny in and of itself; but, when fully grown, it provides shade and a resting place for many birds. This parable certainly applies to an individual who embraces Christ; it also applies to Christianity in the world.

Christianity's roots were small and humble—an itinerant rabbi preached and did miracles for three and a half years around the countryside of subjugated Israel. And today there are more than 1.8 billion professing believers in Him found in most of the nations on earth![2] There are tens of millions today who make it their life's aim to serve Him alone.

Emperors and governors were the men with power in Christ's day. But now their bodies rot in their sepulchres, and their souls await the Final Judgment. They have no followers today. No one worships them. No one serves them or awaits their bidding.

Not so with Jesus! Napoleon, who was well accustomed to political power, said that it would be amazing if a Roman emperor could rule from the grave, and yet that is what Jesus has been doing. (We would disagree with him, though, in that Jesus is not dead; He's alive.) Napoleon said: "I search in vain in history to find the similar to Jesus Christ, or anything which can approach the gospel . . . nations pass away, thrones crumble, but the Church remains."[3]

# A QUICK OVERVIEW

Despite its humble origins, the Church has made more changes on earth for the good than any other movement or force in history. To get an overview of some of the positive contributions Christianity has made through the centuries, here are a few highlights:

- Hospitals, which essentially began during the Middle Ages.
- Universities, which also began during the Middle Ages. In addition, most of the world's greatest universities were started by Christians for Christian purposes.
- Literacy and education for the masses.
- Capitalism and free-enterprise.
- Representative government, particularly as it has been seen in the American experiment.
- The separation of political powers.
- Civil liberties.
- The abolition of slavery, both in antiquity and in more modern times.
- Modern science.
- The discovery of the New World by Columbus.
- The elevation of women.
- Benevolence and charity; the good Samaritan ethic.
- Higher standards of justice.
- The elevation of the common man.
- The condemnation of adultery, homosexuality, and other sexual perversions. This has helped to preserve the human race, and it has spared many from heartache.
- High regard for human life.
- The civilizing of many barbarian and primitive cultures.
- The codifying and setting to writing of many of the world's languages.

- Greater development of art and music. The inspiration for the greatest works of art.
- The countless changed lives transformed from liabilities into assets to society because of the gospel.
- The eternal salvation of countless souls!

The last one mentioned, the salvation of souls, is the primary goal of the spread of Christianity. All the other benefits listed are basically just by-products of what Christianity has often brought when applied to daily living. The rest of this book is devoted to demonstrating how all of these benefits to mankind have their origins in the Christian faith.

When Jesus Christ took upon Himself the form of man, He imbued mankind with a dignity and inherent value that had never been dreamed of before. Whatever Jesus touched or whatever He did transformed that aspect of human life. Many people will read about the innumerable small incidents in the life of Christ while never dreaming that those casually mentioned "little" things were to transform the history of humankind.

# IF JESUS HAD NEVER BEEN BORN

Many are familiar with the 1946 film classic, *It's a Wonderful Life*, wherein the character played by Jimmy Stewart gets a chance to see what life would be like had he never been born. In many ways this terrific movie directed by Frank Capra is the springboard for this book. The main point of the film is that each person's life has impact on everybody else's life. Had they never been born, there would be gaping holes left by their absence. My point in this book is that Jesus Christ has had enormous impact —more than anybody else—on history. Had He never come, the hole would be a canyon about the size of a continent.

Christ's influence on the world is immeasurable. The purpose of this book is to glimpse what we *can* measure, to see those numerous areas of life where Christ's influence can be concretely traced.

# BUT SOME PEOPLE WISH CHRIST HAD NEVER BEEN BORN

Not all have been happy about Jesus Christ's coming into the world. Friederich Nietzsche, the nineteenth-century atheist philosopher who coined the phrase "God is dead," likened Christianity to poison that has infected the whole world.[4] He said of Jesus: "He died too early; he himself would have revoked his doctrine had he reached" greater maturity![5]

Nietzsche said that history is the battle between Rome (the pagans) and Israel (the Jews and the Christians);[6] and he bemoaned the fact that Israel (through Christianity) was winning and that the cross "has by now triumphed over all other, nobler virtues."[7] In his book, *The AntiChrist*, Nietzsche wrote:

I *condemn* Christianity; I bring against the Christian Church the most terrible of all the accusations that an accuser has ever had in his mouth. It is, to me, the greatest of all imaginable corruptions; it seeks to work the ultimate corruption, the worst possible corruption. The Christian Church has left nothing untouched by its depravity; it has turned every value into worthlessness, and every truth into a lie, and every integrity into baseness of soul.[8]

Nietzsche held up as heroes a "herd of blond beasts of prey, a race of conquerors and masters."[9] According to Nietzsche, and later Hitler, by whom or what were these Teutonic warriors corrupted? Answer: Christianity. "This splendid ruling stock was corrupted, first by the Catholic laudation of feminine virtues, secondly by the Puritan and plebeian ideals of the Reformation, and thirdly by inter-marriage with inferior stock."[10] Had Jesus never come, wailed Nietzsche, we would never have had the corruption of "slave morals" into the human race. Many of the ideas of Nietzsche were put into practice by his philosophical disciple, Hitler, and about 16 million died as a result.[11]

In *Mein Kampf*, Hitler blamed the Church for perpetuating the ideas and laws of the Jews. Hitler wanted to completely uproot Christianity once he had finished uprooting the Jews. In a private conversation "shortly after the National Socialists' rise to power,"[12] recorded by Herman Rauschning, Hitler said:

> Historically speaking, the Christian religion is nothing but a Jewish sect. . . . After the destruction of Judaism, the extinction of Christian slave morals must follow logically. . . . I shall know the moment when to confront, for the sake of the German people and the world, their Asiatic slave morals with our picture of the free man, the godlike man. . . . It is not merely a question of Christianity and Judaism. We are fighting against the most ancient curse that humanity has brought upon itself. We are fighting against the perversion of our soundest instincts. Ah, the God of the deserts, that crazed, stupid, vengeful Asiatic despot with his powers to make laws! . . . That poison with which both Jews and Christians have spoiled and soiled the free, wonderful instincts of man and lowered them to the level of doglike fright.[13]

Both Nietzsche and Hitler wished that Christ had never been born. Others share this sentiment. For example, Charles Lam Markmann, who wrote a favorable book on the history of the ACLU, entitled *The Noblest Cry*. said: "If the otherwise admirably civilised pagans of Greece and their Roman successors had had the wit to laugh Judaism into desuetude, the world would have been spared the 2000-year sickness of Christendom."[14]

Interestingly, people living under Nazi oppression, under Stalin's terror, under Mao's cultural revolution, and the reign of the Khmer Rouge were all spared "the 2000-year sickness of Christendom"! As we'll see in chapter 6, contrary to Markmann's armchair philosophizing, civil liberties have been bequeathed by Christianity and not by atheism or humanism.

Stalin and Mao both tried to destroy Christianity in their respective domains.[15] In the process, they slaughtered tens of millions of professing Christians, but they utterly failed in their ultimate objective.

In one sense, the point of this book is to say to Nietzsche, Freud, Hitler, Robert Ingersoll, Lenin, Stalin, Mao, Madalyn Murray O'Hare, Phil Donahue, the ACLU, and other leading anti-Christians of the past and present, that the overwhelming impact of Christ's life on Planet Earth has been positive, not negative.

The next twelve chapters will look at a dozen areas where Christianity has made important contributions to world civilization. Then, after that, we'll deal with the negative aspects of the Church's track record in history. We'll deal with the sins of the Church, trying to come to grips from a Christian perspective with the Crusades, the Inquisition, and anti-Semitism by the Church. In the following chapter, we will deal with the sins of atheism. We will show how the post-Christian West ventured into a much more bloody history precisely because the restraints of Christianity were removed. We'll also put to rest the myth so often repeated that "more people have been killed in the name of Christ than in any other." Then, finally, we will close with a brief chapter on where we go from here.

Church history books generally catalogue the influence of Christianity century by century. I have chosen instead to catalogue Christianity's influence *issue by issue*. From transforming the value of human life to transforming individual lives, the positive impact of Jesus Christ is felt around the globe.

Dr. James Allan Francis put Christ's life and influence into perspective so well in his famous narrative:

### One Solitary Life[16]

He was born in an obscure village, the child of a peasant woman. He grew up in another village, where He worked in a carpenter shop until He was thirty. Then for three years He was an itinerant preacher. He never wrote a book. He never held an office. He never had a family or owned a home. He didn't go to college. He never visited a big city. He never traveled two hundred miles from the place where He was born. He did none of the things that usually accompany greatness. He had no credentials but Himself.

He was only thirty-three when the tide of public opinion turned against Him. His friends ran away. One of them denied Him. He was turned over to His enemies and went through the mockery of a trial. He was nailed to a cross between two thieves.

While He was dying, His executioners gambled for His garments, the only property He had on earth. When He was dead, He was laid in a borrowed grave through the pity of a friend. Nineteen centuries have come and gone, and today He is the central figure of the human race.

All the armies that ever marched, all the navies that ever sailed, all the parliaments that ever sat, all the kings that ever reigned, put together, have not affected the life of man on this earth as much as that one solitary life.

# CHAPTER 2

# IN THE IMAGE OF GOD

## Christianity's Impact on the Value of Human Life

*So God created man in His own image; in the image of God He created him; male and female He created them.*

(Gen. 1:27)

**"W**hat is the most important thing to come out of a mine?" asked a French engineer of his students about a century ago. After the pupils named various minerals, he corrected them: "The most important thing to come out of the mine was the miner."[1] I agree and submit that this view of human life is embraced only where the gospel of Jesus Christ has deeply penetrated.

Prior to the coming of Christ, human life on this planet was exceedingly cheap. Life was expendable prior to Christianity's influence. Even today, in parts of the world where the gospel of Christ or Christianity has not penetrated, life is exceedingly cheap. But Jesus Christ—He who said, "Behold, I make all things new" (Rev. 21:5)—gave mankind a new perspective on the value of human life. Furthermore, Christianity bridged the gap between the Jews—who first received the divine revelation that man was made in God's image—and the pagans, who attributed little value to human life. Meanwhile, as we in the post-Christian West abandon our Judeo-Christian heritage, life is becoming cheap once again.

# CHILDREN

In the ancient world, child sacrifice was a common phenomenon. Archaeologists have unearthed ancient cemeteries, near pagan temples, of babies that had been sacrificed—for example, in what used to be Carthage. Before the Jewish conquest of the promised land, child sacrifice among the Canaanites was commonplace. The prophets of the ancient god Baal and his wife, Ashtoreth, commonly practiced child sacrifice as part of their worship. Earlier this century, the Oriental Institute of the University of Chicago did some excavating in Samaria in "the stratum of Ahab's time,"[2] digging up ruins of a temple of Ashtoreth. Halley states:

> Just a few steps from this temple was a cemetery, where many jars were found, containing remains of infants who had been sacrificed in this temple. . . . Prophets of Baal and Ashtoreth were official murderers of little children. But it wasn't just in the Near East that the value of human life was in low esteem.[3]

That's because life was cheap all over, in the Near East, in the Middle East, in the Far East.

It was a dangerous thing for a baby to be conceived in classical Rome or Greece, just as it is becoming dangerous once more under the influence of the modern pagan. In those days abortion was rampant. Abandonment was commonplace: It was common for infirm babies or unwanted little ones to be taken out into the forest or the mountainside, to be consumed by wild animals or to starve or to be picked up by rather strange people who crept around at night, and then would use them for whatever perverted purposes they had in mind. Parents abandoned virtually all deformed babies. Many parents abandoned babies if they were poor. They often abandoned female babies because women were considered inferior.

To make matters worse, those children who outlived infancy—approximately two-thirds of those born[4]—were the property of their father; he could kill them at his whim. Only about half of the children born lived beyond the age of eight,[5] in part because of widespread infanticide, with famine and illness also being factors. Infanticide was not only legal; it was applauded. Killing a Roman was murder, but it was commonly held in Rome that killing one's own children could be an act of beauty. Furthermore, the father exercised an absolute tyranny over his children. He could kill them; he could sell them as slaves; he could marry them off; he could divorce them; he could confiscate their property.

In his book *Third Time Around*—telling how the Church has twice successfully fought abortion in the past and how today the Church is once again on the forefront in the fight against abortion—George Grant adds further insight into just how valueless human life was in ancient Rome:

> According to the centuries old tradition of *paterfamilias*, the birth of a Roman was not a biological fact. Infants were received into the world only as the family willed. A Roman did not *have* a child; he *took* a child. Immediately after birthing, if the family decided not to *raise* the child—literally, lifting him above the earth—he was simply abandoned. There were special high places or walls where the newborn was taken and exposed to die.[6]

Robin Lane Fox, a fellow of New College, Oxford, points out how common and widespread these practices were in ancient Rome:

> Exposure was only one of several checks on reproduction. Abortion was freely practiced, and the medical sources distinguish precoital attempts at "contraception." The line, however, between the two practices was often obscure, not least in the case of drugs which were taken to "stop" unwanted children. Limitation of births was not confined to the poorer classes. Partible inheritance was universal, and as the raising of several children fragmented a rich man's assets, the number of his heirs was often curbed deliberately. As men of all ages slept with their slaves, natural children were a widespread fact of life. However, they followed the servile status of their mother, while laws of inheritance and social

status did discriminate against any who were born from free parents.[7]

In short, it was dangerous to be conceived and born in the ancient world. Human life was exceedingly cheap.

But then Jesus came. He did not disdain to be conceived in the virgin's womb, but He humbled Himself to be found in fashion as a man. Since that time, Christians have cherished life as sacred, even the life of the unborn. In ancient Rome, Christians saved many of these babies and brought them up in the faith. Similarly, this very day, despite a virtual media black out, Christians are helping thousands of pregnant women through the 3,000 pro-life Crisis Pregnancy Centers around the country.[8]

Abortion disappeared in the early Church. Infanticide and abandonment disappeared. The cry went out to bring the children to Church. Foundling homes, orphanages, and nursery homes were started to house the children. These new practices, based on this higher view of life, helped to create a foundation in Western civilization for an ethic of human life that persists to this day—although it is currently under severe attack. And it all goes back to Jesus Christ. If He had never been born, we would never have seen this change in the value of human life.

A dismal fate awaited the youngsters of ancient Rome, Greece, India, and China. Herod slaughtered the innocents, but the advent of Christ was the triumph of the innocents. Jesus gathered the little children unto Himself saying, "Let the little children come to Me, and do not forbid them" (Matt. 19:14a). His words gave a new importance to children, an importance that bestowed dignified treatment upon them. After Jesus said that God was our Father, not only did this radically alter the attitudes of fathers toward children, but fatherhood in this life asssumed a completely new form as well.

Through His Church, ultimately Jesus brought an end to infanticide. The influence of Christ brought value to human life, and infanticide was outlawed. It lost favor with a Christian population as an outrageous crime. Christian influence in the Roman Empire helped to enshrine in law Christian principles of the sacredness of human life. More than twenty years ago, Sherwood Wirt, at the time the editor of Billy Graham's *Decision* magazine, wrote an important book called *The Social Conscience of the Evangelical*. Wirt points out the positive influences for human life that the Church of Jesus Christ was able to effect, for example, through emperors who were professing Christians:

> Many permanent legal reforms were set in motion by Emperors Constantine (280?–337) and Justinian (483–565) that can be laid to the influence of Christianity. Licentious and cruel sports were checked; new legislation was ordered to protect the slave, the prisoner, the mutilated man, the outcast woman. Children were granted important legal rights. Infant exposure was abolished. Women were raised from a status of degradation to that of legal protection. Hospitals and orphanages were created to take care of foundlings. Personal feuds and private wars were put under restraint. . . . Branding of slaves was halted.[9]

Wirt quotes a second-century "Letter to Diognetus," wherein the writer states that Christians "marry . . . they beget children; but they do not destroy their offspring."[10] The implication in this statement is that child killing was common at the time, except among Christians.

The role of the sixth-century Christian Emperor Justinian on behalf of human life is profound. Put in simplistic terms, Justinian had his top jurists compile what they believed to be the best of previous codes of law and judicial opinions into one summary, which—along with a few of Justinian's own edicts—is now known as "the Justinian Code." The Justinian code was explicit in declaring infanticide and abortion illegal:

> Those who expose children, possibly hoping they would die, and those who use the potions of the abortionist, are subject to the full penalty of the law—both civil and ecclesiastical— for murder. Should exposure occur, the finder of the child is to see that he is baptized and that he is treated with Christian care and compassion. They may be then adopted as *ad scriptitiorum*—even as we ourselves have been adopted into the kingdom of grace.[11]

George Grant points out that in the seventh century, the Council of Vaison met to "reiterate and expand that pro-life mandate by encouraging the faithful to care for the unwanted and to give relief to the distressed."[12] At that time, the Church reaffirmed its commitment to adoption as the alternative to abortion.

Grant demonstrates how, in centuries past, the Church— through word and deed—gave rise to a pro-life view of human life. After reviewing much of the evidence for how the early Church and the early medieval Church impacted the value of human life, Grant sums up:

> Before the explosive and penetrating growth of medieval Christian influence, the primordial evils of abortion, infanticide, abandonment, and exposure were a normal part of everyday life in Europe. Afterward, they were regarded as the grotesque perversions that they actually are. That remarkable new pro-life consensus was detonated by a cultural reformation of cosmic proportions. It was catalyzed by civil decrees, ecclesiastical canons, and merciful activity. . . . Assaults on the bastion of that great medieval legacy have been fierce and furious during the five-hundred-odd years since the fall of Constantinople and the passing of the medieval mantle. But battered and bedraggled as it is, it still stands—vivid testimony to the depth of its foundation.[13]

Today we take many of these ideas for granted in the West because they have been so embedded in our culture for centuries. But had Christ never been born, it would have been a far different story—human life would be quite cheap!

## WOMEN

Prior to Christian influence, a woman's life was also very cheap. In ancient cultures, the wife was the property of her husband. In India, China, Rome, and Greece, people felt and declared that women were not able or competent to be independent (although in Rome, particularly in the third century, some women of the upper class were asserting their independence). Aristotle said that a woman was somewhere between a free man and a slave. When we understand how valueless a slave was in ancient times, we get a glimpse of how bad a woman's fate was back then. Plato taught that if a man lived a cowardly life, he would be reincarnated as a woman. If she lived a cowardly life, she would be reincarnated as a bird.

In ancient Rome we find that a woman's lot was not much better—for those who survived infancy. Little girls were abandoned in far greater numbers than boys. In *Pagans and Christians*, Robin Lane Fox points out that the killing of infant girls was so widespread it affected marriage customs:

> In antiquity, this pattern [the postponement of marriage] is not so evident, because of *the widespread habit of exposing female babies at birth*. Adult girls were in shorter supply and thus their age at marriage tended to be low. . . . Habitual exposure of babies was a further brake on the size of a family and the balance of the sexes.[14]

As we've seen above, over time it was Christianity that stilled the practice of child killing, until its recent revival by the modern pagan in the practice of abortion.

The killing of baby girls simply because of their sex was not just a practice of the ancient world. When missionaries or European explorers came into contact with foreign lands that had not been affected by the gospel, they found similar appalling practices—with baby girls, in particular, being the targets. For example, two Norwegian women missionaries in the last century— Sofie Reuter and Anna Jakobsen—found infanticide of little girls a common practice in late nineteenth-century China. Writing in 1880, they declared:

> It is an exception that a couple would have more than one or two girls. If there would be more born, they would be disposed of immediately. It was done in different ways. She could simply be put out as food for wild dogs and wolves. The father would sometimes take her to a "baby tower," where she would soon die of exposure and starvation and be

discovered by birds of prey. Others again would bury the little ones under the dirt floor in the room where they were born. If there is a river flowing by, the children would be thrown in it.[15]

Adam Smith, writing in 1776, confirms this in his book *The Wealth of Nations*. He states: "In all great towns [of China] several [babies] are every night exposed in the street, or drowned like puppies in the water. The performance of this horrid office is even said to be the avowed business by which some people earn their subsistence."[16] This was just two hundred years ago, and it was before any influence of Jesus Christ was to begin to penetrate China.

However, in the last two centuries, because of the modern missionary movement, the lives of women have been greatly improved in scores of countries and hundreds of tribes as the gospel took root in those cultures. Take the two courageous missionaries mentioned above as an example. Reuter and Jakobsen would daily comb the abandonment places to save Chinese girls from sure death. They would then rear these girls and disciple them into the Christian faith.

Take India as another example. Prior to Christian influences in India, widows were voluntarily or involuntarily burned on their husbands' funeral pyres—a grisly practice known as *suttee*. The word itself literally translates "good woman," implying that the Hindus believed it was a good woman who followed her husband into death. As can be imagined, this practice shocked the Christian missionaries coming from the West.

Furthermore, infanticide—particularly for girls—was common in India, prior to the great missionary William Carey. Carey and other Christians detested seeing these little ones being tossed into the sea. These centuries-old practices, *suttee* and infanticide, were finally stopped only in the early nineteenth century and only through missionary agitation to the British authorities. Tragically, as Christian influence is often felt less and less in modern India, we have seen the rise of sex-selection abortions[17]—killing unborn girls—practiced widely there, a practice that vexes even the most ardent feminist. This is practiced all over the Far East.[18]

India also had "child widows," young girls who grew up to be temple prostitutes. In the twentieth century, Amy Carmichael, a missionary of the Dohnavur Fellowship, fought this practice by weaning many girls out of this situation and into a Christian community. In the last century, Charles Spurgeon told of a Hindu woman who said to a missionary: "Surely your Bible was written by a woman." "Why?" he asked. "Because it says so many kind things for women. Our pundits never refer to us but in reproach."[19]

Prior to Christian influences, Africa had a practice similar to *suttee*. The wives and concubines of the chieftain were killed at his death. Such tribal customs were stopped after Christianity began to penetrate the continent.

In other areas of the globe where the gospel of Christ has not penetrated, the value of women's lives is cheap. Even in my lifetime, I saw in the Middle East four men playing checkers, while another man, presumably of a lower class, was plowing a field with two animals yoked to each other. One animal was an ox, but I couldn't tell what the other animal was until they turned the corner, and I saw that it was a woman! She was probably the wife of one of the men playing checkers on the porch. And I realized in what low esteem and how cheaply the lives of women were held prior to the coming of Christ. Christ did an incredible thing for women, lifting them to a high level—higher than they had ever been before.

How ironic that feminists today do not give any credit to Christ or Christianity; in fact, they say it has oppressed women. In reality, Christianity has elevated women enormously. Had Jesus never come, Gloria Steinem, had she survived childhood, would most likely be wearing a veil today!

# THE ELDERLY

It has often been said that the Chinese and Japanese worship their elders, but only after exposure to Christianity were homes built for them. Throughout history, many tribes and peoples killed off their elderly, much as they have killed off their unwanted babies. The Eskimos used to kill their elderly by setting them adrift in ice floes floating out to sea! Whatever the method, the pattern is the same. Prior to Christ, the value of the elderly was determined by the particular custom of each tribe. With Christ, all human life has value, including that of the elderly.

Of course, it should be pointed out that the care of the elderly wasn't always as much of an issue as it is in modern times. Even as recently as 1892, only one in 100 people worldwide lived to be over the age of 65. Only through modern medicine do we have people living as long as they do today. So this wasn't as much of an issue in past times as, say, child killing.

As we have moved away from God and His principles in this country, we are reverting to a more pagan view of life. We see the move afoot to kill off the elderly—whether it's called mercy killing or euthanasia. Some today are advocating that those elderly persons who lack a certain "quality of life" should die and get out of the way for the younger population! Today there's a hideous way of abandoning the elderly that is common enough to warrant a name: "Granny dumping." This refers to bringing an old person to a hospital or race track or some place crowded with people and abandoning him or her there.[20] We have abandoned the Judeo-Christian view of human life and substituted a tawdry one instead!

## SLAVERY

Half of the population of the Roman Empire was slaves. Three fourths of the population of Athens was slaves. The life of a slave could be taken at the whim of the master. Over the centuries, Christianity abolished slavery, first in the ancient world and then later in the nineteenth century, largely through the efforts of the strong evangelical William Wilberforce. It didn't happen overnight, and certainly there have been dedicated Christians who were slaveowners. Nonetheless, the end of slavery, which has plagued mankind for thousands of years, has come primarily through the efforts of Christians.

The condition of the slave in the ancient world was abysmal. Professor Findlay reminds us that in Athens it was legal to admit into a courtroom the testimony of a slave only under torture; yet the testimony of a free man was admitted under oath. Among the

Romans, if the master of a household was murdered, all of his domestic slaves were put to death without legal inquiry. It was a common mark of hospitality to assign a female slave to a guest for the night, as one would any other convenience. Thus we see the crushing tyranny and degradation of the ancient, humanistic world, manifested in slavery.

This is even more disturbing when we consider what a large percentage of the population of the ancient world was made up of slaves. Wirt comments on the horrors of their condition:

In Sparta there was systematic terrorizing of slaves. Primitive tribes around the world considered the slave to be utterly without dignity or rights. For millions upon millions of enslaved people in past centuries, and even down to the present day in outlying pockets of civilization, survival has been a matter of supreme indifference because of their condition of bondage. The warrior who preferred death to capture was not necessarily being brave or noble; he was being realistic. Even in sophisticated Athens and Rome, where household slaves received humane treatment and were accorded special privileges, their lives were never out of jeopardy. Four hundred slaves belonging to the Roman Pedanius Secundus were ordered put to death because they were under their master's roof when he was murdered.[21]

People of even the same race enslaved each other in ancient times. The deities had no concern for the slaves. Slaves had no rights, no relation to society, none to the state, and none to God. But when the gospel began to take root in people's hearts, that changed over time. In that brief book of the Bible called Philemon, Paul writes from prison to Philemon, a wealthy Christian slaveowner. Paul sends the letter to Philemon with Onesimus, Philemon's runaway slave who was a fellow prisoner with Paul. Paul had led both men to Christ and in his letter tells Philemon, "Receive him (Onesimus) not as a slave, but as a brother beloved."

Millions of people in modern America have read that statement and have not been touched at all. Yet that was among the most revolutionary concepts the world had ever heard—a slave, an "animated tool," was a brother, beloved! Absolutely unthinkable and incredible! Such a simple statement, along with the concept of Christian brotherhood, melted away the fetters of slavery, like icicles before the rising sun!

Critics of Christianity like to point out that the lack of direct challenge of the institution of slavery from Paul or other leaders in the early Church constitutes a Christian complicity of sorts with slavery. In *Asimov's Guide to the Bible: The New Testament*, the late secularist Isaac Asimov wrote:

> Nevertheless, while Paul urges kindness to the slave Onesimus, who is now Philemon's brother in Christianity, there is no hint anywhere in Paul that slavery might be wrong and immoral as an institution. Indeed, Paul even admonishes slaves to obey their masters, so that Christianity, however novel some of its tenets, was by no means a doctrine of social revolution.[22]

Other secularists also make a similar point. Oxford scholar Robin Lane Fox writes that Christian leaders in the second and third centuries did nothing to disturb the institution of slavery.[23] Of the early Church, Fox observes:

> Its priorities are not those of a faith concerned to free slaves from their masters, or to urge masters to let them be released. . . . At most, Christian slaves were consoled and comforted. . . . Christian masters were not specially encouraged to set a slave free, although *Christians were most numerous in the setting of urban households where freeing was most frequent.*[24]

Fox summarizes all this by his statement: "Christians aimed to reform the heart, not the social order."[25] Both Asimov and Fox miss the big picture, however, because Christians don't assert that the Christian religion abolished slavery overnight. If Christianity totally disallowed slavery, the gospel could not have spread as it did in the early Church. Once the gospel did spread, the seeds were sown for the eventual dissolution of slavery. Thus by reforming the heart, Christianity, in time, reformed the social order! Furthermore, as Latourette points out, "Christianity undercut slavery by giving dignity to work."[26]

Alas, slavery did rear its ugly head again in more recent times at the hands of the Portuguese and the Spanish. When they discovered the black man in Africa, we had another bout with slavery. But it wasn't until men devoted their whole lives to abolishing the slave trade that action was taken. A strong evangelical, William Wilberforce, who was a member of the British Parliament for decades, was such a man. And Wilberforce gathered other like-minded evangelicals to help him in the fight, they were known as "the Clapham Sect," since they met in Clapham, England.

The model Christian statesman in the history of the world, William Wilberforce worked tirelessly to halt the slave trade from Africa to the West Indies. After he spent twenty years diligently crusading against it, Parliament finally passed his bill to halt the slave trade. Then he worked indefatigably to free the slaves in the British territories; this battle was to last twenty-five years! Despite constant opposition and derision, he pursued his course as a service to Jesus Christ.

Wilberforce had undergone a dramatic conversion as a young man which changed his life from one of trivial pursuit to one of freeing the slaves. On his deathbed he received word that Parliament had acted and twenty million pounds had been delegated to release the remaining slaves of England. And on that day in 1833, 700,000 British slaves were freed. Wilberforce was greatly moved to know that a whole lifetime of effort on his part had finally seen fruition, and he thanked God for bringing it to pass.

Thirty years later, at far greater cost of war, after the thunderous indictments from the pulpits of the North, slavery disappeared from America. Wirt points out:

In eastern and midwestern United States the evangelicals were often drawn into the struggle against slavery. Calvinist and Methodist alike were giving spiritual support to the abolition movement in the 1840's and 1850's. The town of Oberlin, Ohio, founded by Charles G. Finney as a college for the training of evangelists, became . . a main connecting point on the "underground railroad." President Finney himself was not above hiding fugitive slaves in his attic.[27]

We know that two-thirds of the members of the abolition society in 1835 were ministers of the gospel.[28] It is well-known that many of the leading practitioners of the Underground Railroad were Quakers. Abraham Lincoln's Christianity is well-documented; his writings are filled with Bible quotes. Ultimately, Christianity and slavery are incompatible. Robert E. Lee, who freed the slaves he had inherited by marriage, once wrote that the War between the States was needless bloodshed in terms of ending slavery, for he believed the evil institution would have eventually withered away because of Christianity.

## THE GLADIATORS

Does boxing strike you as cruel? As vicious as it may seem, prior to Christ's influence, people used to kill other humans for sport! The spilling of human blood thrilled the masses. Rome was cruel. Gladiators (who were slaves) would fight to the death. After one opponent pinned the other down at sword point, he would look up to Caesar, who would then usually give a thumbs down signal. Then the victorious gladiator would plunge his sword into the loser, and the crowds would go wild! That this was a *staple* of entertainment before Christian influence was felt on the culture cannot be underscored enough. Perhaps, the climax of this orgy of blood was when Emperor Trajan held a spectacle wherein 10,000 gladiators were killed in a span of only four months.[29]

It is also well known that many early Christians were mauled and eaten by the lions before cheering and jeering crowds. Author Dinesh D'Souza writes, "Among the animals used in the arenas were lions, panthers, bears, wild boars, and bulls goaded with red-hot irons."[30] Tacitus tells us that Nero held parties in his gardens, in which the entertainment for the evening would be the torturous killing of Christians by wild beasts, by crucifixion, or by being lighted on fire as human torches. Nero would often mix with the crowd, sometimes in disguise. Many spectators felt sorry for these Christians, realizing this orgy of blood was "not for the public good but to satisfy one man's mania."[31] Indeed, human life was cheap prior to Christ's influence!

But when Christianity began to spread in the Roman Empire, gladiatorial contests eventually ceased. Church historian Kenneth Scott Latourette writes:

> Under the influence of his new faith, the Emperor Constantine forbade gladitorial shows and abolished the legal penalties which required criminals to become gladiators. . . . We are told that the gladitorial combats persisted in Rome until, in the fifth century, a monk, Telemachus, leaped into the arena to stop the combatants and the mob, presumably nominally Christian, stoned him to death for interfering with their pleasure. Thereupon the Emperor ordered that the spectacles be stopped and Telemachus enrolled among the martyrs.[32]

Today, in the Colosseum, in the very amphitheater where tens of thousands of Christians were sacrificed for sport, there stands a large cross—a silent testimony to the victory of Christianity over the brutality of the ancient world.

Eminent historian Will Durant, who has written a definitive, multi-volume survey of world history, comments on the conquering of the cross over the Roman Empire:

> There is no greater drama in human record than the sight of a few Christians, scorned or oppressed by a succession of emperors, bearing all trials with a fiery tenacity, multiplying quietly, building order while their enemies generated chaos, fighting the sword with the word, brutality with hope, and at last defeating the strongest state that history has ever known. Caesar and Christ had met in the arena, and Christ had won.[33]

## CANNIBALISM

If life is seen as of no value higher than a T-bone steak or a roast beef sandwich, then it is truly worth very little. When Christ made statements like, "Are you not of much more value than these [referring to sparrows]?" (Matt. 6:26), then He certainly distinguished humans from animals. The influence of Christianity —even within the last few decades—stopped cannibalism in those regions where the gospel of Christ has penetrated.

James C. Hefley provides a telling anecdote about the end of cannibalism in one tribe because of Christ. During World War II, on a remote island in the Pacific, an American G.I. met a national who could speak English carrying a Bible. "The soldier pointed to the Bible and grinned knowingly. 'We educated people don't put much faith in that Book anymore,' he said. The islander grinned back. 'Well, it's a good thing for you that we do,' he said while patting his stomach, 'or else, you'd be in here by now.' "[34]

Ted Baehr and Dr. Bonnie Harvey wrote a critique of the movie *Alive*, which dealt in part with cannibalism, for *Ted Baehr's Movie Guide: A Family Guide to Movies and Entertainment*. Here is what they said about cannibalism:

> Historically, before the advent of Christianity, cannibalism was widespread. The flesh pots outside the walls of ancient cities were repositories of the bodies of the dead, cooked for the ingestion of the poorest of the poor. Throughout the ages, beyond the boundaries of the spread of the Gospel, peoples ate each other in the cruel delusion that they would thereby triumph over their enemies and incorporate the strengths of their enemies into themselves. Thus, the Aztecs consumed tens of thousands in their perverted quest for power. However, wherever the Gospel was preached, cannibalism was abolished as men were born again to see with new eyes the sanctity of life.[35]

As the modern missions movement of the last two centuries has spread the gospel, it has wrought great changes. Those changes include the virtual elimination of cannibalism. In describing what happened in the Fiji Islands, one scholar sums up well in a phrase what took place in most areas where cannibalism was eradicated: "From Cannibalism to Christianity."[36]

# SUICIDE

The sin of suicide is mentioned five times in the Bible. In over 4,000 years of biblical history, only five people took their own lives, and all five of them were wicked men, like Judas, who sold the Savior for thirty pieces of silver.

In contrast to Jewish history, many of the Roman leaders committed suicide.[37] This includes Pontius Pilate,[38] Senators Brutus and Cassius, Antony and Cleopatra (though she wasn't a Roman leader), Emperor Nero, Stoic philosopher Seneca, several gladiators in training, Emperor Hadrian, and on it goes. Durant writes of the average Roman living by the popular Stoic philosophy, that "life itself was always to remain within his choice."[39] Thus suicide was not uncommon in ancient Rome prior to Christian influences.

Christianity has long been a foe of suicide, in the ancient world and now in the modern world. Today the neo-pagan view is cheapening the value of human life all over again. Recently, one of the nation's best-selling books was a how-to manual on suicide! But God's wisdom says, "All those who hate me love death" (Prov. 8:36).

# ANIMAL RIGHTS

Evolution, which simply reduces man to the animal kingdom and ultimately makes him no different from an animal, leads to the kind of thinking today which prompts people to go to enormous lengths to save the eggs of turtles but do nothing to save an unborn human being! We have vastly greater penalties for anybody breaking or touching endangered turtle eggs than we have for killing a fetal human being, who is also in a sense in an egg. I am all in favor of people caring for animals, but the irony is that usually these people care little about the slaughter of millions of unborn children.

Humanist Ted Turner spoke at a conference in Miami Beach in the spring of 1992. According to eyewitness Marvin Olasky, professor at the University of Texas, Austin, Turner said: "Overpopulation is the 'cause of drive-by shootings' and other social ills, but the root of the problem is Christianity, which posits that people are more important than sea otters and elephants."[40] In the Christian world view, human beings will always be of greater value than animals.

An environmentalist magazine, *Wild Earth*, contained an article in its summer 1991 edition that demonstrates to what extremes some people are willing to take these pro-animal—but anti-Christian and anti-human life—ideas:

> If you haven't given voluntary human extinction much thought before, the idea of a world with no people in it may seem strange. But, if you give it a chance, I think you might agree that the extinction of Homo Sapiens would mean survival for millions, if not billions, of Earth-dwelling species. . . . Phasing out the human race will solve every problem on earth, social and environmental.[41]

What a contrast with the Judeo-Christian concept that man is made in the image of God.

# SANCTITY OF LIFE VS. QUALITY OF LIFE

In modern times, we have drifted from a sanctity of life ethic to a quality of life ethic. The concept of sanctity of life is a spiritual concept; it is a religious concept. The word *sanctity*—which comes from the Latin word *sanctitas* from *sanctus*—means "holy or sacred unto God, inviolable, that which God has declared is of great value." It is, therefore, a spiritual concept.

However, for a humanist or an atheist or an unbeliever of most any kind, there is no such thing as sanctity of life. Unless there is a God who has given us a spirit and who sanctifies us, there cannot be a sanctity-of-life ethic.

With such a low view of man as that introduced in the last century, should it surprise us that man has killed more of his own during the twentieth century than in all the other centuries combined? As the saying goes, "Ideas control the world." Only by the resurgence of modern paganism, in a post-Christian culture, do we find the Nazi concentration camp, the Soviet gulag, the American abortion chamber.

Quality of life is a physical concept. No one can look at another and determine the quality of that person's soul. If life is merely molecules in motion, then we can have a quality-of-life ethic. But if we are Christians and believe that there is an infinite, eternal, and unchangeable God who is Spirit, who has given us an eternal soul; and if we have an inalienable right to life, we cannot buy that kind of an ethic.

When Supreme Court Justice Harry A. Blackmun wrote *Roe v. Wade* he appealed to religion. However, he said, "If I were to appeal to religion, I would appeal to the religions of Rome and Greece"—which, of course, practiced and encouraged abortion, infanticide, euthanasia, suicide, and all of the rest, including the Colosseum! He would appeal to pagan religion for support of *Roe v. Wade*! We are reverting, in the Western world, to heathen paganism, and most people don't even know that it is happening!

## CONCLUSION

The morality of any society can be easily judged by the view it holds of human life. In 1844, H. L. Hastings visited the Fiji Islands. He found there that life was very cheap and that it was held in low esteem. You could buy a human being for $7.00 or one musket! That was cheaper than a cow. After having bought him you could work him, whip him, starve him, or eat him, according to your preference—and many did the latter. He returned a number of years later and found that the value of human life had risen tremendously. One could not buy a human being for $7.00 to beat or eat. In fact, you could not buy one for seven million dollars. Why? Because across the Fiji Islands there were 1,200 Christian chapels where the gospel of Christ had been proclaimed, and people had been taught that we are not our own; that we have been purchased with a price, not with silver and gold, but with the precious blood of Jesus Christ.

Remove Jesus Christ from the history of the world and the value of life would indeed be just as Jack London's character Wolf Larsen put it: "Life? Bah! It has no value. Of the cheap things it is the cheapest." You who are reading this book might very well not be alive today if Christ had not been born!

# CHAPTER 3

# COMPASSION
# AND MERCY

## Christianity's Contribution to Helping the Poor

*He who despises his neighbor sins;*
*But he who has mercy on the poor, happy is he.*

(Prov. 14:21)

**S**aint Laurence was a deacon in the Christian Church, who was quite generous, especially to the poor. He lived in Aragon of the Roman Empire of the third century. During one of the persecutions, he was ordered to bring to a Roman official some of "the treasures of the Church." What he brought were some poor, downtrodden and lame people, and he said of them, "These are the treasures of the Church." For this response, he was roasted to death on a gridiron.[1]

Today in the Ft. Lauderdale, Florida, area there is a day shelter for homeless people named after him—St. Laurence Chapel. This shelter feeds the homeless, provides a mailbox, job counseling and referrals, a shower and bathroom, chapel services, a telephone, and more.

While poverty has always been a part of life on earth, the Church of Jesus Christ has done more—and often *still* does more —than any other institution in history to alleviate poverty. Furthermore, it has set the pattern for relief that is copied worldwide. From Mother Teresa helping the destitute on the streets of Calcutta to the Salvation Army providing shelter for a family whose home just went up in flames, the sun never sets on

Christians—individually and corporately—meeting human needs in the name of Jesus. It was He who gave us the example in the first place, and He taught us to imitate Him.

# PRIOR TO CHRIST'S COMING

The world before Christianity was like the Russian tundra—quite cold and inhospitable. One scholar, Dr. Martineau, exhaustively searched through historical documents and concluded that antiquity has left no trace of any organized charitable effort. Disinterested benevolence was unknown. When Christ and the Bible became known, charity and benevolence flourished.

Will Durant writes about ancient Rome, which was the zenith of civilizations in antiquity: "Charity found little scope in this frugal life. Hospitality survived as a mutual convenience at a time when inns were poor and far between; but the sympathetic Polybius reports that 'in Rome no one ever gives away anything to anyone if he can help it'—doubtless an exaggeration."[2]

# THEN JESUS CAME

Jesus set the great example of helping the poor, of caring for the poverty-stricken and downtrodden. He bid His followers to go and do likewise. One of His best-known parables is that of the good Samaritan, the kindly gentleman who stopped and cared for the stranger in need when neither the priest nor the Levite would (Luke 10:25–37). This parable has had a great impact on Western civilization. So also has His parable of the sheep and the goats, wherein Christ says, "Inasmuch as you did it [help the poor] to one of the least of these My brethren, you did it to Me" (Matt. 25:40). This teaching has introduced the idea of "Christ's poor," where the poor are treated as if they are Jesus Christ Himself!

Jesus encouraged generosity toward the poor. And in some cases, He even invited a few individuals to give all they had to the poor. Through the ages, some Christians have felt the calling to do that, and they've experienced great joy. This was the case of St. Francis of Assisi and those who followed in his footsteps—taking vows of poverty for the sake of the gospel. But it is not the calling of every Christian. There have been other great Christians through the centuries who have given away their wealth to help the poor in the name of Christ, such as Pope Gregory I (the Great) or C. T. Studd, an evangelical missionary from nineteenth-century England.

The early Christians made history through generosity to their own, and to nonbelievers as well. The late Yale historian Dr. Kenneth Scott Latourette wrote that "in the use of money for the general welfare, Christianity brought five significant innovations."[3] The first of these innovations, wrote Latourette, is that giving was an obligation of all who joined the ranks, rich or poor, each according to ability.

Also, the motive of Christian giving was new. It was done out of love for Christ, for the Christian teaching is that Jesus was rich but became poor for our sakes, so that we might become rich (2 Cor. 8:9). Furthermore, the *objects* of giving changed:

> The Christian community stressed the support of its widows, orphans, sick, and disabled, and of those who because of their faith were thrown out of employment or were imprisoned. It ransomed men who were put to servile labour for their faith. It entertained travelers. One church would send aid to another church whose members were suffering from famine or persecution. In theory and to no small degree in practice, the Christian community was a brotherhood, bound together in love, in which reciprocal material help was the rule.[4]

Christian giving was also personalized—from individuals to individuals, not to "masses of men, although often, as in times of famine, it dealt with large numbers."[5]

Another innovation of Christian charity, according to Latourette, was that it was not limited to church members. They extended their giving to non-Christians as well, so much so that Emperor Julian "the Apostate," the last Roman emperor to try to stamp out the Christian faith, marveled at how the Christians loved even the pagans, even their enemies. Dr. Richard Todd, history professor at Wichita State University, writes, "It was the church's care for its own poor and for outsiders that so impressed the pagan Emperor Julian."[6] Julian wrote: "For it is disgraceful that, when no Jew ever has to beg and the impious Galileans [Christians] support both their own poor and ours as well, all men see that our people lack aid from us."[7]

Historian after historian verifies the same thing: The early Church had a great record of helping the needy. Will Durant says that the early Church attracted converts by providing a way out of Rome's harshness. These converts, declares Durant, "turned from Caesar preaching war to Christ preaching peace, from incredible brutality to unprecedented charity."[8] Oxford scholar Dr. Robin Lane Fox adds:

> To the poor, the widows and orphans, Christians gave alms and support, like the synagogue communities, their forerunners. This "brotherly love" has been minimized as a reason for turning to the Church, as if only those who were members could know of it. In fact, it was widely recognized. When Christians were in prison, fellow Christians gathered to bring them food and comforts: Lucian, the pagan satirist, was well aware of this practice. When Christians were brought to die in the arena, the crowds, said Tertullian, would shout, "Look how these Christians love one another." Christian "love" was public knowledge and must have played its part in drawing outsiders to the faith.[9]

Fox also points out the contrast between the charity of the pagans versus the charity of the Christians: "Whereas the corn doles of pagan cities had been confined to citizens, usually to those who were quite well-off, the Christians' charity claimed to be for those who were most in need."[10]

Furthermore, Fox points out that whereas some pagan emperors, prior to Constantine, may have had marginal feeding programs for the less fortunate, these were very limited and were clearly earmarked for those who would later serve in the army.[11] In contrast, the first Christian emperor, Constantine, became the first emperor in history to widen the scope of charity.

> He [Constantine] also acknowledged the new ideal of charity. Previous Emperors had encouraged schemes to support

small numbers of children in less favoured families, the future recruits for their armies. Constantine gave funds to the churches to support the poor, the widows and orphans.[12]

## CHARITY IN THE MIDDLE AGES

Through the centuries, there has been a perpetual witness on the part of Christians to help those in need. During the Middle Ages, monks—who carried on the practical Christianity of their day—helped the poor on a regular basis. They lived very modestly, they worked the land they had cleared, and they cared for the needy in their area, including orphans.[13]

Will Durant says that the Church's charity to the poor achieved "new heights" in the later part of the Middle Ages. Virtually all parts of society were helping the needy—including "individuals, guilds, governments, and the Church." Feeding took place at the gates of barons' estates a few times a week. Ladies of the upper class took part in active charity. A quarter of the tithes of the local parish was commonly set aside for helping the destitute and the sick. Durant sums up, "In one aspect the Church was a continent-wide organization for charitable aid."[14]

The administration of charity by the Church was so widespread during the Middle Ages that it outweighed the cruelty of the Crusades, the Inquisition, and witch hunts. So writes the skeptic and historian W. E. Lecky in his *History of European Morals*: "All through the darkest period . . . amid ferocity and fanaticism and brutality, we may trace the subduing influence of Catholic Charity."[15]

## THE EXAMPLE OF THE PURITANS

The Puritans had few poor among them, and those who were needy were taken care of. Dr. Leland Ryken, a scholar on the Puritans, pens these words:

What did the Puritans actually do to help the poor? The Anglican divine Lancelot Andrewes noted in 1588 that the

Calvinist refugee churches in London were able "to do so much good as not one of their poor is seen to ask in the streets." . . . W. K. Jordan has assembled an enormous quantity of data about patterns of philanthropy in England during the Reformation era. . . . "A very large proportion [of the donors] were Puritans," concludes Jordan, and he lists as one of "the great moving impulses" behind the growth of voluntary charity "the emergence of the Protestant ethic."[16]

## CHRISTIAN CHARITY IN THE NINETEENTH CENTURY

Christian charity continued beyond the Industrial Revolution. There are countless examples of Christians in the nineteenth century helping the needy in the name of Christ:

- George Mueller and his famous orphanages in England that were run by faith, which helped thousands of children and sparked similar ministries.
- The Young Men's Christian Association (YMCA), founded in 1844, and the Young Women's Christian Association (YWCA), founded in 1855. These greatly ministered to the physical and spiritual needs of millions of poor in the urban areas of the world (although the spiritual emphasis seems to be played down in most of the chapters today).
- Lord Shaftesbury, Anthony Ashley Cooper (1801–1885), who did for the poor in Great Britain what Wilberforce did for the poor people of Africa.[17]

And the list goes on.

## CHARITY IN OUR DAY

Everyone living in America, and the Western world for that matter, has caught something from the Spirit of Christ. Even the most virulent atheists still live and operate within that Christian world view, whether they know it or not, and are indebted to it. This is similar to the Communists in the United States, who have lived lives of comparative ease and well-being produced by capitalism, while at the same time they rail against it. So also the secular agencies of our time have inadvertently taken pages from the Bible and used them to create many of today's charities.

Many of our charities today began with a Christian base, and over time they have become secular. They continue on today with little or no reference to their Christian roots, as if they were purely secular organizations, having their origins in the secular mind-set. Even the names of a number of charities reveal their Christian roots: Our Daily Bread Food Bank, Providence House, Covenant House, and so on.

Co-author Jerry Newcombe remembers seeing a bulletin-board announcement seeking volunteers to operate a hotline with the name "Samaritan." The announcement stated the organization wanted only people who were not religious to apply. The irony is that not only does that idea deny the fact that such goodwill projects were motivated by Christianity in the first place, but the very name "Samaritan" comes from Christ's parable of the "good Samaritan."

## CHARITY DONE TODAY IN THE NAME OF CHRIST

Much of the charity that goes on today is fueled by the love of Christ. Take the case of the Salvation Army, which is in scores of countries, constantly helping the very poor. Whether ministering to a drunken, homeless person in the inner-city or helping provide immediate shelter after a hurricane or tornado, the Salvation Army provides a constant, shining witness to the love of Christ—day in and day out. The love of Christ has undergirded the activities of the Salvation Army from its inception to the present. The Salvation Army was founded by General William Booth. In 1887 Booth, seeing homeless men sleeping outdoors on London Bridge, decided to do something practical. After intense research he set out the facts in a best-selling book, *In Darkest England—and the Way Out*:

[he was] appealing for a fighting fund of 100,000 pounds. Cheap food debts, an unofficial employment exchange, a missing persons bureau, night shelters, a farm colony, soup kitchens, leper colonies, woodyards in the USA, home industries in India, hospitals, schools, and even a lifeboat for the fishermen of Norway—these marked successive stages in the Army's massive program of social action. Permeating it all was *the basic concern for personal salvation which had been the motivation of its beginnings.*[18]

Internationally, much of the work to help the needy is carried on by the Church through missions agencies, such as the work of various denominations. This is also true with groups like World Relief Corporation, which works directly with churches to help the poor. And it is true with parachurch groups like World Vision, International; Samaritan's Purse; Food for the Hungry; Christian Children's Relief Fund; and Compassion, International.

Here in America, churches and agencies diligently meet human needs in imitation of Christ. Christian rescue missions, which proclaim the gospel and feed and clothe the homeless, can be found in the poorest neighborhoods.

No doubt millions of things happen every single week right here in America and around the world, where people—taking a page from the New Testament—go out of their way to help others in need. They visit the sick in the hospital. They provide food and clothes for the impoverished. They help tutor an inner-city child. Ultimately, this all gets back to the teaching and example of Jesus Christ. Thousands of volunteers, many of them Christians, traveled down to help rebuild South Dade County after Hurricane Andrew. In fact, on Easter Morning 1993, several months after the nation's worst storm, *The Miami Herald's* headline story on April 11, 1993, was devoted to these volunteers: " 'Holy Sweat' Church volunteers prove a blessing." Christians responded similarly to the widespread flooding in the Midwest during the summer of 1993 in what was dubbed "Operation Noah."

Churches are often the hub of such social programs—having food pantries, Thanksgiving projects, collecting and distributing gifts for the needy at Christmas time. We see it right here in our own church, the Coral Ridge Presbyterian Church of Ft. Lauderdale. Every day of every week, the "Channel" (of God's blessing) ministers to the needs of people—providing food or job leads or meeting whatever kind of need they have. We have a thrift shop that provides clothing and other goods at practically no cost. And all of this derives from the Spirit of Christ.

A few years ago, co-author Jerry Newcombe was conducting some interviews for a Miami TV station of homeless people being helped by St. Laurence Chapel, the ministry to the homeless mentioned above. He'll never forget what one middle-aged homeless man said: "If it weren't for these churches, there'd be a lot more of us in jail because we would be out stealing food." "If it weren't for these churches" translates into "if it weren't for Jesus Christ."

## MODERN SURVEYS ON RELIGION AND GIVING

Modern surveys provide solid evidence for what common sense would dictate: Religious people tend to be more generous. They also show that often the poor give more relatively than the wealthy, and often charity depends on "the widow's mite."[19] Religion in American Life, a survey group in Princeton, New Jersey, founded by the Gallup organization, discovered that churchgoers tend to be more generous in their giving to charity. A report they put out in 1990, entitled "Religion and the Public Interest," found that "churches and synagogues contribute to America's social services more than any other non-governmental institution, including corporations."[20] They also found that every year, relgious institutions contribute $19 billion to "care for children and the elderly, education, health, food for the hungry, housing for the homeless." Furthermore, the dollar value from church volunteers adds up to more than $6 billion per year. The study also found that churches and synagogues topped the list of organizations "regarded among the top 24 that improve urban life"; they are also found to be "among the most cost-effective charitable institutions in society."

Another survey uncovered similar findings. This study was put out by Independent Sector in conjunction with Gallup. Independent Sector is a "coalition of 650 corporate, foundation, and voluntary organizations."[21] According to *Christianity Today,* one of the study's most important findings was that:

religious belief is a major fact in contributions of time and money. . . . Those who attended religious services weekly "were clearly the most generous givers of both time and money, compared with all other groups," said the report. It continued, "People who attended church regularly were far more likely to give a higher percentage of their household income to charitable causes."[22]

Does this surprise anyone? It shouldn't. It's just a modern example of what the Church has been doing all along.

Mother Teresa, one of the world's most admired women, embodies the Christian ideal of one who helps the poor in the name of Christ. Motivated by the love of Christ, she helps the utterly destitute on the streets of Calcutta. She writes: "Today God has sent us into the world as he sent Jesus, to show God's love to the world. And we must sacrifice to show that love, just as Jesus made the greatest sacrifice of all."[23]

Take Jesus Christ away, and there would be no Mother Teresas.

## SANTA CLAUS—
## A CHRISTIAN MYTH

Even the mythical character of Santa Claus ultimately points back to Christ. Although he often regrettably upstages Christ at Christmas time, St. Nick unquestionably arose within the Christian tradition; and the legend is symbolic of the spirit of giving that marks the coming of Christ. The first Christmas gift was the Son of God Himself, given to us by the Father. The next Christmas gifts were those the wise men brought to the Christ Child. Christians have been giving gifts ever since.

According to *The New International Dictionary of the Christian*

*Church*, we know very little about the real St. Nicholas (from whose name we get Santa Claus). He lived in Myra in the fourth century and was reported to have given gifts to children on his feast day, December 6.[24]

Take away Jesus and you take away Santa Claus. Had Jesus never come, there would be no Christmas. People like Nietzsche and Hitler, who wished that Jesus had never come, and groups like the ACLU—that do their best to stop Christmas (or totally privatize it)—are reminiscent of the Grinch who unsuccessfully tried to steal Christmas. How sad it would be, to paraphrase C. S. Lewis, if it were "always winter but never Christmas," which is a good description of life on earth had Jesus never come!

# ATHEISM AND HELPING THE POOR

From a purely secular, atheistic perspective, there is no reason why a person should be concerned about the poor, or anybody else for that matter. In 1855, the *New York Observer* reported, "Infidelity makes a great outcry about its philanthropy, but religion does the work."[25] That was true in 1855, and it is still true today.

Many people have been so imbued today with the Christian spirit that they fail to grasp that. I have challenged people to try to show me why, from an atheistic point of view, there is any better reason for me to help an elderly woman across the street, rather than run her over with my car if she gets in the way. Or steal her purse and knock her teeth out (apart from the consequences of getting caught). People don't realize that from an atheistic point of view, you can make no solid case for doing the one or the other. This has been recognized by the leading atheistic, existential philosophers, like Camus and Sartre.[26] They say all that matters is that you act. Whether you knock her down or help her across the street is really immaterial; what counts is that you exercise your own will.

A person will say, "Well, we should care for other people." Why should I care for other people? They have no answer for that. If you take God away, and if you take away a future life and a future judgment, why should I go out of my way to help any-body? Someone might say, "Because it makes me feel good." Well, maybe it makes me feel better to spend my time at the beach, rather than visit a shut-in. Another might say, "Well, it's good for society." Well, you tell that to the Mafia boss and see what kind of guffaw you get out of him. Society? What does he care about society? Society is just something he is plucking for himself. A world without Christ is a world without charity!

## CONCLUSION

All charity points back to Jesus Christ, whether people recog-nize it or not. Jerry Lewis raising money for muscular dystrophy is a reminder of Christ. I assure you that if there had been televi-sion in 100 B.C., there would have been no such program as that!

Meanwhile, the overall witness of the early Church was very positive in terms of sharing. Even some pagans commented on the ways in which Christians helped the poor. As one writer put it, "Look how these Christians love one another." That was astonishing to them—more astonishing than it would be today because everybody has been taught in this so-called Christian civilization that they're supposed to love one another.

There's probably no one in America who hasn't heard that they ought to love one another, whether they do or not. But in the ancient pagan society that was an astonishment—that these people loved one another! You didn't love other people or give to them; you got as much as you could out of them—until Christ came.

What if Jesus had never been born? Then I think that probably we would wish that we had never been either. It would be a very cruel world, as was the ancient pagan world. But Jesus did come and Christian history is rich in people showing care and compas-sion for the poor and needy—"the treasures of the Church"—in the name of Christ.

# CHAPTER 4

# EDUCATION
# FOR EVERYONE

## Christianity's Contribution
## to Education

*"And these words which I command you today shall be in your heart; you shall teach them diligently to your children, and shall talk of them when you sit in your house, when you walk by the way, when you lie down, and when you rise up."*

Moses (Deut. 6:6, 7)

**E**very school you see—public or private, religious or secular—is a visible reminder of the religion of Jesus Christ. So is every college and university. This is not to say that every school is Christian. Often the exact opposite is true. But the fact is that the phenomenon of education for the masses has its roots in Christianity. Nor is this to say that there wasn't education before Christianity, but it was for the elite only. Christianity gave rise to the concept of education for everyone. Furthermore, the phenomenon of the university has its roots in the Christian faith as well; the greatest universities worldwide were started by Christians for Christian purposes. While many of them may be quite hostile today to the Christian faith, the fact is that it was through the sweat and sacrifice of Christians that Oxford, Cambridge, Harvard, Yale, Princeton, and others were created.

## JEWISH ROOTS

From the beginning of Christianity, there has been an emphasis on the Word of God. This grows out of its strong Jewish roots, since Christianity is derived from Judaism. Christians have often been called the "people of the Book," which implies a literate people. Dr. J. D. Douglas, general editor of *The New International Dictionary of the Christian Church*, writes: "From its beginning the religion of the Bible has gone hand in hand with teaching. . . . Christianity is par excellence a teaching religion, and the story of its growth is largely an educational one. . . . As Christianity spread, patterns of more formal education developed."[1]

Even during the Dark Ages, when most people were illiterate, it was Christian priests and monks who kept alive what learning there was. And, following the lead of Cassiodorus (c.477–c.570), Christian monks painstakingly hand copied many classics from antiquity, both Christian and pagan. We would not have many of these writings today were it not for them.

## THE CODIFYING OF LANGUAGES

Many of the world's languages were first set to writing by Christian missionaries in order for people to read the Bible for themselves. That is still true today. Many tribal languages are being codified by Christians out in the field; for example, Wycliffe Bible Translators are carrying this work out in obscure areas of the world. This is an ongoing challenge, and, according to Wycliffe, at this present time more than 300 million people "still do not have a way to write their own language."[2] By providing the Bible in people's own language, missionaries are also promoting worldwide literacy as a natural by-product. This is a trend that began hundreds of years ago.

In the fourth century, the brave Ulfilas (c.311–c.381) became a missionary for forty years and, later, a bishop, to the fierce Goths. In his work he was repeatedly "hampered by persecution."[3] Although he was an Arian,[4] he was the first to introduce any form of Christianity to the Germanic tribes. His missionary work paid off, for "it was much due to the work of Ulfilas that these plunderers became peacemakers."[5]

Ulfilas studied their language carefully in order to set it to writing, so that he could translate the Bible. This was "an unwritten language for which he had to devise an alphabet."[6] Ulfilas's translation work was important, as eminent historian Kenneth Scott Latourette points out that this was "probably the first or second instance of what has since happened for hundreds of tongues—their reduction to writing by Christian missionaries and the translation into them by that medium of a part or all of the Scriptures."[7]

A famous example of Christians setting an unwritten language to writing is the work of St. Cyril (d. 869) and St. Methodius (d. 885). These two brothers came from Thessalonica to Moravia (central Czechoslovakia) and became known as "the Apostles of the Southern Slavs."[8] They are reported to have developed an alphabet known to this day as the "Cyrillic alphabet" in order to translate the Bible and liturgy into the Slavic tongue. We see these letters sometimes in news reports from Russia or on the side of Aeroflot planes. Cyril once said, "Do you not feel shame at authorizing only Latin, Greek, and Hebrew and condemning other peoples to blindness and deafness?"[9] Cyril himself may or may not have been the one who developed this alphabet that bears his name, but tradition and the "legendary" *Life* of Cyril ascribe it to him. "Today more than 200 million people, representing more than 100 languages, communicate nationally using the Cyrillic alphabet."[10] During the days of the atheistic Soviet Union, most of their writing was done with an alphabet developed by a Christian to translate Christian writings! Indeed, the Christian faith has helped to promote education and literacy worldwide.

## EDUCATION FOR EVERYBODY

The idea of education for everybody grew directly out of the Reformation, even though there were sporadic attempts at educational reform before the sixteenth century. The most notable of these was under Charlemagne's reign in ninth-century France.

Charlemagne hired Alcuin (735–804) to provide as much education for the people of the Holy Roman Empire as he could. But after the death of Charlemagne, the whole attempt died out. It wasn't until the Bible became the focal point of Christianity again that education for the masses was born.

# THE GUTENBERG BIBLE AND THE PRINTING PRESS

The invention of the printing press helped to pave the way. A monumental development in the field of human learning, the printing press was given birth in the printing of the Gutenberg Bible. Although Johann Gutenberg (c. 1398–1468) was not the first Westerner to develop a movable type printing press, he was the first to do it in a way that made the mass production of books possible. Gutenberg is reported to have said, "I know what I want to do: I wish to manifold [print] the Bible." To achieve this, he "converted a wine press, so it pressed pages onto the type blocks"[11] Yale Church historian Philip Schaff comments: "The art of printing, which was one of the providential preparations for the Reformation, became the mightiest lever of Protestantism and modern culture."[12]

# THE REFORMATION AND EDUCATION FOR EVERYBODY

Prominent American educator and author Dr. Samuel Blumenfeld has researched the origins of public education for his provocative book, *Is Public Education Necessary?* He demonstrates that the roots of education for the masses goes back to the Reformation and, especially, to John Calvin. The Reformers believed that the only way the Protestant Reformation would hold would be for people themselves—laypeople—to read the Bible. Blumenfeld states:

> The modern idea of popular education—that is, education for everyone—first arose in Europe during the Protestant

Reformation when papal authority was replaced by biblical authority. Since the Protestant rebellion against Rome had arisen in part as a result of biblical study and interpretation, it became obvious to Protestant leaders that if the reform movement were to survive and flourish, widespread biblical literacy, at all levels of society, would be absolutely necessary.[13]

Interestingly, Blumenfeld has come to believe in Christianity because of reading Calvin's *Institutes of the Christian Religion*. As Blumenfeld did his research on the origins of public education, he found that when it came to the concept of education for the masses, all roads led to Calvin. So feeling the need to read primary source documents, he read the *Institutes* and put his faith in Christ.

## CALVIN AND EDUCATION

The evangelical Christian Comenius is known as "the Father of Modern Education." Comenius was a seventeenth-century Moravian bishop. Luther contributed heavily to widespread education in countries where his views held sway, as in Scandinavia, and the same holds for Calvin. The Reformer of Geneva could be viewed as the *de facto* father of modern education in numerous countries, including America. Dr. Loraine Boettner, the late American theologian, wrote:

Again, history bears very clear testimony that Calvinism and education have been intimately associated. Wherever Calvinism has gone it has carried the school with it and has given a powerful impulse to popular education. It is a system which demands intellectual manhood. In fact, we may say that its very existence is tied up with the education of the people.[14]

Calvin has left for us a tremendous memorial in his educational theories and also in the practical application of them, which we find in the Academy at Geneva, the model for many of the early colleges and universities established by the Puritans and their successors in America.

Calvin advocated that the purpose of education is for people to know God and glorify Him as God—that in our vocation and in our life we might know God. He wrote, "The true wisdom of man consists in the knowledge of God the Creator and Redeemer."[15] Therefore, what is to be the content of education? It begins with God's first book, the Scriptures. And then, realizing that all truth comes from God, Calvin saw that we should also study the truth that is revealed in God's second book, nature.

In Geneva, Calvin promoted education for everybody, which has become a pattern for our day throughout the world. Thus when John Knox visited Geneva from Scotland he returned to say that in Geneva there had been produced the greatest school of Christ since the time of the apostles. Everything was to be done according to the Scriptures, and this was the legacy left to and carried by the Pilgrims and Puritans to America.

Calvin also strongly emphasized that education must have a moral relevance. Calvin would never have been so naive as to say what Socrates said: that knowledge is virtue. He had too deep a concept of human depravity and the sinfulness of the human heart to ever suppose that knowledge, in itself, necessarily would make people better. It must be connected with the spiritual teachings of Jesus Christ, the renewing power of the grace of God, the redemption that is in the cross of Christ. And if these factors are not present, then indeed education will produce Frankenstein monsters. We have seen that in this century. You may note very well that in 1941 the most literate country on the face of this earth was Nazi Germany. The highest standard of education in the world was found there. Yet this did not prevent Auschwitz!

Calvin also had strong opinions as to whose responsibility it was to educate children. He declared that the Bible makes it plain that the ultimate responsibility rests with the parent—not with the state, not with the Church, but the control of education should be with the parent. The Bible makes it very clear that it is the responsibility of parents to see that their children receive a godly education. Scripture teaches that children are a gift from God. They are loaned to us for a little while, and we, as parents, are responsible to give them a godly education. We are to rear them in the nurture and admonition of the Lord; line upon line, precept upon precept, His truth is to be taught to them.

Because of the emphasis on the Word of God in the countries most influenced by Calvin and Luther, these nations were better educated. By the turn of this century, before cultures had been smeared over, a survey of literacy rates of the diverse nations of the world was taken. The pagan nations, such as China and India, with little exposure to the Word of God had a literacy rate ranging from 0 to 20 percent. The groups of nations with a predominantly Roman Catholic outlook had a much higher range of 40 to 60 percent. Note that over the centuries, a strong emphasis was not placed on reading the Word of God in those countries—a trend repudiated by Vatican II. Where such an emphasis existed, as in the third group of countries of largely Protestant influence, the literacy rate ranged from 94 to 99.9 percent!

## EDUCATION IN AMERICA

Consider the history of education in this country for a moment; it provides a telling description of how Christianity has promoted education. When the Pilgrims and Puritans first came to this country, education was a high priority. It wasn't long before they legally required education in their colonies. As early as 1642 the Puritans passed a law to require education for all children; and in 1647, they passed the "Old Deluder Satan Act," establishing public schools (not in the same sense as modern public education). This mandated towns to hire and pay teachers.[16] The name of the Old Deluder Act was a reference to the devil, who gets his foothold into people's lives because of their ignorance of Scripture. The Old Deluder Act was the first law in the English colonies to require education:

It being one chief project of that old deluder, Satan, to keep man from the knowledge of the Scriptures, as in former times, keeping them in an unknown tongue. . . . It is therefore ordered by this Court and authority thereof, that every township within this jurisdiction, after the Lord hath

increased them to the number of fifty householders, shall
then forthwith appoint one within their town to teach all
such children as shall resort to him, to write and read, whose
wages shall be paid, either by the parents or masters of such
children, or by the inhabitants in general, by way of supply,
as the major part of those who order the prudentials of the
town shall appoint; provided that those who send their children
be not oppressed by paying much more than they can
have them taught for in other towns.[17]

The Puritans, having first come in 1630, hadn't even been in the
American colonies for twenty years before they mandated that
the children among them be educated. Why? So that they would
know the Scriptures for themselves. This is the origin of public
education.

The materials the Puritans used to teach the children to read
and write were, of course, the Bible and other Christian materials.
*The New England Primer* utilized Bible themes to teach the
alphabet. For example, here are many of the letters in one common
version of that primer:

A — In Adam's Fall,
    We sinned all.

B — Heaven to find,
    The Bible Mind.

C — Christ crucify'd
    For sinners dy'd.

D — The Deluge drown'd
    The Earth around.

E — Elijah hid
    By Ravens fed.

F — The judgment made
    Felix afraid.

G — As runs the Glass, [i.e., Hourglass]
   Our Life doth pass.

H — My Book [the Bible] and Heart
   Must never part.

. . . . . . . .

M — Moses was he
   Who Israel's Host
   Led thro' the Sea.

N — Noah did view
   The old world & new.

. . . . . . . .

P — Peter deny'd
   His Lord and cry'd.

. . . . . . . .

S — Young Sam'l dear
   The Lord did fear.

. . . . . . . .

X — Xerxes did die,
   And so must I.[18]

The Puritan children were also taught reading and writing through something known as a "hornbook." The beginning students studied the alphabet and the Lord's prayer from a text that was covered by a sheet of horn and mounted on a board that had a handle attached to it.

This close link between Christianity and education continued beyond the colonial period in America. For instance, the first Congress of the United States passed the Northwest Ordinance in 1787, wherein they declared: "Religion, morality and knowledge, being necessary to good government and the happiness of mankind, schools and the means of education shall forever be encouraged."[19]

For 217 years—from 1620, when the Pilgrims landed, until 1837—virtually all education in America was private and Christian. (The public educational system is only 150 years old.) The basis of America lay with private and Christian education. What was the result of over 200 years of private Christian education? Education historian Lawrence A. Cremin who has written several books about American education has concluded that literacy rates among American whites were as high or higher than in provincial England, and significantly above those in Ireland. "At a time when estimates of adult male literacy in England ran from 48 percent in the rural western midlands to 74 percent in the towns, on the basis of signatures on marriage registers, adult male literacy in the American colonies seems to have run from 70 percent to virtually 100 percent, on the basis of signatures on deeds and wills, militia rolls and voting registers." (See *Traditions of American Education,* Basic Books, New York 1977, and *American Education: The Colonial Experience,* Harper and Row, New York, 1970.) John Quincy Adams said in the early 1800s that only four people out of 1,000 were illiterate, or 4/10th of 1 percent!

Alexis de Tocqueville, the famous French philosopher, when he came here in 1835, said that he was amazed at how much responsibility Americans placed on an enlightened citizenry. And he pointed out that unless the people of this country were educated there would be no hope for such a system of government as ours.

## McGUFFEY'S READERS

Many are familiar with McGuffey's readers. William Holmes McGuffey, a Presbyterian minister, authored *McGuffey's Eclectic Reader,* which sold 120 million copies. For many decades, these provided the backbone of grammar school education for this country. The earlier editions of the McGuffey readers were distinctly Christian. The later ones were moralistic, with a Christian morality at base. Dr. John Westerhoff III, a professor of religion and education at Duke University Divinity School, wrote a biography of McGuffey, entitled *McGuffey and His Readers*. Writing about the first editions, Westerhoff says:

> Basically, the McGuffey Readers directed persons to live for salvation—for eternal life with God in another world—a life goal connected closely to righteousness. . . . First religion, then morality, and last knowledge—that was their focus of content. . . . We should not be surprised, therefore, to learn that McGuffey's Readers read more like a theology textbook than a children's elementary schoolbook. . . . While we are born in sin and destined to damnation, God, in Christ, reconciles those who repent to himself and rewards them with eternal life. Salvation and righteousness are therefore life goals of the faithful. That, simply, is the theistic world view and value system of McGuffey's Readers.[20]

The influence of these readers in the last century cannot be overestimated. They had a profound impact in raising millions in the Christian faith in this country. But there was a move to secularize the readers. Six years after the death of McGuffey, new readers, bearing his name, were published that were "severely secularized."[21] Westerhoff writes:

> Calvinistic theology and ethics have been replaced by American middle-class civil religion, morality, and values. Nevertheless, for those who deplore the urbanization, secularism, social and ethnic pluralism, situation ethics, and prophetic character of schoolbooks of today, this 1879 edition of McGuffey's Readers seems like a breath of fresh air, a blessing from God.[22]

Overall, whether it was the first edition or the later, secularized versions, McGuffey's readers were influential in the teaching of four-fifths of America's school children for seventy-five years.[23] In 1928, Henry Ford issued a reprint of the 1857 version of McGuffey's readers because of his high esteem of them. Ford wrote: "Most youngsters of my day were brought up on the *McGuffey*

*Readers*. Most of those youngsters who still survive have a profound respect for the compiler of the *Readers*."[24]

Education, then, in early America was Christian and highly successful. We'll see in a moment where it went wrong.

# THE UNIVERSITY: A CHRISTIAN PHENOMENON, WITH THANKS TO THE GREEKS

Lower education alone is not the only gift of Christians to the world in the realm of academia; the phenomenon of the university also comes from the Christian Church. Universities did not begin until the later part of the Middle Ages. Former New York University historian, Joseph Reither, wrote that "universities were the creation of the Middle Ages."[25] The late J. K. Hyde, professor of medieval history at the University of Manchester until his death in 1986, pointed out that all universities in the world go back to three prototypes: Oxford, Paris, and Bologna.[26] All three of these universities date back to A.D. 1200, plus or minus a decade. At Oxford and Paris, Christian theology, and to a lesser degree Aristotelian thought, were the chief subjects. At Bologna, the chief study was canonical (translate "Church") and civil law.

Prior to these three, there were other academic institutions that have been called "universities," for example, in ancient Greece or in medieval Islam (in Spain at Cordova). While it is also true that at Salerno, Italy, a school of higher learning was started by Muslims, it was exclusively a medical school. As the scholar H. Rashdall, author of *The Universities in the Middle Ages*, writes, "Nothing approaching a regular university ever existed there."[27]

The generally accepted definition of a university comes from Rashdall: "A scholastic guild, whether of masters or students engaged in higher education and study."[28] By this definition, the origin of the university is in the Christian West and its chief study is Christian theology and, in the case of Bologna, Christian and civil law. Soon to appear after these three universities was Cambridge in England. Other universities began to appear in medieval Europe when the chancellor of the cathedral in the area or some other official allowed masters to start schools other than the cathedral school in the neighborhood of his church.

At other early universities, the main studies were the doctrines of the Church Fathers and the great doctors of the Church, as well as the most difficult points of Christian doctrine. Aristotle and Greek philosophy were also studied. But, overall, Christian theology was the basis of the schools, which were run by Christians for Christian purposes.

Isn't it amazing that the pursuit of the knowledge of God in a systematic, philosophical, and in-depth way gave rise to the phenomenon of universities, all around the world, when we consider that many, if not most of them, today present a world view quite contrary to the Christian faith? But it was the Christian faith that gave rise to idea of higher education.

## AMERICA'S UNIVERSITIES

Almost every one of the first 123 colleges and universities in the United States has Christian origins. They were started by Christians for Christian purposes, to train ministers. Dr. Paul Lee Tan declares:

Every collegiate institution founded in the colonies prior to the Revolutionary War—except University of Pennsylvania —was established by some branch of the Christian church. Even at the University of Pennsylvania, the evangelist George Whitefield played a prominent part.[29]

Harvard, Yale, William and Mary, Brown, Princeton, New York University, Northwestern University, and other schools have thoroughly Christian roots. Harvard got its start from the donation of money and books from the Rev. John Harvard. Engraved in stone at the entrance of Harvard is the message:

After God had carried us safe to New England, and we had built our houses, provided necessities for our livelihood, reared convenient places for God's worship, and settled the civil government; one of the next things we longed for, and looked after was to advance learning, and perpetuate it to posterity; dreading to leave an illiterate ministry to the churches, when our present ministers shall lie in the dust.[30]

Dartmouth was founded to train missionaries to the Indians. William and Mary was created "that the Christian faith might be propagated."[31] An early advertisement for King's College, which opened in 1754 and is now Columbia University, read: "The chief thing that is aimed at in this college is to teach and engage children to know God in Jesus Christ."[32] The president of Princeton, Rev. John Witherspoon, said: "Cursed be all learning that is contrary to the cross of Christ."[33]

Just about all of these schools are so secularized today that it is hard to picture them being founded for the glory of God and the advancement of the Christian faith and yet many of the buildings on these campuses testify to their Christian origins. I read a statement recently on the rules and principles of a school which stated that the great end of all education is to know the Lord Jesus Christ who is eternal life. It was Harvard![34] How tragic that the majority of these institutions have since apostatized. Today, for the most part, God's Word is mocked in the very schools that were founded by the sweat of Christians!

## EDUCATION BECOMES PUBLIC AND EVENTUALLY SECULARIZED

In 1837, modern public education was born in Massachusetts under the influence of Horace Mann. He is revered as the "Father of modern public education." Mann was president of the Massachusetts Legislature and chairman of the new state board of education of America's first public school system. He was a Unitarian, who denied the Trinity and the deity of Christ. He did not believe in the inspiration and authority of the Bible. The fact that the entire educational system for all of the children of America was in the hands of the Christian Church was deplorable to him. He thought something must be done to remedy that situation. His answer was state education, education run, operated, and controlled by the state. Hence, the modern, public educational system was begun in an effort to deliver children from the Christian religion!

However, what Mann planted did not come to full fruition until the twentieth century, and that principally under the influence of another name well-known to public education: John Dewey. Who was John Dewey? He was a professor at New York's Columbia University. During the early years of this century Dewey's school of education became the philosophic touchstone for all of the government-financed state colleges and other teacher-training institutions across America. His ideas of so-called "progressive education" became absolutely dominant in America.

Dewey was the first president of the American Humanist Association. He was a signer of the *Humanist Manifesto I*. He did not believe in Christianity; in fact, he felt that Christianity was the principle problem that needed to be solved by our public educational system.

It is interesting that one hundred years ago, at a time when most people were totally oblivious to the direction the public educational system was moving, Dr. A. A. Hodge of Princeton saw with an eagle eye the direction it was taking. Dr. Hodge and his father, Dr. Charles Hodge, are considered two of the most outstanding theologians America has ever produced. He had a voluminous education. He had a tremendous intellect and was a great scholar. And here is what he prophetically declared a century ago:

> I am as sure as I am of Christ's reign that a comprehensive and centralized system of national education, separated from religion, as is now commonly proposed, will prove the most appalling enginery for the propagation of anti-Christian and atheistic unbelief, and of anti-social nihilistic ethics, individual, social and political, which this sin-rent world has ever seen.[35]

He is saying that a state public educational system separated from religion will become the most atheistic, anti-Christian, nihilistic system the world has ever seen. How remarkably accurate a prediction!

While more than 200 years of Christian education in this country produced a .04 percent illiteracy rate, what has public and increasingly secularized education succeeded in doing? In spite of the fact that more than a trillion dollars have been poured into the educational system, what has happened? The illiteracy rate has increased 32 times. Today, we have 40 million illiterates! In addition there are an estimated 30 million more functional illiterates in this country.

The September 12, 1993 Ft. Lauderdale *Sun-Sentinel* announced the disheartening results of the "Adult Literacy in America" study. According to researchers, nearly half of all adult Americans are barely literate.

Education Secretary Richard Riley said these findings are a "wake up call to the sheer magnitude of illiteracy in this country" (*Washington Times,* September 9, 1993).

The literacy rate in America is rapidly approaching that of Zambia! The modern, secular educator would sneer at the biblical notion that the fear of the Lord is the beginning of wisdom. Yet reality upholds the verity of this 3,000-year-old axiom.

Just how bad is our current, secularized state education? A report entitled *A Nation at Risk*, released by the U.S. Department of Education in the 1980s, sums it up well: "If an unfriendly foreign power had attempted to impose on America the mediocre educational performance that exists today, we might well have viewed it as an act of war. . . . we have, in effect, been committing an act of unthinking, unilateral educational disarmament."[36]

Much more could be said about the secularization of American education and its resultant decline in quality. More could be said about the grave moral problems facing the schools—like robberies, assaults, rape, teen pregnancy, abortion, suicide, and homicide. But our focus here is on the Christian roots of education. The main reason for bringing up modern education is the contrast it provides to the Christian education that shaped the founders of this country.

# EDUCATION WORLDWIDE

Christianity not only helped to educate America and the West, but in the last two centuries, it was primarily Christian missionaries who educated countless millions in Third World countries. Christians have established schools in remotest jungles, converted unwritten languages to writing, and taught reading and writing to the nationals. In numerous countries, prior to decolonization (which occurred in the 1950s, 60s, and 70s), it was Christian missionaries who did most of the teaching.[37]

One American missionary to the Philippines, Frank Laubach (1884–1970), developed a literacy training program that has been used around the world for sixty years now to teach people— including adults—how to read and write. Laubach was a "literacy pioneer," whose slogan was "Each One Teach One,"[38] and who established Laubach Literacy International. It's estimated that more than 100 million people have been taught to read by the Laubach method in at least 200 nations, including many illiterates in this country. Indeed, Christianity has helped promote education and literacy more than any other force in the world!

# CONCLUSION

Much more could be said on how Christianity has promoted education and literacy worldwide. For instance, consider the Sunday school movement of the late eighteenth century, founded by Robert Raikes of Gloucester, England. The purpose of this was to provide Bible-oriented schooling for poor children who otherwise would not have received it. Here again, Christianity made education available for the masses. Or think of the excellent Christian schools (particularly Catholic ones) in our decayed urban areas which provide a lifeline for many poor children out of the ghetto.

Had Jesus never been born, man would yet remain in the darkness of sin and the darkness of ignorance. It's unlikely that there would be education for the common man. Unfortunately, as we move away from the Light of the gospel in the West, we are reverting back to the darkness—both of sin and of ignorance.

# CHAPTER 5

# GOVERNMENT OF THE PEOPLE, FOR THE PEOPLE, BY THE PEOPLE

## Christianity's Impact on the Founding of America

*Righteousness exalts a nation,*
*But sin is a reproach to any people.*

(Prov. 14:34)

In late 1992, Mississippi Governor Kirk Fordice raised a firestorm of controversy by publicly declaring that America is a "Christian nation." So much so that by the end of the week of his declaration, he felt forced to apologize. One newspaper, in commenting on the whole story, summed it up well: "The label 'Christian nation' has become fighting words."[1]

Many years ago, a leading American had the audacity to say something similar to what Gov. Fordice said:

I believe no one can read the history of our country without realizing that the Good Book and the spirit of the Saviour

have from the beginning been our guiding geniuses. . . .
Whether we look to the first Charter of Virginia . . . or to
the Charter of New England . . . or to the Charter of
Massachusetts Bay . . . or to the Fundamental Orders of
Connecticut . . . the same objective is present; a Christian
land governed by Christian perspectives.[2]

Who made this outlandish, politically incorrect statement? Jerry
Falwell? Billy Graham? Dan Quayle? No, it was no less than Earl
Warren! Warren, who was then Governor of California, spoke
these words in 1954. He later became Chief Justice of the
Supreme Court and ironically did much, whether inadvertently
or purposefully, to chisel away America's Christian heritage,
which he had apparently admired earlier in his life.

Exactly how much is—or *was*—America a "Christian nation"?
The purpose of this chapter is to show how the Christian faith
played a vital role in the development of the United States of
America and has given the world a great model of good
government. Had Jesus never been born, there never would have
been an America. And as we move away from Christ in this
nation, we are cutting off the very root of what has made this
nation great in the first place. Two resources that are quite
helpful on this subject are David Barton's *The Myth of Separation*
(Aledo, TX: WallBuilders, Inc., 1992) and John Eidsmoe's
*Christianity and the Constitution: The Faith of Our Founding
Fathers* (Grand Rapids: Baker Book House, 1987).

In the history of the world, there has never been a nation like
the United States of America in terms of the religious, political,
and economic liberties we've enjoyed. Like no other country
before it, the United States has helped pave the way for similar
representative governments around the world. America has been
a beacon to the world. Even today, people voting with their feet
will risk death (e.g., on the open seas) to take advantage of the
opportunities and freedoms we enjoy here. What is the true
source of these freedoms? Take away Christianity, and there
would be no America as we know it. Although Christianity has
brought much good in the political shaping of other nations, we
want to focus on the United States in this chapter because it

seems to have emerged in the last two hundred years as the world's best hope and as the highest model for freedom.

Today there are those who gnash their teeth at the very mention of the fact that America was founded as a Christian nation. But the facts of history are not easily dismissed, though they are certainly ignored in our schools and in many of our modern, revisionist history books.

## ALL NATIONS HAVE A THEISTIC OR ATHEISTIC BASE

All nations that have ever existed have been founded upon either a theistic or an anti-theistic principle—here we think of the Hinduism of India, the Confucianism of China, the Judaism of Israel, the Islam of Saudi Arabia, or the atheism of the former Soviet Union. If we are historically literate, we know that America was founded upon Christ and His Word.

But the true sources of America's greatness have recently been blotted out for the most part by the miasmic fog of secularism. Credit is not being given where it is due. From whence do most of the streams of thought—the basic principles of life that have made this country great—originate? What man in history, in your opinion, made the greatest—certainly not the sole, but the greatest—contribution to the sources of American liberty, government, economics, education, and its general thought?

Let me suggest to you the man I believe history clearly gives the decision to. He is a humble reformer from Geneva, Switzerland, and his name is John Calvin. If we are going to get back to the principles that made America great, then we are going to have to get back to the principles of John Calvin, because it is precisely his principles that made this nation great. John Calvin is considered to be one of the greatest original thinkers of all time; however, this is really not accurate, because Calvin was not so much an originator as he was an expositor of the Scriptures— an expounder of the teachings of Jesus Christ. So, in an indirect sense, the virtual founder of this nation was Jesus Christ and His teachings. Now, of course, many other strands have been involved, and since all human activities are performed by sinful human hands, they are defiled in the process.

A number of historians have declared that Calvinism played a pivotal role in the founding of America and in the birth of the republican form of government enjoyed in America:

German historian von Ranke said: "John Calvin was the virtual founder of America."[3]

French historian Taine said concerning the Calvinists, "These men are the true heroes of England. . . . They founded Scotland; they founded the United States."[4]

D'Augibne, another French scholar and historian, said, "Calvin was the founder of the greatest of republics,"[5] and he listed America as one of them.

One of America's greatest historians ever, George Bancroft, in the nineteenth century called Calvin simply "the father of America" and added: "He who will not honor the memory and respect the influence of Calvin knows but little of the origin of American liberty."[6] The tragedy is that the popular education in the last half century has left the average American knowing little of the origin of American liberty!

It should be noted that Calvin's influence is far broader than the Presbyterian Church. Two or three centuries ago not only were the Presbyterians Calvinists, but so were all of the Pilgrims, Anglicans or Episcopalians, Congregationalists, Baptists, Puritans, the Reformed of Holland, Germany, and Switzerland, and the Huguenots of France.

Some suppose that all Calvinist influence was gone by the time of the American War for Independence, but that's not true at all. Bancroft says: "The Revolution of 1776, so far as it was affected by religion, was a Presbyterian measure."[7] This was not referred to as the American Revolution in England; it was called the "Presbyterian Rebellion." And one ardent colonial supporter wrote to King George III the following words: "I fix all of the blame for these extraordinary proceedings upon the Presbyterians. They have been the chief and principal instruments in all of these flaming measures."[8] And when these "extraordinary proceedings" reached the ears of England, Prime Minister Horace Walpole rose in Parliament and made this statement: "Cousin America has run off with a Presbyterian parson."[9] Do you know the parson's name? Rev. John Witherspoon, president of Princeton, the only minister who signed the Declaration of Independence.

At the time of the American Revolution, over half of the soldiers and officers in the Revolutionary army were Presbyterians. And though there were few officers' ranks in the Revolutionary army, one of those was "colonel," and all of the colonels in the American Revolution, except one, were Presbyterian *Elders*.[10] A Presbyterian rebellion!

Yes, they were there! And why? Because of the form of government Presbyterianism fosters. When tyranny in the Church government is destroyed, it inevitably leads to freedom in the civil government. Presbyterianism has always been understood to be contrary to both tyranny and to all forms of monarchical government. This was clearly understood, for example, by King James I of England, who said this: "Presbytery agreeth with monarchy like God with the Devil."[11]

Bancroft again speaks of the political character of Calvinism as one that monarchs instinctively judge to be that of republicanism. The form of government that exists in the Presbyterian Church, which was the only republic existing on this continent for seventy-five years before 1776, is what the American government, to a great extent, is simply a copy of.

The American government is a republic. Everywhere Presbyterianism has gained dominion, it has produced a republic. Every republican government that exists in the world was produced by the influence of Presbyterianism and Calvinism. This is a statement made by innumerable historians.[12] In the Church, laypeople are given the right to govern the church. It is not governed from somewhere up above. And freedom has been restored to the Church. Politically, "Calvinism has been," said Boettner, "the chief source of republican government."[13]

Calvinism and republicanism are related to each other as cause and effect. This nation (though some are not aware of it) has a republican form of government that has nothing to do with the Republican Party, but has to do with a government by law—by elected representatives. It is exactly the kind of government we have in our country today.

# THE MAYFLOWER COMPACT

Despite the denial of the modern secularist, this nation began as a Christian nation. We remember the words of the Mayflower Compact, written by the first settlers of Plymouth as they sat in the captain's quarters on their ship before setting foot on these shores. That famous document, also known as the "birth certificate of America," affirmed that they set out in this great undertaking "for the glory of God, and the advancement of the Christian faith." That is why those settlers came. What they wrote in 1620 was a political covenant that directly mirrored the spiritual covenant that they had written up in 1606. It will be helpful for us to back up and provide the historical background of the Pilgrims. Their story is well-chronicled in one of the first books written in the New World, *Of Plymouth Plantation*, by Governor William Bradford. It was he, through citing of the Bible, who named them "pilgrims." Bradford quoted from 1 Peter 2:11, which says, "Beloved, I beg you as sojourners and *pilgrims*, abstain from fleshly lusts which war against the soul" (emphasis mine).

The Pilgrims, as they are now known, were a single congregation, which secretly formed in 1606 in the large manor home of William Brewster in the sleepy town of Scrooby, in Nottinghamshire, England. Considering that they were literally just one congregation, they were one of the most remarkable congregations that ever existed on the face of this earth. Their main leader through the years was the Rev. John Robinson, who unfortunately was never able to come to the New World, although he laid down many of the vital principles that helped those who did come over.

The Pilgrims were part of the Separatist movement, a group of Christians who despaired that the Church of England could ever be reformed. The Separatists stand in contrast to the Puritans, whose name derives from their desire to purify the Church of England from within.

The manner in which the Pilgrims started is most significant. As we mentioned, they began their underground congregation by making a covenant, which became known as the Scrooby Covenant. In doing this, they framed "one of the first written covenants for local church self-government, pledging to obey God and His law, and to walk together in Christian fellowship."[14] Religious freedom was nonexistent in England, so under intense persecution, they soon left for the Netherlands, where there was religious freedom. In Holland, however, they faced many different hardships, including the falling away of their children because of the influence of a worldly environment. So they eventually left for America but not all at the same time, the first group arriving in 1620 on the *Mayflower*. When this group arrived in the New World—but before they disembarked—they voluntarily agreed to Christian self-government by writing up the Mayflower Compact, which states:

> In the name of God, Amen. We, whose names are underwritten, the loyal Subjects of our dread Sovereign Lord, King James. . . . Having undertaken for the Glory of God, and Advancement of the Christian Faith, and the Honour of our King and Country, a voyage to plant the first colony in the northern Parts of Virginia; do by these Presents, solemnly and mutually in the Presence of God and one of another, covenant and combine ourselves together into a civil Body Politick, for our better Ordering and Preservation, and Furtherance of the Ends aforesaid.[15]

The significance of the Mayflower Compact to our constitutional form of government cannot be stressed enough. Nor can the link between their church covenant and the Mayflower Compact, which was a political echo of their church charter. *The World Almanac 1991* says of the Mayflower Compact: "The voluntary agreement to govern themselves was America's first written constitution."[16]

Scholar Dr. Robert Bartlett, who is a direct descendent of the Pilgrims and who has written *The Pilgrim Way*, writes: "This compact was to play a role in the development of American democracy. It repudiated the aristocratic system which exalted the privileges of the few and established a small community based on a signed, mutual agreement."[17]

After the first Pilgrims came over on the *Mayflower,* succeeding waves of additional Pilgrims came. Then, in 1628, the first contingent of Puritans arrived. Although the Puritans intended to stay in England and purify the Church from within, their hopes were not realized. King James I, who hated the Pilgrims and the Puritans, said of all religious dissidents: "I will make them conform themselves, or else I will harry them out of the land, or else do worse!"[18] So in the next few decades after the arrival of the Mayflower, wave upon wave of Pilgrims and Puritans came and settled New England. They interchanged ideas, and many of the Puritans came to adopt many of the Pilgrims' ideas. Meanwhile, the Puritans numerically overwhelmed the Pilgrims and eventually the distinctions were blurred. As legal scholar John Eidsmoe puts it: "By 1700 the Pilgrims had been completely absorbed into Puritan society, and there was no distinction between the two groups thereafter."[19]

Over the course of the next 150 years, these dedicated Christians in New England wrote up about 100 different compacts, covenants, and constitutions. Like the Mayflower Compact, they reflect the Christian motivation of these early Americans. For example, in 1643, for the first time, for mutual protection, delegates from the colonies joined together and signed the New England Confederation. Here is what they said was the singular reason for their coming into these parts of America as stated in the New England Confederation: "We all came into these parts of America, with one and the same end and aim, namely, to advance the Kingdom of our Lord Jesus Christ."[20]

The numerous constitutions, covenants, and compacts that these early settlers wrote up paved the way for the constitutional form of government we enjoy in America, and it all began with the church covenants of the Calvinists. As historian Dr. Charles Hull Wolfe puts it:

> under their Biblical-type covenant, the Pilgrims experienced religious, political and economic freedom. Then in 1636, they used that covenant as the foundation on which they framed a complete, detailed constitution. This led to the framing of almost a hundred other Biblically-based covenants, compacts and constitutions by the year 1776, and laid the groundwork for a uniquely free and Christian America.[21]

No one can argue with the Christian character of the Puritans and Pilgrims. However, instead of holding them up as examples and instead of being grateful for the contributions they made to our nation, the modern secularist holds them up merely as objects of ridicule. They don't recognize the incredible character that these stalwart Christians displayed. They don't see the link between their stern faith and the strength that enabled them to leave everything in the Old World behind to bring their families to the risky unknown, and to pave a way in the hostile wilderness. The brave Pilgrims and Puritans deserve our gratitude, not our mockery. Every single day, we enjoy the contributions they made to civilization. Alas, this message is largely lost on the secularist of today.

After trivializing the legacy of the Pilgrims and Puritans, today's secularist then attempts to convince us that by the time of Independence, Christian influence had totally waned. Secularists tell us that the Founding Fathers were by-and-large secularists giving us a secular government. When I debated with Sam Donaldson on the "Merv Griffin Show" a few years ago, he brought forth this argument. But the facts totally refute this thesis.

First of all, in 1776 the founders of this country never heard or thought of any such thing as a secular nation. There had never existed anywhere on the face of this planet such a thing as a secular nation. When it finally did come into existence in France shortly after the founding of America, the Founding Fathers of this country were appalled. They were horrified by what they saw taking place in France. It was an unmitigated disaster, as attempts were made there to throw off religion completely. Soon it led to a river of blood and then the tyranny of Napoleon—an inevitable result. They were forced to abandon their atheistic and secularistic foundation.

Now, let's examine in the next several pages the role Christianity played in the official founding of this nation. We have to begin a few decades prior to the American Revolution with what is known today as "the Great Awakening." Jonathan Edwards, one of the greatest theologians and philosophers America ever produced, played a critical role in sparking this revival.

# THE GREAT AWAKENING

During the 1730s and 1740s, a major revival swept through many of the colonies. This Great Awakening helped to bond the disparate colonies and united them in one spirit. It reinforced the vital importance of the Bible in the life of the Americans of that era. Dr. Ellis Sandoz, who heads the Eric Voegelin Institute at Louisiana State University, affirms:

> The denominational differences are minimized partly as a result of the homogenizing and democratizing effects of decades of revivalism from the Great Awakening and its rumbling echoes and aftershocks. That the leading lights of the Revolutionary Congresses and the Federal Convention were generally men of faith can no longer be doubted.[22]

Furthermore, the Great Awakening helped to reconfirm the republican form of government the colonists saw in their Bibles. Sandoz quotes Alice Baldwin, who studied the clergy in Virginia and North Carolina during the Great Awakening and afterward:

> Southern Presbyterian ministers based their political concepts on the Bible. The idea of a fundamental constitution based on law, of inalienable rights which were God-given and therefore natural, of government as a binding compact made between rulers and peoples, of the right of the people to hold their rulers to account and to defend their rights against oppression, these seem to have been doctrines taught by them all. . . . In the South as in New England, the clergy helped in making familiar to the common people the basic principles on which the Revolution was fought, our constitutional convictions held, our Bill of Rights written and our state and national constitutions founded.[23]

Thus liberty thundered forth from the colonial pulpits, mostly in New England, and ignited the War for Independence.

## THE IMPORTANCE OF CHRISTIANITY TO KEY PATRIOTS

So many of those involved in the fashioning of American Independence were committed Christians. We want to highlight a few of them:

# Samuel Adams

The firebrand of the American Revolution was Samuel Adams, a devout believer. He saw himself as "the Last of the Puritans."[24] He is often called "the Father of the American Revolution." For more than twenty years, he indefatigably gave himself to the cause of liberty. Adams formed the Committees of Correspondence. "These Committees provided the unity and cohesion necessary for the Colonies to stand united during a time when communication was difficult and unreliable."[25] Adams, according to multiple sources, was the most important figure in starting the War. *Encyclopaedia Britannica* declares: "Samuel Adams did more than any other American to arouse opposition against English rule in the Colonies."[26] From what source did Samuel Adams say free citizens could learn of their rights? He wrote: "These [rights] may be best understood by reading and carefully studying the institutes of the great Law Giver and Head of the Christian Church, which are to be found clearly written and promulgated in the New Testament."[27]

When the Declaration of Independence was being signed in 1776, Samuel Adams declared: "We have this day restored the Sovereign to whom all men ought to be obedient. He reigns in heaven, and from the rising to the setting of the sun, let His kingdom come."[28] And along this same theme, the published battle cry of the American Revolution was "No King but King Jesus!"[29]

# Patrick Henry

Patrick Henry, a Christian patriot, was the golden-tongued orator of the Revolutionary period. Henry is perhaps best known for his history changing, impassioned speech before the Virginia House of Burgesses, where he declared, "Give me liberty or give me death!" Henry recognized the tremendous contribution Christianity made to the founding of this country. He said: "It cannot be emphasized too strongly or too often that this great nation was founded, not by religionists, but by Christians; not on religions, but on the gospel of Jesus Christ! For this very reason peoples of other faiths have been afforded asylum, prosperity, and freedom of worship here."[30]

# John Witherspoon

The only clergyman who signed the Declaration of Independence was Rev. John Witherspoon, the president of the College of New Jersey, which is today Princeton University. At that time, this college was a stalwart Presbyterian institution. Witherspoon had emigrated from Scotland. He helped to shape the political thinking of many key Americans, including James Madison, who attended Witherspoon's college, while preparing for the ministry. Witherspoon befriended the young man and had a profound impact on Madison's life. Obviously Madison chose a political career, but his theological training served him well. John Eidsmoe writes: "One thing is certain: the Christian religion, particularly Rev. Witherspoon's Calvinism, influenced Madison's view of law and government."[31]

But Madison is not the only shaper of America whose thinking Witherspoon helped shape. Eidsmoe also states: "John Witherspoon is best described as the man who shaped the men who shaped America. Although he did not attend the Constitutional Convention, his influence was multiplied many times over by those who spoke as well as by what was said."[32]

# George Washington

Some people have written that the father of our country was not a Christian, but a Deist. I believe an honest examination of the facts shows otherwise. For example, a book of prayers that Washington used on a regular basis was found in April 1891 among many of his papers. This twenty-four-page, manuscript book, titled "Daily Sacrifices," was in his own hand-writing. Whether he had originated these or whether he had merely copied them, historians note that they were important to him.[33] Here is a representative sample of his book of prayers:

O most Glorious God, in Jesus Christ my merciful and loving father, I acknowledge and confess my guilt, in the weak and imperfect performance of the duties of this day. I have called on thee for pardon and forgiveness of sins, but so coldly and carelessly, that my prayers are become my sin and stand in need of pardon.[34]

Washington was a vestryman in good standing in the Episcopal Church, at a time when their doctrine conformed closely to evangelical teaching. He was well-known for his godly disposition and his fervent prayer life, for instance when he was spotted kneeling in prayer at Valley Forge. His prayers were answered as God sovereignly helped the fledgling nation in its struggle against the most powerful nation on earth. So much so that Washington wrote this to Thomas Nelson in a letter dated August 20, 1778: "The hand of Providence has been so conspicuous in all this, that he must be worse than an infidel that lacks faith, and more than wicked, that has not gratitude enough to acknowledge his obligations."[35]

When Washington was inaugurated, which occurred in 1789 in New York City, he got down on his knees and kissed the Bible. Then he led the entire Senate and House of Representatives to an Episcopal Church for a two-hour worship service. Why, that is enough to give the ACLU collective apoplexy!

When Washington left office, he gave a lengthy farewell address, considered one of the greatest speeches in American history. Listen to what he said about the place of religion in our national life:

Of all the dispositions and habits which lead to political prosperity, religion and morality are indispensable supports. In vain would that man claim the tribute of patriotism, who should labor to subvert these great pillars of human happiness. . . . And let us with caution indulge the supposition that morality can be maintained without religion.[36]

# RELIGIOUS AFFILIATION OF THE POPULATION OF 1776

The Christian actions of America's leaders in those days should not surprise us when we look at the religion of the leadership and the constituency of that day. Research has determined that of the fifty-five men who met in Philadelphia in the Constitutional Convention to write our Constitution, fifty of them were unquestionably Christians, and possibly fifty-two. The late Dr. M. E. Bradford of the University of Dallas has documented this fact in his book on the framers of the Constitution, *A Worthy Company*. He has also researched the signers of the Declaration of Independence. He concludes that of the fifty-six men who signed the nation's birth certificate, definitely fifty, maybe fifty-two, were Christians.[37]

Furthermore, let us look at the constituency of this country in 1776. At that time, 98 percent of Americans were Protestant Christians; 1.8 percent were Catholic Christians; .2 percent, or two tenths of 1 percent, were Jewish. Therefore, 99.8 percent of the people in America in 1776 claimed to be Christians. Who, then, with even a modicum of historical knowledge would dare claim that what they founded was not a Christian nation?

# THE IMPORTANCE OF THE BIBLE TO THE FOUNDING FATHERS

The book the Founding Fathers cite the most in their writings and speeches is the Bible. After that are other Christian sources. Eidsmoe brings this out in his book *Christianity and the Constitution*:

> Two professors, Donald S. Lutz and Charles S. Hyneman, have reviewed an estimated 15,000 items, and closely read 2,200 books, pamphlets, newspaper articles, and monographs with explicitly political content printed between 1760 and 1805. They reduced this to 916 items, about one-third of all public political writings longer than 2,000 words.
>
> From these items, Lutz and Hyneman identified 3,154 references to other sources. The source most often cited by the founding fathers was the Bible, which accounted for 34 percent of all citations. . . .
>
> The most cited thinkers . . . were not deists and philosophes, but conservative legal and political thinkers who often were Christians.[38]

They include, in order of the frequency of citation, Montes-quieu, Blackstone, and Locke—all of whom were professing Christians.[39]

# THE BIBLE AND THE CONSTITUTION

Secularists argue that Christianity has absolutely nothing to do with the Constitution or the Bill of Rights. This is one of the most egregious fallacies of our time. Amazingly, the secularist misses the crucial point, developed earlier, that the form of constitutional government we enjoy comes from Christians—namely, the Pilgrims and the Puritans, and their church covenants! Besides, the Constitution must be recognized as a how-to document, whereas the other founding document, the Declaration of Independence, provides more of the rationale for the creation of the new nation. In the latter, there are several references to God; whereas there is only one direct one in the former, "in the Year of Our Lord." Nonetheless, as Sandoz points out, "the Constitution owes a great debt to the spiritual convictions of the country and to its Christian traditions."[40]

The Constitution of the United States, declared the skeptical historian H. G. Wells, is "indubitably Christian."[41] Because the overwhelming majority of the creators of the Constitution were practicing Christians[42] who derived their political philosophy from the Bible and other Christian sources, it should come as no surprise that they enshrined numerous biblical principles in the Constitution. Here are some highlights:

1. The Constitution is based on government by law and not by men—on the idea that both the citizens and the public officials who represent them must be governed by a fundamental law in keeping with the law of God. The founding fathers, including Madison, chief framer of the constitution, believed this view, which would later be articulated so well by de Tocqueville:

> Despotism may govern without faith, but liberty cannot. Religion is much more necessary . . . in democratic republics than in any others. How is it possible that society should escape destruction if the moral tie is not strengthened in proportion as the political tie is relaxed?[43]

2. The Constitution is based on equality under the law. The Bible says "God shows no partiality." (Acts 10:34). The Declaration of Independence expresses this truth when it says that God is the Creator, and "all men are created equal." It may have taken another one hundred years before that principle was fully implemented, but it was established in the Constitution.

3. The Constitution is based on the Declaration's assertion that all are "endowed by their Creator with certain inalienable rights." Where were these rights first expressed? In the Ten Commandments.

4. The Constitution is committed to the protection of individual liberty. As Christians, the framers believed that "where the Spirit of the Lord is, there is liberty" (2 Cor. 3:17).

5. The Constitution rests on the Founders' understanding that man is sinful. Therefore, they separated powers—the executive from the legislative branch, the legislative from the judicial—so that no one group would lord it over another. Madison wrote in *The Federalist Number 51*:

> But what is government but the greatest of all reflections on human nature? If men were angels, no government would be necessary. If angels were to govern men, neither external or internal controls on government would be necessary. In framing a government which is to be administered by men over men, the great difficulty lies in this: you must first enable the government to control the governed; and in the next place oblige it to control itself.[44]

Thus the Christian doctrine of man's sinful nature led to the Constitution's division of powers, so excessive power would not be in the hands of any one or few men. How were these powers to be divided? The founders knew that Isaiah 33:22 said: "For the LORD is our judge, the LORD is our Lawgiver, the LORD is our king," and they divided the functions of government in just this way—into judicial, legislative, and executive branches.

6. The Constitution is based on the conviction that a hereditary monarchy is not a truly Christian form of civil government. The framers held that no man is entitled to be a monarch; only

Christ is King. Again, one of the slogans of the American Revolution was: "No King but King Jesus!"[45]

# ACTIONS OF THE NEW NATION

If the founders of the new nation intended this to be a secular state, then why did they, when governing, perform so many religious acts which were officially part of the government? The first act of the first Congress—the same men who wrote the first amendment—was to hire chaplains to say prayers before the sessions of the House and the Senate. The leaders of the new nation called for national days of fasting, prayer, and thanksgiving. No less than sixteen such days were called during the Revolutionary War alone. Even the patron saints of the ACLU, Jefferson and Madison, made national proclamations for days of fasting and prayer.

At the very time the first Congress was passing the First Amendment to the Bill of Rights, that same Congress passed one of what is called the "four most important documents in American history": the Northwest Ordinance of 1787. It states: "Religion, morality and knowledge being essential to good government and the happiness of mankind, schools and the means of education shall forever be encouraged."[46] Notice that *schools* were to be established to teach religion, morality, and knowledge!

# AMERICA, A CHRISTIAN NATION

In the Trinity Decision of 1892, the Supreme Court examined literally thousands of documents that had anything to do with the founding of this country—every state constitution, all of the compacts that led up to 1776, all of the various decisions of the courts. Finally, they said: "This is a religious people. This is historically true. From the discovery of this continent to the present hour, there is a single voice making this affirmation. . . . These are not individual sayings, declarations of private persons; they are organic utterances; they speak the voice of the entire people. . . . these and many other matters which might be noticed, add a volume of unofficial declarations to the mass of organic utterances that this is a Christian nation."[47]

## HISTORICAL REVISION

Alas, the religious foundations of America have been completely expurgated from our history textbooks. I recently read one that is used in a local school, and I was astounded by the distortions, omissions, perversions, and downright lies that filled this textbook, which high school students are being forced to read today. A classic example is a history textbook from the 1970s that contains more than seven pages on Marilyn Monroe and a couple of paragraphs on George Washington! With books like this, our children won't learn much about our history—much less our Christian heritage. For further reading on this, we recommend the Gablers' *What Are They Teaching Our Children?* (1985) and Dr. Paul Vitz's *Censorship: Evidence of Bias in Our Children's Textbooks* (1986).

## MISINTERPRETATION OF THE FIRST AMENDMENT

Much of the misunderstanding in the area of "the separation of Church and State" hinges on the interpretation of the first amendment. The religion clauses (actually, clause) of the first amendment states: "Congress shall make no law respecting an establishment of religion or prohibiting the free exercise thereof." Traditionally, it has always been understood that this meant that in America there would be no State Church, like the one they had in England. Historically, it has been understood that there is a separation of the function of the Church from the function of the State. But that does not mean there is to be a separation of God or Christianity from the State, which we find taking place in our country today.

Since 1947 a relatively new interpretation of Church-State relations emerged to gain national prominence with the Supreme Court's decision in *Everson v. the Board of Education*. Justice Hugo Black quoted an 1802 letter from Thomas Jefferson to the Danbury Baptists, wherein Jefferson described "a wall of separation between church and State."[48] Over time, this interpretation came to gain wide circulation, so much so that today the average person on the street most likely thinks the Constitution even teaches the separation of Church and State. What this misinterpretation of the first amendment has done is effectively to turn it into a search-and-destroy mission against any vestige of religion in public. How far we have come from George Washington's inauguration and the prayer service for the new nation that followed it!

The only way that modern secularists can come to the conclusion that the founders of this country intended a purely secular state, where the state is "neutral" (translate "hostile") to religion is by *selective history*. They base their decisions on a few selected passages from our history and ignore a mountain of evidence to the contrary.

An eminent legal scholar in the early nineteenth century who taught at Harvard Law School and eventually become an Associate Justice of the United States Supreme Court was Joseph Story, a Unitarian. He was appointed to the Supreme Court by President Madison. Story wrote the first great commentary on the Constitution. In that commentary, dated 1851, he has this to say about the first amendment:

> Probably at the time of the adoption of the Constitution, and of the amendment to it now under consideration [first amendment], the general if not the universal sentiment in America was, that Christianity ought to receive encouragement from the State so far as was not incompatible with the private rights of conscience and the freedom of religious worship. An attempt to level all religions, and to make it a matter of state policy to hold all in utter indifference, would have created universal disapprobation, if not universal indignation.

> The real object of the First Amendment was not to countenance, much less to advance, Mahometanism, or Judaism, or infidelity, by prostrating Christianity; but to exclude all rivalry among Christian sects, and to prevent any national ecclesiastical establishment which should give to a hierarchy the exclusive patronage of the national government.[49]

# CONCLUSION

Much more could be said about America's Christian roots. There have been numerous incidents where God's protective hand seemed to intervene at just the right moment. His hand can even be seen in leading some of the courageous explorers who opened up the New World. For example, Christopher Columbus saw his voyage as fulfillment of what Isaiah had prophesied about the heathen turning to the true God. About a decade after his expedition, he wrote:

It was the Lord who put into my mind (I could feel His hand upon me) to sail to the Indies. All who heard of my project rejected it with laughter, ridiculing me. There is no question that the inspiration was from the Holy Spirit, because He comforted me with rays of marvelous illumination from the Holy Scriptures. . . . Our Lord Jesus Christ desired to perform a very obvious miracle in the voyage to the Indies . . .[50]

Columbus' death-defying voyage was a milestone in history. It's entirely possible that had Jesus never been born, we might never have come over to this continent.

Today, America needs to return to God. We need to be recommitted to the great principles our Founding Fathers gave us in the founding documents of this nation; to strive by our prayers, by our efforts, by our evangelization, to make ours a Christian nation once more. Because of the abandonment of those principles, all manner of ills, plagues, and problems have descended upon this country. Our only hope is to go back to the foundations and to rebuild the Christian heritage that made this nation great. As President Abraham Lincoln put it:

It is the duty of nations as well as of men to own their dependence upon the overruling power of God . . . and to recognize the sublime truth, announced in the Holy Scriptures and proven by all history, that those nations only are blessed whose God is the Lord.[51]

# CHAPTER 6

# FREEDOM FOR ALL

## Christianity's Contribution to Civil Liberties

*Now the Lord is the Spirit; and where the Spirit of the Lord is, there is liberty.*

The apostle Paul (2 Cor. 3:17)

**R**adio commentator Paul Harvey tells of an experiment involving a chimpanzee to which scientists were determined to teach written communication. For fourteen years, project directors labored diligently and patiently with this chimpanzee, providing things in its cage to enable it to form certain syllables.

Finally, the day arrived when it seemed that the chimpanzee was actually going to construct a sentence from the symbols it had been learning. Word went out, and other scientists crowded into the room and gathered around the cage. They watched breathlessly as symbols were formed into words and into a sentence. At last, the first message from the world's most pampered, most cared for, most patiently trained chimpanzee was about to come forth. The scientists could hardly contain themselves as they pressed around the cage to read the history-making sentence.

Said the chimpanzee: "Let me out!"

All of the training, all of the pampering, all of the feeding does not mean a thing as long as there is no freedom. And Christianity has contributed so greatly toward human freedom and civil liberties that had Jesus never been born, I daresay freedom would not exist at all, or if it did, it would be the exclusive domain of the elite.

Jesus Christ is the greatest emancipator in the history of the world. What freedom we have in this world we owe to Christ and to His Word. "Where the Spirit of the Lord is, there is liberty." Wherever the Word has gone, tyrants have trembled. Despots have been cast from the throne, and people have become free. The tremendous liberties and freedoms we own in this country we owe primarily to the Word of God. Andrew Jackson said, "That book, sir, is the rock on which our Republic rests." When that book falls, I assure you that the liberties you enjoy will go with it.

## LIBERTY—A CONSTANT THEME OF THE BIBLE

Many people don't realize that liberty is a constant theme throughout the Bible. The Old Testament tells the story of the fall of man into slavery; God's deliverance of His people; their bondage in Egypt; then God bringing them out after 430 years of slavery. Again, they fell into idolatry in their own land and were taken away by the Babylonians into seventy years of captivity, only to be delivered again. All of this is but mere foreshadowings of the great deliverance and of the great emancipator, Jesus Christ, who came to deliver us from bondage unto freedom, from slavery unto liberty, to set free the slaves and those who are imprisoned.

## THE IRONY OF "THE AMERICAN INQUISITION"

The irony of the civil libertarians who are carrying on the "American Inquisition" against any vestige of the nation's Christian heritage is that civil liberties are a by-product of the Christian faith. You find them only in the countries that began with a Christian base. In modern America, Judeo-Christian beliefs are often held up to ridicule and disdain by the media. How ironic that the free speech forum that they utilize is ultimately a gift of Christianity—a fact that you could easily miss on Donahue, Sally, or Oprah! If you went to Saudi Arabia, you'd never hear a talk show discussing whether Mohammed was really the prophet of Allah. Muslim converts to Christianity are summarily executed in Muslim lands. At last check, Salman Rushdie (author of *Satanic Verses*) was still in hiding. If you went to Israel, you wouldn't hear a broadcast discussing whether Jesus was the Christ (Messiah). Messianic Jews (who believe Jesus is the Christ) have even been expelled or threatened to be expelled from Israel.[1] If you were in India, you wouldn't hear an open discussion on whether sacred cows should be eaten. And if you were in China, with its atheistic base, you wouldn't hear a discussion on whether citizens should be allowed to leave or return to China at will. We enjoy free speech and other civil liberties, *precisely* because of our Christian heritage.

When it comes to free speech, in many countries, even to this day, people don't have any freedom to criticize their government. You can land yourself in jail in a hurry by speaking out against the government. Freedom of speech probably was realized to a greater degree in America than anywhere ever before—keeping in mind that since 1776, many other countries have emulated what we have. If you were to go back to 1776 England and publicly criticize the king, you might find yourself in Australia before you knew what happened.

# THE ULTIMATE CIVIL LIBERTARIAN

Jesus Christ is the ultimate civil libertarian. Prison reformer Chuck Colson once made that point when he was commenting on the ACLU, a group with which he has occasionally found himself on the same side (when it comes to trying to curb abuses against prisoners):

> But the very name itself, civil libertarian, I kind of resent that being taken over by one organization. I consider myself a civil libertarian of the highest order because I pay homage

to that one individual in all of human history who brought dignity and liberty to the individual. And so I find myself a bit offended by the name, to be perfectly honest with you. I don't think they have any corner on civil liberties. The greatest civil libertarian of all time was Jesus Christ.[2]

## THE JEWISH BASE OF CIVIL LIBERTIES

Christianity did not invent civil liberties per se because God—in the Old Testament, dealing with the Hebrew people—entered into a covenant with them and gave to them His commandments. Inherent or implied in these commands are civil liberties. For example, the command that prohibits murder also protects life. The commandment that forbids theft also guarantees private property. The commandment that forbids adultery also protects the institution of marriage. So those liberties existed among the Hebrew people. However, these were a very tiny group of people in the world as a whole and were largely despised by the Gentile world. Christ expanded on those liberties and made them the view and the possession of most of the world. And they have gone with Him into every nation on earth. Where His message in its purity has gained dominance, those liberties have flowered and flourished as well.

## A CONTINUUM FROM ABRAHAM TO THE AMERICAN CONSTITUTION

Historian Dr. Charles Hull Wolfe observes that constitutional government and liberty are a heritage passed on from God, beginning with the Abrahamic covenant and climaxing with the American Constitution. When Moses made the covenant between God and the Hebrew people, it was the beginning of political liberty. For example, in Exodus 19:5, God said to Israel: "If you will indeed obey My voice and keep My covenant, then you shall be a special treasure to Me, above all people." The people agreed to do this, as recorded in verse 8. Because of the significance of this covenant and the line that can be traced from it to our freedom today, we quote at length from a script that Dr. Wolfe wrote for a Coral Ridge Ministries television special on liberty:

> As a result of their initial obedience, the Israelites became a free people—the first free people in history. As Moses said, they were to "proclaim liberty throughout all the land unto all the inhabitants thereof" (Lev. 25:10). . . . In God's good time, through Jesus Christ, God fulfilled the Old Testament's promise to make a new covenant with His people. Christ not only fulfilled the Old Covenant but confirmed and universalized the Law, and showed men how to obey it better—by receiving Him as their Lord and King. Even more, Christ showed men how to be free—by being governed by Him from within, instead of being tyrannized by men from without! In turn, St. Paul, who knew that "where the Spirit of the Lord is, there is liberty" took the Gospel and the principles of the Mosaic Covenant Westward again, from Israel across the Mediterranean to Greece and to Rome.
>
> Soon other believers took it Westward once more—to England and then to Ireland. In the year 432 A.D., Patrick—using a Latin document known as "Liber Ex Lege Moisi," i.e., Book of the Law of Moses, in cooperation with the Irish leaders whom he had converted, made the Ten Commandments the foundation on which Britons would base their civil law. In 890, King Alfred—the only monarch the English ever called "the Great"—made the Mosaic decalogue and Jesus' Golden Rule the basis of his code of law for England, and the foundation of British freedom.
>
> In 1215, Archbishop Stephen Langton, drawing on Britain's heritage of Bible-based law, framed the Magna Carta. A forerunner of the U.S. Constitution, it asserted the God-given rights of the English people and the Christian Church and is remembered today for its contribution to freedom under law.[3]

But it wasn't until the Protestant Reformation with Luther in 1517 and later, Calvin with his great intellectual contributions, that many Christians rediscovered the importance of God's covenant and law. In 1555, Calvin applied his knowledge of biblical covenant and law in framing a charter for the Geneva City Council. Wolfe continues: "Soon after, John Knox, one of Calvin's most gifted students, took what he learned in Geneva to his native Edinburgh, and launched a famous series of covenants defending the religious freedom of Scotsmen."[4]

After Knox, the Biblical Covenant was put into practice by the devout believers we know today as the Pilgrims, whom we discussed in the previous chapter. Beginning with their church covenant of 1606, they ultimately formed a political covenant that was the Mayflower Compact. From the Pilgrims, the covenant concept can be traced to the Founding Fathers. And so Wolfe concludes:

And when the Founding Fathers formed a strictly limited government in the Constitutional Convention, they were following the Biblical views of Calvin who said, "Civil government has its appointed end . . . to cherish and protect the outward worship of God . . . to reconcile us with one another, and to promote the general peace and tranquility."[5]

## FREEDOM FROM SIN LEADS TO POLITICAL FREEDOM

Christianity first set people free from the shackles of sin. Then, having experienced spiritual liberty, there was set in motion an inevitable quest for civil liberty as well. In the United States, where Christianity had its greatest impact, we have experienced civil liberties of a form and degree that had never been seen in any other country of the world. As John Quincy Adams once put it, "The highest glory of the American Revolution was this: it connected in one indissoluble bond, the principles of civil government with the principles of Christianity."[6] This is light–years away from the so-called "separation of church and state."

# THE BLACK REGIMENT

The road to American freedom was paved in large part by the pulpits of New England. Sermons from the colonial era helped to shape the American understanding that "resistance to tyranny is obedience to God." Thus the New England clergy helped lay the intellectual and theological foundation for liberty. Dr. Ellis Sandoz has compiled a book of influential political sermons, entitled *Political Sermons of the American Founding Era, 1730–1805*. Sandoz writes:

I discovered that the "pulpit of the American Revolution"— to borrow the title of John Wingate Thornton's 1860 collection—was the source of exciting and uncommonly important material. . . . Religion gave birth to America, Tocqueville observed long ago. . . . Of the Americans on the eve of the Revolution Carl Bridenbaugh has exclaimed, "who can deny that for them the very core of existence was their relation to God?"[7]

Sandoz says that the clergy, particularly in New England, have been called by some "the Black Regiment" because of the color of their robes and because of the role they played in spurring on the patriots to resist tyranny.

One example is the work of Rev. Jonas Clark. He was the minister of the church in Lexington. "Throughout that period [1762–1776], he was the most influential politician as well as churchman in the Lexington-Concord area."[8] His home was a meeting place for many important patriots; in fact, the night of Paul Revere's ride, Clark was entertaining John Hancock and Samuel Adams. When asked if the men of Lexington would fight, he replied that he had trained them for that very hour.

The next day, the American Revolution began with the Battle of Lexington in the "shot that was heard around the world." Author Franklin Cole, who has compiled biographical sketches of the New England clergy intimately involved in the American Revolution in his book *They Preached Liberty*, writes:

It was but a few rods from the parsonage that the first blood of the Revolution was shed on the following day, April 19, and the men who fell were his parishioners. Upon seeing the slain, Clark observed: "From this day will be dated the liberty of the world."[9]

And so, it was from the pulpits of New England that there thundered forth the great proclamations concerning liberty and freedom and the sovereignty of God and the nature of man which led to the foundation of the American Revolution and our Constitution.

## RELIGIOUS FREEDOM

Ironically, the inter-denominational fighting among Christians in the American colonies, prior to the founding of the country, helped to create the massive freedom of religion enjoyed in this nation. Two Christians of the seventeenth century who helped to pave the way for greater freedom of conscience were the Baptist Roger Williams, a dissenting Puritan who founded Rhode Island, and the Quaker William Penn. Although Roger Williams was apparently unable to get along with some people, his view "that the state must not coerce the conscience of the individual"[10] has significantly contributed to civil liberties in America. William Penn, whose name is enshrined in the territory he founded (Pennsylvania), gave freedom of conscience for all residents, and he treated the Indians with Christian charity and justice. He called Pennsylvania "the Holy Experiment."[11] Penn established a law, known as the Frame of Government, that "held out a greater degree of religious liberty than had at that time been allowed in the world."[12]

In the eighteenth century, the founders of this country were weary of one denomination lording it over another. They had seen the Quakers persecuted. They were alarmed at Baptists in Virginia being jailed for preaching the gospel without a license—since in that colony, there was a state church, which was a branch of the Church of England. The founders of this country—though mostly Christian men, as discussed in the last chapter—did not want to see any one denomination have a state monopoly.

In fact, there was a seldom-mentioned threat perceived by the American patriots, which sheds more light on what was at stake for the Americans in the War for Independence. The late Dr. M. E. Bradford of the University of Dallas said that the patriots feared that if they lost the war, one of England's retaliatory punishments against the colonies would have been to impose the Church of England upon the whole land, including those states founded by the Pilgrims, the Puritans, and the Quakers.[13] All of the religious freedom gained in 150 years of American history would have been thrown out the window! Furthermore, the Americans feared that should the English win the war, they would send over British Bishops to rule over the Americans. The Americans didn't want it—including devout Anglicans, like George Washington. So the American patriots of different denominations fought together—the Presbyterians with the Baptists, the Congregationalists of New England with the Anglicans, the Catholics of Baltimore with the Huguenots of Pennsylvania. And after they won the war, religious freedom and freedom of conscience were so important to the founders of this country that acceptance of the Constitution was conditional upon religious liberty being guaranteed in the document. That's why religious freedom is the first one listed in the Bill of Rights.

There was to be no state church in America but freedom of conscience. Nineteenth-century Supreme Court Justice Joseph Story pointed out that the First Amendment was able to solve a centuries-old problem that has plagued Christendom: "It [the First Amendment] thus cut off the means of religious persecution (the vice and pest of former ages) and of the subversion of the rights of conscience in matters of religion which had been trampled upon almost from the days of the Apostles to the present age."[14]

Unfortunately, the civil libertarians of our day have totally twisted the meaning of the religious clauses of the First Amendment—as we saw in the last chapter—and turned them into a virtual search-and-destroy mission against any vestige of religion in the public square.

The Founding Fathers gave us a system, built on Christian

principles, where the atheist, the Muslim, the Jew, the Christian, the Buddhist, anybody was able to build a church, worship God, stand on a street corner or housetop and proclaim his or her views, publish books, and do anything without any kind of repression from government in a Christian nation.

A few hundred years ago, there was nothing like the religious freedom we have enjoyed in the United States. The Pilgrims fled the religious persecution of England, which we look at as a very free nation. But it certainly was not. There was no nation on earth 218 years ago in which there existed anything vaguely resembling the civil freedoms that were built into the Constitution by the founders of this country. And this is a bequest of Christianity to the world! As John Quincy Adams asseverated:

> The birth-day of the nation is indissolubly linked with the birth-day of the Saviour [and] forms a leading event in the progress of the gospel dispensation . . . the Declaration of Independence first organized the social compact on the foundation of the Redeemer's mission upon earth [and] laid the corner stone of human government upon the first precepts of Christianity.[15]

The idea that civil liberties were somehow inconsistent with Christianity is not what the founders felt. They believed that this was the civil blossoming of the principles of Christianity found in the Bible.

The perfections of this religious freedom did not spring full blown like Athena from the head of Zeus. Rather, it took some time and experimentation and trial and error to work out the flaws and perfect the system that was developing from 1620 for the next 160 years. It went through various stages as it progressed those many decades, and it climaxed with the first amendment to the Constitution with its guarantee of religious freedom.

## WHAT ABOUT SLAVERY?

But what about slavery? How can we meaningfully discuss civil liberties when hundreds of thousands of Americans were in bondage solely because of the color of their skin? At the founding of America and at the Constitutional Convention, there was considerable discussion about this. And there were many in the North who wanted to write slavery out of the Union by disallowing it in the Constitution. There were those in the South who actually wanted it written into the Constitution. We almost had the Civil War in 1787—except there would not have been a war; there just would not have been a union. In order to preserve and create a United States of America, they compromised on this issue and allowed slavery to continue. In the process of enlightenment, it would take the next eighty years for that compromise to be finally resolved in the Civil War. The Constitution was then amended so that blacks were citizens just as much as whites. Even then, after the war, discrimination against blacks was still embedded in American life. It would take another hundred years and the courage of a Baptist minister, Dr. Martin Luther King, Jr., before a semblance of fairness would be achieved.

Full liberty and full truth have never leaped from humanity in a complete form. For example, scientific truth did not leap from the mind of Francis Bacon in a complete form, nor did it from any of the other founders of the branches of science. There are no Athenas, but there is one Christ, Jesus of Nazareth, who has inspired civil liberties like no one before Him or since. In the same way that in science each generation passes down its collected body of knowledge, so in Christianity, each generation passes down its accumulated knowledge, ever tweaking the Christian conscience. We have a revelation that came to us complete, but even within that revelation there is a progress of revelation, from Genesis to the book of Revelation. And then our understanding of that revelation has grown over the centuries.

# OBSERVATIONS OF DE TOCQUEVILLE

Alexis de Tocqueville, a Frenchman who traveled throughout America in 1830, was astonished to see that though the American people were quite religious, they were also most free. He wrote: "The Americans combine the notions of Christianity and of liberty so intimately in their minds, that it is impossible to make them conceive the one without the other."[16] And in another passage, he observed:

> There is no country in the whole world in which the Christian religion retains a greater influence over the souls of men than in America and there can be no greater proof of its utility, and of its conformity to human nature, than that its influence is most powerfully felt over the most enlightened and free nation on earth.[17]

This was the result of the pure proclamation of the gospel of Christ, over against the situation in France. "In France I had almost always seen the spirit of religion and the spirit of freedom pursuing courses diametrically opposed to each other, but in America I found that they were intimately united, and that they reigned in common over the same country."[18]

## CONTRAST OF THE AMERICAN REVOLUTION WITH THE FRENCH REVOLUTION

When it comes to liberty of conscience, religious liberty, and civil liberty, it is interesting to note the vast difference between the American Revolution and the French Revolution. As de Tocqueville pointed out, in France religion and liberty were seen as antithetical; the only way to gain liberty was to break the chains of religion.

So, in their revolution, the French cracked down on the Church and confiscated its properties. They desecrated the altar at Notre Dame by placing atop it a naked woman—the symbol of reason. They did away with *Anno Domini*, the Year of Our Lord, and made 1792 their year one, the first of the Republic—a Republic without God, and soon a Republic that was subject to chaos, anarchy, and finally tyranny.

As always happens when religion is banished, tyranny resulted. In Paris, more than 20,000 were killed in a wave of terror brought on by the Revolution. The streets ran with blood. They did not find liberty; they found tyranny, and the country was plunged into desperate wars and a time of great bondage. But in America, where we did not sever faith and freedom, we found the greatest liberty.

# LIBERTY VS. LICENSE

However, we are approaching in this country today a situation somewhat similar to France of the 1780s—where sin becomes flagrant and the morals debased. Many people today are beginning to look at Christianity as an impediment to the continuation of their "freedom"—to sin. But they have transformed liberty into license, and in the worst form of licentiousness, they don't want anybody speaking against that or in any way restraining them. Hence, the modern hedonist views Christianity as repressive and not liberating.

Setting out to set themselves free—to fulfill all of their lusts—the hedonists find themselves ultimately in bondage to tyranny. As Edmund Burke said, "There must be some restraining influence upon the wills and passions of men, and the less there is from within, the more there must be from without."[19]

# CONCLUSION

Civil liberties are a gift of Christianity to the world, and even at this time, on the eve of the year 2000, those countries that enjoy the most civil liberty are generally those lands where the gospel has penetrated most. After a Christian foundation was laid for this nation, people of *all* faiths were welcome and given freedom of conscience as they could find in no other place on earth. America became a refuge for the persecuted, the downtrodden, the poor. "In the process of time thousands have come among us," said the great Charles Hodge of Princeton. He continued:

All are welcomed; all are admitted to equal rights and privileges. All are allowed to acquire property, and to vote in every election, made eligible to all offices, and invested with equal influences in all public affairs. All are allowed to worship as they please, or not to worship at all, if they see fit. No man is molested for his religion or for his want of religion. No man is required to profess any form of faith, or to join any religious association. More than this cannot reasonably be demanded. More, however, is demanded. The infidel demands that the government should be conducted on the principle that Christianity is false. The atheist demands that it should be conducted on the assumption that there is no God. And the positivist on the principle that man is not a free moral agent. . . . The sufficient answer to all is that it cannot possibly be done.[20]

# CHAPTER 7

# THINKING GOD'S THOUGHTS AFTER HIM

## Christianity's Impact on Science

*Then God blessed them, and God said to them, "Be fruitful and multiply; fill the earth and subdue it; have dominion over . . . every living thing that moves upon the earth."*

(Gen. 1:28)

**O**urs is pre-eminently the scientific age, where science has come to its mastery of the world. It used to be said that we live in the age of the steam engine or the electric age. Now, more properly, it is called the nuclear age, the atomic age, the electronic age, the computer age, the information age, or the space age. All of which is simply to say that we live, unquestionably, in the age of science.

It may seem strange to many people that we would include a chapter on science in a book on the blessings Christianity has bequeathed to the world. Hasn't religion always been the enemy of science? No! Furthermore, many scholars agree that the scientific revolution that gained great momentum in the seventeenth century was birthed for the most part by Reformed Christianity.[1] If Jesus had never been born, science would likely not have come into being.

Think of all the ways in which our lives have been improved by the scientific revolution. I believe that had Christ never come, you would not be reading this book by electric light. You would not have a microwave oven, a television, or a radio. If Christ had never been born, there would be no computer or microchips, no planes or rocket ships. If Christ had never been born, we would never have had the scientific revolution that came into being when people began to "think God's thoughts after Him."

A number of scholars have commented on how Christianity gave birth to modern science. Francis Schaeffer mentions a few of them:

Both Alfred North Whitehead (1861–1947) and J. Robert Oppenheimer (1904–1967) have stressed that modern science was born out of the Christian world view. Whitehead was a widely respected mathematician and philosopher, and Oppenheimer, after he became director of the Institute for Advanced Study at Princeton in 1947, wrote on a wide range of subjects related to science. . . . Whitehead [in his 1925 book, *Science and the Modern World*] said that Christianity is the mother of science because of "the medieval insistence on the rationality of God."[2]

What is science and what is the Christian view of it? *Science* comes from the Latin term *scientia*, which simply means "knowledge." God is said to be *omniscientia*, or omniscient—all knowing. But modern science is that peculiar blend of deduction and induction, of rationalism and empiricism that came into being in the sixteenth century and has given rise to what we know as the Scientific Age.

## SCIENCE AND CHRISTIANITY

What is the relationship between science and Christianity? Books and articles have been written *ad infinitum, ad nauseum,* for many years by skeptics and various unbelievers, stating that science and Christianity are antithetical; they are opposites and can have nothing to do with one another. A person had to choose either to be a superstitious religionist, as they would describe a Christian, or a scientist; but never the twain could meet. And all manner of unbelieving scientists were wont to describe it in those terms.

It is interesting how the worm has turned and things have changed. Science, in the last few decades, has come upon, in some ways, some very difficult times with the advent of ecology and with the whole new generation of hippies in the 1960s and 1970s that rose up to declare that science is a Frankenstein monster that is destroying the planet. Rather than being a sacred cow, science—according to many of these people—is more like a rampaging bull in an earthly china shop, threatening to destroy everything. So the ecologist has blamed the ills of humankind on science. It is very interesting how attitudes toward the relationship of Christianity to science have changed. I have one book after another, written by ecologically minded people, who are also unbelievers, who now point out that it is because of Christianity that we have science and that Christianity is to blame for the whole thing.

## THE ORIGINS OF SCIENCE

Where did science really come from? It all began about six hundred years before Christ with the Greek philosophers who began to seek a nontheological answer for the existence of life and the arrangement of the natural world. Efforts were made in a protoscientific direction. However, the Greeks never developed anything like modern science or we might have had the nuclear and space age in 100 B.C.! The Greek mind looked upon the natural world largely as simply an exercise for the magnificent Greek reason. The world was not to be changed. It was not to be used; it was simply to be understood. It was a mental gymnastics game. So they applied the rational deduction systems they developed to nature and came up with many great and interesting facts. But it never developed into "the scientific age."

Dr. Malcom Jeeves ponders the question why the Greeks never went further in their scientific queries in his book *The Scientific Enterprise and the Christian Faith*. He points out that a unique blend of Greek thinking with a specific strand of Christianity—namely, the Reformed faith—birthed modern science. Jeeves writes:

It was with the rediscovery of the Bible and of its message at the time of the Reformation . . . that a new impetus came to the development of science. This new impetus, flowing together with all that was best in Greek thinking, was to produce the right mixture to detonate the chain reaction leading to the explosion of knowledge which began at the start of the scientific revolution in the sixteenth century, and which is proceeding with ever-increasing momentum today.[3]

Not only did science not *develop* with the Greeks, but it is also true that science would not have originated among the Hebrew people—it did not and would not—for the simple reason that to the Hebrews, as you recall in the Psalms, the natural world was simply an occasion for praise to the Creator. "The heavens declare the glory of God; and the firmament shows His handiwork" (Ps. 19:1).

Nor could modern science ever have come into existence among the Arabs, because of the Muslim religion. The writings of Aristotle, when lost to the Western world from about A.D. 500 to A.D. 1100, were kept by the Arabs of north Africa and finally reintroduced into Europe in the 1100s and 1200s. Aristotle—unlike Plato—had a philosophy that would lend itself to the scientific type of study because it was more inductive than Plato's deductive kind of reasoning. Plato would get an ideal and *deduce* all manner of things from it. Aristotle would tend to look at the particulars and *induce* principles from them. Because of the Aristotelian thought they had access to, the Arabs—including the Nestorian Christians—generally made greater scientific and mathematical advances than the Europeans during the Middle Ages.

But during all of that time the Arabs never introduced nor ever created any real science. Why? Because of their religion. Because of the fatalism that dominates the Muslim religion. Since everything is fatalistically determined, obviously there is no point in trying to manipulate the natural world to change anything, because all things are unchangeable.

Science could never have come into being among the animists of central or southern Africa or many other places in the world because they never would have begun to experiment on the natural world, since everything—whether stones or trees or animals or anything else—contained within it living spirits of various gods or ancestors.

Nor could science have originated in India among the Hindus, nor in China among the Buddhists, for both Hinduism and Buddhism teach that the physical world is unreal and that the only reality is that of the world's soul and that the greatest thing anyone has to learn is that the physical world is not real. Therefore, there would have been no point in spending one's life fooling with that which had no reality in the first place.

It waited for Christianity to come and take several of the different strains and weave them together to produce in the sixteenth century the phenomenon we know as modern science. It was because of a number of basic teachings of Christianity. First of all is the fact that there is a rational God who is the source of all truth, and that this world is a rational world. This gave rise to the possibility of scientific laws.

It is interesting to note that science could not originate in the philosophical view prevalent in the world today. The prevailing philosophy of the Western world today is existentialism, which is irrational. It would not be possible for science to develop in an irrational world because science is based on the fact that if water boils at 212 degrees today, it will boil at 212 degrees tomorrow, and the same thing the next day, and that there are certain laws and regularities that control the universe. This all stems from the Christian concept of the God who created a world—a God who is rational and who created a rational world.

## THE CULTURAL MANDATE

Another concept that Christianity brought to light was the "cultural mandate" from Genesis that we quoted in the beginning of this chapter, where God said to man at the beginning to have dominion over the earth. The Christians in the sixteenth century, for the first time, took seriously and systematically worked out the implications of the Lordship of Christ over all realms of the earth. If Jesus Christ were to be King of all of the earth; if He were Lord of lords and King of kings; if His kingdom were to rule over all of the earth; if this kingdom were not only to be over the hearts of men but over every sphere of human society; if Christ were to be all in all; and if all of the things found in the natural world were there for the glory of God and for the well-being of his fellow man; then man was to have dominion over them. He was to take them and shape them and use them for his own well-being, the well-being of his neighbor, and the glory of God. The world was not here simply to be understood as the Greeks thought, nor merely to be a cause for worship as the Hebrews thought, nor merely to be denied in its existence as the Hindus thought, nor to be worshiped as the animists thought, but it was here as a creation of a great Creator, made for His glory and our good.

Another basic concept that led to science was the doctrine of sin. It became clear that man was sinful, and that man's sinfulness and his total depravity were taken seriously for the first time. It was realized by the Reformers of the sixteenth century that every faculty of man, including the mind, was depraved; therefore, human reason could not be depended on to come to all truth, as the Greeks had proudly supposed. Because of man's sinfulness and his propensity to twist things to his own desires, it was necessary for reason to be backed up with experimentation. Science, you may remember, is a blend of reason and experimentation, rationalism and empiricism. It is this combination of deduction and induction that leads to science and to all of its achievements. Therefore, all rationalism was to be backed up by experimentation. But the Christian, especially the Calvinistic Christian, taking very seriously the total depravity of man, thought that even the experimentation of man could be twisted to sinful ends. Therefore, it was to be always evaluated in the light of the Scriptures, for the Christian believes that God has revealed Himself in two books—the book of nature and the book of Scripture—in general revelation and in special revelation. The man who is credited with developing the scientific method, Francis Bacon, said as much when he wrote: "There are two books laid before us to study, to prevent our falling into error; first, the volume of the Scriptures, which reveal the will of God; then the volume of the Creatures, which express His power."[4]

And so, the deep study of these two books—the creation and the written word of the Creator—gave rise to modern science.

# THE CHRISTIAN ROOTS OF MODERN SCIENCE

Modern science began, observes Francis Schaeffer, when the Aristotelian view of the universe was questioned scientifically.[5] What was at stake in the Copernican revolution? Many modern secularists will tell you it was a biblical cosmology. In reality it was an Aristotelian cosmology that was shaken to the core by Copernicus. Only by imposing Aristotelian thought on the Bible did the Church mistakenly, misguidedly, censure Galileo in 1632. Schaeffer elaborates:

> The foundation for modern science can be said to have been laid at Oxford when scholars there attacked Thomas Aquinas's teaching by proving that his chief authority, Aristotle, made certain mistakes about natural phenomena. . . . When the Roman Church attacked Copernicus and Galileo (1564–1642), it was not because their teaching actually contained anything contrary to the Bible. The church authorities thought it did, but that was because Aristotelian elements had become part of church orthodoxy, and Galileo's notions clearly conflicted with them. In fact, Galileo defended the compatibility of Copernicus and the Bible, and this was one of the factors which brought about his trial.[6]

In recent years, the Roman Catholic Church issued a public apology for its censure of Galileo, and the pope affirmed the important place of science in our lives.

## PROTESTANTISM AND SCIENCE

James Moore of the Open University, Milton Keynes, England, writes that there is "distinct and plausible evidence that Protestantism gave rise to modern science."[7] For example, Lutherans were intimately involved in the subsidization, publication, and dissemination of Copernicus's book, *De Revolutionibus*.[8] Moore points out that in the sixteenth century the Lutherans (including Johannes Kepler) helped to pave the way to scientific development, and in the seventeenth century it was the Calvinists who led the way.

One of the great organizations that helped to propel science and scientific advances was the Royal Society of London for Improving Natural Knowledge, founded in 1660. Most of its members were professing Christians. The Royal Society began in a Christian College, Gresham College of London. In fact, Gresham was a Puritan college; therefore, it was purely Bible-oriented. Moore writes:

> There [at Gresham College] in 1645, Theodore Haak, inspired by the Moravian educator J.A. Comenius,[9] commenced informal gatherings which in 1661 became the Royal Society of London. Seven of the ten scientists who formed the nucleus of those meetings were Puritans. In 1663 sixty-two per cent of the members of the Royal Society were clearly Puritan by origin—at a time when Puritans were only a small minority in England.[10]

Moore concludes that the exact *reason* why Protestantism "encouraged the birth of modern science" is disputed, but that some historians view the Protestant emphasis on the priesthood of all believers as a significant factor. He also points out that there were important scientists of the sixteenth and seventeenth centuries who were Roman Catholic.[11]

# PIONEERS OF SCIENCE— COMMITTED CHRISTIANS

Some of the greatest pioneers of science were committed Christians. Johannes Kepler (1571–1630) coined the phrase that is the title of this chapter: "Thinking God's thoughts after Him." When a scientist is engaged in the study of nature, he is looking for what laws God set up in nature. Kepler wrote: "Since we astronomers are priests of the highest God in regard to the book of nature, it befits us to be thoughtful, not of the glory of our minds, but rather, above all else, of the glory of God."[12] Kepler wrote in *The Mystery of the Universe*: "Now, as God the maker played, He taught the game to Nature, Whom He created in His Image."[13]

Another godly pioneer of science was Blaise Pascal (1623–1662), whose work was so great he now has a computer language named after him. Pascal not only made innovations in mathematics and probability science and invented the first working barometer, but he was also a devout Christian of a particular sect in France, known as the Jansenites. The Jansenites were a "Calvinistic quasi-Protestant group within the Catholic Church."[14] Pascal wrote a Christian devotional classic, known as the *Pensees*, which is a defense of the Christian faith. Pascal wrote: "Faith tells us what the senses cannot, but it is not contrary to their findings. It simply transcends, without contradicting them."[15]

Pascal used his probing, scientific mind to make a compelling apologetic for Christianity. He wrote: "Jesus Christ is the only proof of the living God. We only know God through Jesus Christ."[16] Pascal points out that the knowledge we have about God goes beyond what we can detect in our minds.

The Christian's God does not merely consist of a God who is the Author of mathematical truths and the order of the elements. That is the notion of the heathen and the Epicureans. . . . But the God of Abraham, the God of Isaac, the God of Jacob, the God of the Christians, is a God of love and consolation.[17]

Another great scientist who viewed science as thinking God's thoughts after Him was Isaac Newton (1642–1727), who wrote voluminously on theology as well as science. Newton is well-known for his piety, although he harbored some doubts. While he is sometimes classified as a Unitarian,[18] he professed to believe in Christ and in the message of salvation.[19] Newton had a strong faith in God that undergirded his scientific world view. He wrote in *Principia*: "This most beautiful system of the sun, planets, and comets, could only proceed from the counsel and dominion of an intelligent and powerful Being."[20] Francis Schaeffer points out that humanists regret that Newton spent so much time near the end of his life writing about the Bible rather than studying the creation independent of the Creator.[21] This criticism is predicated on their assumption that science and Scripture conflict, whereas it was the Bible that gave rise to modern science! Newton said: "I have a foundational belief in the Bible as the Word of God, written by men who were inspired. I study the Bible daily."[22]

This great scientist had this to say on the subject of unbelief: "Atheism is so senseless. When I look at the solar system, I see the earth at the right distance from the sun to receive the proper amounts of heat and light. This did not happen by chance."[23]

Another great scientist who was a Christian was Michael Faraday (1791–1867). Faraday made his greatest contributions in the study of electricity. He discovered electromagnetic induction and invented the generator.[24] Schaeffer observes that Faraday belonged to a Christian fellowship group of scientists whose position was "Where the Scriptures speak, we speak; where the Scriptures are silent, we are silent."[25] He was an active member of his Bible-oriented church and is reported to have had a strong "abiding" faith in the Bible and in prayer.[26]

# SCIENTISTS WHO WERE CREATIONISTS

In a debate on creation-evolution held in our church several years ago, the evolutionist-scientist made the incredible claim not only that creationism wasn't scientific, but that creationists, therefore, were not scientists. The truth is that creationists gave the world science! Creationists invented science! Without creationists there wouldn't be science.

Here is a list of some of the outstanding Bible-believing scientists who *founded* the following branches of science, some of whom we've already met.[27]

Antiseptic surgery, Joseph Lister
Bacteriology, Louis Pasteur
Calculus, Isaac Newton
Celestial Mechanics, Johannes Kepler
Chemistry, Robert Boyle
Comparative Anatomy, Georges Cuvier
Computer Science, Charles Babbage
Dimensional Analysis, Lord Rayleigh
Dynamics, Isaac Newton
Electronics, John Ambrose Fleming
Electrodynamics, James Clerk Maxwell
Electromagnetics, Michael Faraday
Energetics, Lord Kelvin
Entomology of Living Insects, Henri Fabre
Field Theory, Michael Faraday
Fluid Mechanics, George Stokes
Galactic Astronomy, Sir William Herschel
Gas Dynamics, Robert Boyle
Genetics, Gregor Mendel
Glacial Geology, Louis Agassiz
Gynecology, James Simpson
Hydrography, Matthew Maury
Hydrostatics, Blaise Pascal
Ichthyology, Louis Agassiz
Isotopic Chemistry, William Ramsey
Model Analysis, Lord Rayleigh
Natural History, John Ray
Non-Euclidean Geometry, Bernard Riemann
Oceanography, Matthew Maury
Optical Mineralogy, David Brewster

And on it goes. All of these founders were Bible believers and believers in creation.

Creationists are not scientists? Creationists invented science! Therefore, to say that creationists are not scientists or that creationism is not science is not only totally false, but it is ludicrous as well. Creationism violates none of the laws of science as evolution does, but is in complete harmony with them.

# THE GLASSES HAVE BEEN THROWN AWAY

Calvin said that the Bible—God's special revelation—was spectacles that we must put on if we are to correctly read the book of nature—God's revelation in creation. Unfortunately, between the beginning of science and our day, many scientists have discarded these glasses, and many distortions have followed.

What has been the result? In the beginning, science was looked upon as the handmaiden of theology; the study of the creation was to lead men to the adoration of the Creator. It was not inconsistent, then, for someone like Isaac Newton, who was an incredible innovator in science, to write as much about theology as he did about science. Yet we know that in the last century, especially with the advent of the theory of evolution, science has fallen to a large extent into hands that are inimical to the Christian faith and has instead been forged into a weapon that has perhaps been the most deadly ever forged against Christianity.

A clear example that evolution proved fatal to many people's belief in Christianity is what happened in Victorian England. Prior to Darwin's ideological revolution, evangelicalism in England was vibrant and flourishing. Missionaries were sent across the globe. With the appearance of Darwinism, many Victorians lost their faith in evangelicalism because they were presented with a false dichotomy; science *or* the Bible. Today, fewer than 5 percent of people in England attend church. According to Ravi Zacharias, the very church in England that sent William Carey (the father of the modern missionary movement) to India two centuries ago was recently converted to a Hindu temple to accommodate Indian immigrants![28] Christianity has suffered greatly in Mother England, a country that has played a critical role in the history of Christianity. Although there may be many other factors to this, Darwin's theory appears to be one of the biggest causes of this apostasy.

Many young people today, when asked about Christianity, assume that science has disproved God. Asked why they do not believe the Bible, they say that the Bible has been disproved. When this is further probed, it turns out that the main area in which they feel the Bible has been disproved is the creation of man, or the creation of the world—the creation of life. They say that supposedly evolution has been proved; it has overthrown the doctrine of creation; it is believed by all intelligent scientists, therefore, that the Bible is not true.

Now, since we base our faith on the Scriptures, what then is the attitude we should have as far as science and the Scriptures are concerned? Do they contradict each other? One thing we should note: A complete harmony of science and the Bible is not possible. Many people fail to see this. That is because they do not understand the nature of science. Science, unlike revelation, is always progressing in its search for the truth. It never arrives at final or absolute truth. It is always seeking to know more. It presents one hypothesis and then replaces it with another and then another.

All one has to do is trace the various hypotheses and theories that have been put forth by science in all sorts of fields over the last fifty or one hundred years to see how true this is. In any science book written fifty years ago, we might find that half of its conclusions are discarded today. For example, at the beginning of this century evolutionists said that the entire human endocrine system, including the pituitary, the thyroid, and all of the other glands of the endocrine system, were totally without present function and that they were vestigial remains of some previous ancestry. Today we know that they simply run the entire chemical process of the body.

The atomic age also destroyed an age-old scientific belief that the atom was indivisible. In fact, the word *atom* comes from the Greek word *atomos*, from *tomos*, "cut," and the privative *a*. Together they mean "that which cannot be cut." Yet we know today that this is not true. Many are the theories that have been set forth, and then abandoned.

## "THE BIBLE'S NOT A SCIENCE TEXTBOOK"

Every once in a while, you'll hear someone say that the Bible is not a science textbook. It is basically a book of religion. Therefore, we are to believe it when it speaks on matters of faith and duty, but when it gets into scientific or historical areas, we are to recognize that "these people did the best they could, but they were speaking from their own age and their own limitations."

This view has been very palatable to many because it seems to solve the problem by taking science and locking it into an airtight room over here, and taking the Bible and locking it into an airtight room over there, and thus we have taken care of the combatants in this way. But it really doesn't solve anything at all, I believe, for the simple reason that science and history and theology, as has been well pointed out, are not three distinct branches of knowledge. They are simply three different ways in which we view the reality we find around us, just as length and breadth and depth are three different ways we view any physical object. Since they are not three distinct branches of knowledge, they cannot be separated.

Take, for example, the central and cardinal doctrine of the Christian faith: the resurrection of Jesus Christ. Is that theological? Historical? Or scientific? Why, a moment's reflection would tell you that it is obviously all three. Almost every branch of science is involved in the resurrection of Christ, from anatomy and biology to physics and chemistry. Obviously, it is a historical fact; it is the most important historical fact in the world. It was recorded by eyewitnesses and testified to by many others, and histories have been written about it. It is the basis and centrality of the Christian theological viewpoint that Jesus Christ was dead and He rose again. Yet if we remove from that truth its scientific and historical aspects, what do we have left? A myth and nothing more. With this view the Bible is destroyed as a basis for sound belief. It is interesting to note that the churches that have based their views on this approach to science and religion have progressively lost their congregations because they instinctively know that there is nothing there but froth, and they will not tolerate being deceived.

The only approach is the one Christ took: The Bible is the very Word of God and cannot be broken, whether it speaks upon historical or scientific matters. When it speaks, it speaks the truth. It is not a scientific textbook. It is not a textbook on religion. It is not a textbook at all; it is a revelation from God! But it does touch on scientific matters in a very embryonic form, and when it does, those statements are true.

## THE ISSUE OF ORIGINS

The main reason why people today fail to see the connection between Christianity and the creation of science is because of the misunderstanding on origins. We have been told for so long that evolution is a proven fact that many people have bought this lie —hook, line and sinker. They forget the fact that the basic tenets of the scientific method are that it must be observable, testable, repeatable, and falsifiable. The fact of the matter is that neither evolution nor creationism fully meets the rigorous demands of science. Therefore, neither really falls into the realm of objective science.

Our purpose in this chapter is not to address the creation-evolution debate, but rather to show the link between Christianity and the creation of modern science. For the reader who wants to know more about creation-evolution, a wide variety of books now document how there are no known transitional forms, from amoeba to trilobites, from birds to reptiles, from ape to man. There are no intermediate links. These books include *Evolution: The Fossils Say No*, by Duane Gish; Luther Sunderland's *Darwin's Enigma*; and Wm. R. Fix's *The Bone Peddlers*. Fix is a nonevangelical who believes in theistic evolution (even though he refutes much of the evidence for evolution!). There are numerous other books we could recommend, such as Wendell Bird's monumental work *The Origin of Species Revisited: The Theories of Evolution and of Abrupt Appearance* (1987), Ian Taylor's

*In the Minds of Men* (1987), and Michael Denton's *Evolution: A Theory in Crisis* (1986).

## CONCLUSION

All sorts of good things have been harnessed by modern science for our everyday use. Had Jesus never come, it is unlikely science would ever have come to be. Take a break from reading this book and look around you. What do you see? Electric lights? An electric clock? A stereo? A television? A computer? If Jesus had never come, I strongly doubt these would have ever been invented.

There would be no satellites; there would be no airplanes. If you went to work today, you would probably have gone by foot or horse or donkey or camel. You would not have fixed your breakfast on an electric stove or in a microwave oven, for such things would not exist. You would not have fixed your toast in a toaster. Countless other benefits of science would not exist if Christ had not been born.

# CHAPTER 8

# FREE ENTERPRISE AND THE WORK ETHIC

## Christianity's Impact on Economics

*"Thou shalt not steal, . . . Thou shalt not covet."*

(Exod. 20:15, 17)

**F**idel Castro has on occasion reluctantly admitted that he admires many of the evangelicals in Cuba. This is because they are hard workers; they show up to work on time; they don't cheat the system. In short, although he would vehemently disagree with their world view, the Communist dictator recognizes the *utilitarian* value of their putting into practice the Christian work ethic. This is the same ethic that helped to bring about prosperity in America, which he so often vilifies.

If Jesus had never been born, it is unlikely that capitalism and the free enterprise system—which has brought unparalleled prosperity to billions of people—would ever have developed. In this chapter, I will trace the links between the Christian faith and the prosperity enjoyed in the West, particularly in the United States. As John Chamberlain writes in *The Roots of Capitalism*, "Christianity tends to create a capitalistic mode of life whenever siege conditions do not prevail."[1]

## AS A NATION THINKETH

Why has America—and for the most part, the West—enjoyed such material abundance? Why have some of the Asian countries also prospered *after* they adopted economic ideas from the West? If you look at the poor nations around the world, you will find that what the Bible says is true: They are what they are because of what they believe. "As a man thinketh in his heart, so is he" (Prov. 23:7 KJV). Look at India, a nation that has stagnated in its poverty for several millennia. Why? Because of what its people believe. Its Hindu religion teaches that there is no reality to matter. The external, visible world is unreal; therefore, you do not try to correct an unreal world; you try to escape from it. Consequently, progress dies. And the belief in reincarnation has also had a devastating effect on the nation's poverty. Or consider North Africa, which for centuries has been sunk in poverty, superstition, and ignorance. Why? Because of what its people believe. The fatalism of Islam has kept the Muslims from progress because human initiative can accomplish absolutely nothing, and all that is, Allah has fated; therefore, they are left in perpetual stagnation. Or consider the many nations of the East (prior to Western influence) whose religion is Buddhism, which teaches that life is irreparably evil and cannot be changed. Man's only hope is to rid himself of all desire for any improvement in this life. The goal is not a more abundant life, but it is extinction—absorption into the world-soul—and so the very roots of social amelioration are severed. Not so with the nations that have had a Christian base, especially when they have applied a more biblical interpretation of economics.

## THE BIBLICAL FOUNDATION

Larry Burkett, the founder and director of Christian Financial Concepts, points out that the Bible—with more than 700 references to money[2]—says more about economics than many other subjects. He writes:

Money is such an important subject that nearly two-thirds of the parables that Christ left us deal with the use and handling of it. That alone should tell us the importance of understanding God's plan for finances.[3]

What does the Bible say about economics? In the Decalogue (the Ten Commandments) alone, we have a sound endorsement of private property, the foundation for all good economics. The commandment "Thou shalt not steal" (Exod. 20:15), as virtually every theologian for twenty centuries has declared, is a divine guarantee of private property. I cannot steal something from you if you do not own it. Furthermore, in the Decalogue, we even have the command, "Thou shalt not covet thy neighbor's house . . . nor anything that is thy neighbor's" (Exod. 20:17). Again, a clear teaching of private property.

This is a critical point because private property is the foundation of capitalism, which is often defined as "the private ownership of the means of production." Author John Chamberlain, in *The Roots of Capitalism*, expounds:

> "Thou shalt not steal" means that the Bible countenances private property—for if a thing is not owned in the first place it can scarcely be stolen. "Thou shalt not covet" means that it is sinful even to contemplate the seizure of another man's goods—which is something which Socialists, whether Christian or otherwise, have never managed to explain away. Furthermore, the prohibitions against false witness and adultery mean that contracts should be honored and double-dealing eschewed. As for the Commandment to "honor thy father and thy mother that thy days may be long," this implies that the family, not the State, is the basic continuing unit and constitutive element of society.
>
> By extension, or deduction, the Lockean creed is all here: the right to life, the right to liberty and property necessary to sustain life, and the importance of the free family unit as the guarantor, through its love and possessions, of "long" days in the land given by the Lord.
>
> The Bible-reading colonists, then, had no actual need for the sophisticians of late Seventeenth Century political science. They were the children of antiquity, heirs to the oldest wisdom known to western man.[4]

Some people, however, argue that the Bible teaches socialism —the antithesis of private property. For a proof-text, they point to the passage in Acts 5, where Ananias and his wife sold a piece of land and gave the money to the apostles, but kept back a part of the price for themselves. Many liberal theologians and economists use this and other New Testament passages concerning the early Christians, who often pooled their resources, to imply that the Bible teaches socialism. Is private property repudiated here or is it taught? Notice what Peter said to Ananias: "While it [this property] remained, was it not your own?" (Acts 5:4). It is difficult for me to imagine any clearer statement of the ownership of property than that! While it remained . . . before you sold it . . . was it not your own? Did you not own it? Could you not do with it whatever you wanted? Even after you sold it, was not the money your own? he said, showing Ananias that he even controlled the capital he had earned from the sale.

Another biblical foundation that contributed to the rise of capitalism is the fact that labor is a God-given responsibility. Work is neither a curse to be avoided nor an activity to be pursued only when necessary. On the contrary, God ordained work before the fall. It is *not* a part of the curse. Adam was commanded to tend the garden before he fell into sin. Even after sin (although it is greatly aggravated by the results of the fall and the curse), it is still true that work occupies a very important position in man's life.

Prior to Christ, the nations of antiquity despised honest work and consigned it to slaves. As we saw in chapter 2, three-quarters of Athens and half of the Roman Empire were made up of slaves. We get a taste of how "gentlemen" did no labor in ancient Greece in Acts 17, when Paul visited the Athenians to spread the gospel there: "For all the Athenians and the foreigners who were there spent their time in nothing else but either to tell or to hear some new thing" (Acts 17:21).

But Jesus revolutionized labor. By picking up the saw, the hammer, and the plane, he imbued labor with a new dignity. Over the centuries, where the gospel worked its way into and throughout a land, it transformed the slaves and serfs into people of the working classes. Without work, it is impossible for any human being to fulfill the probation that God has given in this life.

# THE FATHER OF ACCOUNTING

Another contribution of Christianity to economics was double-entry bookkeeping and accounting, bequeathed to the world by an Italian Franciscan monk of the Renaissance. Fra Luca Pacioli, who is recognized as the father of modern accounting, published a revolutionary book in 1494, *Summa de Arithmetica, Geometria, Proportioni et Proportionalita*. The book deals primarily with mathematics, but contains a chapter on double-entry bookkeeping that is the basis for our modern accounting. Goethe said that this was "one of the finest discoveries of the human intellect."[5] An economist and sociologist, Werner Sombart, said, "Double-entry bookkeeping is born with the same spirit as the system of Galileo and Newton."[6]

Pacioli's work was dedicated to the glory of God. His goal was to write on the science *and theology* of mathematics—to take it "out of the library" and see it put into practical use in the marketplace. He wrote in the *Summa* that people should begin all their economic transactions "in the name of God." The methodology he developed changed the future of business forever and led to the development of spread sheets. His ingenious accounting equation of "Assets = Liabilities + Owner's Equity" is used worldwide today. This humble servant of Jesus Christ has provided the world a vital tool for business—to the greater glory of God.

# THE ROOTS OF FREE ENTERPRISE

The Protestant work ethic, which has helped bring about great prosperity, arose mostly through John Calvin and his followers. So also do we trace free enterprise back to the Master of Geneva. Historian Richard Dunn writes:

Was it mere coincidence that the most dynamic businessmen were to be found in Protestant Holland and the most vigorous industrial growth in Protestant England, both states heavily tinctured with Calvinism? Why were the Huguenots [French Calvinists] so prominent in the business community of Catholic France? Or Protestant Brandenburg-Prussia under the Calvinist Great Elector almost the only seventeenth-century German state to exhibit increasing prosperity?[7]

As historians know, John Calvin has often been credited with being the founder of capitalism. So tremendous was his influence in the economic realm that he has been accused by his enemies (such as the famous work by Max Weber) of all of the inequities of capitalism and all of its distortions.

# MAX WEBER'S THESIS

Max Weber wrote a famous book on this subject. In 1904–1905, he first published his classic *The Protestant Ethic and the Spirit of Capitalism*. He begins with the observation that business leaders, higher-trained workers, and the owners of capital were overwhelmingly Protestant. He then traces the link between the two, with few positive comments about Calvinism. For instance, Weber refers to "the motive to constant self-control and thus to a deliberate regulation of one's own life," which was a natural outworking of "the gloomy doctrine of Calvinism."[8] Weber also wrote: "Calvinism, in comparison [to Pietism], appears to be more closely related to the hard legalism and the active enterprise of bourgeois-capitalistic entrepeneurs."[9] Calvinists practiced what Weber describes as "worldly asceticism,"[10] which set the stage for the capitalist revolution. The Puritans, followers of Calvinism, viewed the attainment of wealth "as a fruit of labour in a calling" as "a sign of God's blessing."[11] Weber continues:

The religious valuation of restless, continuous, systematic work in a worldly calling, as the highest means to asceticism, and at the same time the surest and most evident proof of rebirth and genuine faith, must have been the most powerful conceivable lever for the expansion of that attitude toward life which we have here called the spirit of capitalism.[12]

Ernst Troeltsch also blamed all of capitalism on John Calvin. These historians, Weber and Troeltsch, who were opponents of capitalism and Calvinism, saw that John Calvin was, indeed, the great prime mover in this.

It is true that capitalism began to rise, at least in a nascent form, in the northern cities of Italy and the southern cities of Germany, prior to Calvin's time. But John Calvin was the first theologian who saw to the very heart of the matter and was willing to depart from the view that had been held for all of these centuries by the Roman Catholic Church, which was influenced by the teachings of Aristotle through Thomas Aquinas, who tried to harmonize Christian teaching with the views of Aristotle.

In about 400 B.C. Aristotle taught that money was sterile and nonproductive. This was the view of the Roman Catholic Church. Calvin saw that this was not true; in fact money could be exceedingly productive. The Roman Catholic Church had defined usury as any interest at all. This was the view of the Church for centuries.

A case can be made that the Church did this to help protect people from exploitation. Chamberlain writes:

Far from being the source and protector of the political and economic institutions of the Middle Ages, the Church was the buffer which defended the individual against the more abrasive trends of the times. Naturally, the church took a stand against usury in a period when there was no opportunity for money loans to expand into a fruitfulness that would reward both lender and borrower. Because money was quickly "used up" by the small-time medieval borrower, it seemed monstrous to Thomas Aquinas and other Catholic philosophers to compel men to pay interest on what was no longer there.[13]

But circumstances were changing.

Calvin saw that classifying usury as any interest was neither right nor biblical, and he redefined usury into the sense in which we know it; that is, that usury is the charging of *excessive* interest. Calvin also felt that no interest should be charged to the poor. Above all, the golden rule is to be the standard as to how economic transactions are to be conducted. Calvin writes:

> Reason does not suffer us to admit that all usury is to be condemned without exception. . . . I reply, that the question [as to when usury is to be prohibited] is only as to the poor, and consequently, if we have to do with the rich, that usury is freely permitted. . . . usury is not now unlawful, except in so far as it contravenes equity and brotherly union. Let each one, then, place himself before God's judgment-seat, and not do to his neighbour what he would not have done to himself, from whence a sure and infallible decision may be come to.[14]

In his classic book *Religion and the Rise of Capitalism*, R. H. Tawney writes of John Calvin:

> He assumes credit to be a normal and inevitable incident in the life of society. He therefore dismisses the oft-quoted passages from the Old Testament and the Fathers as irrelevant, because designed for conditions which no longer exist, argues that the payment of interest for capital is as reasonable as the payment of rent for land, and throws on the conscience of the individual the obligation of seeing that it does not exceed the amount dictated by natural justice and the golden rule.[15]

Calvin freed money from the bondage in which it had been held for centuries, and he unleashed the powers that capitalism has produced. And what are they? Well, there is no reason to question the fact that the free enterprise system in America has generated the highest standard of living of any nation on the face of the earth since the creation of the world. Even poor people in an industrialized nation are far better off than the average person in Third World nations. People on welfare in America would be considered rich in many nations of the world. Most of us do not realize that.

Calvin upheld the right of private property. He also taught the biblical concept of stewardship, that we are mere stewards of money entrusted to us by God, for which we will one day give account.

# THE PROTESTANT WORK ETHIC

When I was unregenerate, I made a C-average my first two years in college; after my conversion I made straight A's. The same thing is true in business: When people become Christians, they often begin to prosper. Why?

First, we are not concerned about anxiety. Worry, which so frustrates and limits people's ability, is taken away. The Scripture tells us: "Be anxious for nothing" (Phil. 4:6). Christ is going to provide for us.

Second, we have the aid and help of God who gives us additional strength to perform our tasks.

Third, we have new wisdom and ideas that come from God. "If any of you lacks wisdom, let him ask of God, who gives to all liberally" (James 1:5).

Fourth, the redeemed are given the power to persevere and continue on when others may fall to the side.

Fifth, we have a purpose for what we do. Our work, whatever that may be, is done to the glory of God. "Excellence in all things, and all things for the glory of God" is our motto at Coral Ridge Presbyterian Church.

Now, may I say there is a name for those five concepts I just mentioned? It is called the Puritan Work Ethic, the Protestant Work Ethic, or simply the Christian Work Ethic.

Because the redeemed have been given these enhanced abilities, they actually produce more. They produce more than they even want of this world's goods. Therefore, they are enabled to give far more. They are enabled to save far more. They are able to invest in tools. That is why, one hundred years after the founding of our country, Americans were saving more than any people in the world. We were investing more in tools. American workers in factories and on farms had more and better tools per capita, and used these tools more effectively, than the people of any other nation. Therefore, we enjoyed the world's highest standard of living.

The experience repeats itself today in Latin American countries. People often become wealthy, compared to their neighbors, as a by-product of becoming evangelicals or Christ-centered Catholics. They no longer drink or gamble away their money, and often for the first time they begin to save for the future. This same trend has been repeated throughout Church history.

In fact, it can even become a *problem* clearly stated in Deuteronomy: As people become more prosperous, they tend to forget God as their source for wealth (see Deut. 6:10–12). John Wesley warned:

> I fear, wherever riches have increased, the essence of religion has decreased in the same proportion. Therefore I do not see how it is possible, in the nature of things, for any revival of true religion to continue long. For religion must necessarily produce both industry and frugality, and these cannot but produce riches. But as riches increase, so will pride, anger, and love of the world in all its branches.[16]

The great Puritan minister Cotton Mather put it more succinctly when he said, "Religion begat prosperity and the daughter hath consumed the mother!"

## THE WEALTH OF NATIONS

Adam Smith wrote his famous foundational work *The Wealth of Nations* in 1776, the birthday of America. We were, in a way, born together. Though the Bible laid out some of the principles upon which such a free system should be built, people never did put them all together. The Reformers, particularly Calvin, helped to bring to light many of them. On that basis, Adam Smith, a professor of Christian moral philosophy at the University of Glasgow, finally put the pieces together in *The Wealth of Nations*. This has impelled scholars to say that around 1780 modern capitalism began. The essence of one of Smith's main arguments can be found in his famous comments about the "invisible hand":

Every individual necessarily labours to render the annual revenue of the society as great as he can. . . . he intends only his own gain, and he is in this, as in many other cases, led by an invisible hand to promote an end which was no part of his intention. Nor is it always the worse for society that it was no part of it. By pursuing his own interest he frequently promotes that of the society more effectually than when he really intends to promote it. I have never known much good done by those who affected to trade for the public good.[17]

In short, a market economy is much better than a planned economy. Writing from the vantage point of the end of the twentieth century, we have the benefit of experience to appreciate the truth of Smith's observations. Planned economies do not work, because they fail to take into account man's sinfulness. The right of private property and free enterprise is not an end in itself, as it has been made to be by many in our day. No one is free to use property as he or she sees fit—not a part of it, not any of it— without realizing that he or she shall give an accounting to the God of creation for every penny ever kept, as well as that given away.

# THE FRUITS OF FREE ENTERPRISE

A few centuries ago, four-fifths of the French expended 90 percent of their income for food. With only what you and I consider a marginal tip to a waitress, they had yet to provide for all their other needs. Europe had been in like condition for several thousands of years. It was thus little different from modern Africa with the vast majority of people living on subsistence wages, eking out an existence from hand to mouth. Even as recently as 1780 in Germany, fewer than 1,000 people earned $1,000 a year or more. At last scriptural principles, re-enunciated by the Reformers and articulated by Adam Smith, were put into place and took effect.

The greatest growth, therefore, dates beyond 1776. From 1800 to 1850, with inflation out of the picture, real wages quadrupled. From 1850 to 1900 real wages, after inflation, quadrupled again so that in the nineteenth century actual wealth and income increased sixteen times over. The world had never seen anything like that before! This was true in England; it was more true in America, where free enterprise had its freest reign.

In Egypt, as we find in other Third World countries, the economy is based mostly on animals—donkeys, mules, and water buffalo—which pull carts loaded with all sorts of things. It is interesting to note that one of these animals costs about eighty-five dollars. The average income of people in Egypt is about a hundred dollars a year. Therefore, it is an exceedingly grievous thing when an animal dies. Here is a land that is decapitalized. If someone could save enough money to buy a truck, he would be able to make far more than a hundred dollars. He would be able to make ten, fifty, a hundred times that much because of what he would be able to do.

Accumulated capital or profit is transformed into tools and implements, which is what separates the technological twentieth century from the poverty of the Middle Ages or the conditions that exist in India, a decapitalized country. To decapitalize any nation would be to reduce it to the plight of India, where people eke out a living pushing a plow just as in the Middle Ages.

Jesus said that "whoever desires to become great among you, let him be your servant" (Matt. 20:26). And in the parable of the talents, Jesus said that God has given us certain amounts of wealth, as He has seen fit in His sovereign will, and we are responsible for how we use it. It is incredible to me that we—who have achieved the greatest materialistic, economic civilization the world has ever known that, even in the midst of a depression, we are so vastly better off than most of the nations on the face of this earth—are willing to trade this in and to adopt the system of socialism, which over and over again has reduced the level of living of the average person greatly.

# WELFARE: A CHRISTIAN HERESY

In this century, we've seen government eat away some of our prosperity by trying to carry out by force the Christian ideal of helping the poor. We believe this has been a misguided effort that has hampered prosperity and has actually hurt the poor by hurting productivity. Because state-sponsored welfare has not considered what the Bible says about human nature and what it says about economics, these programs have overall been an abysmal failure. We have more poor per capita than when we started! Because of its messiah complex, today the government preempts the work of the Church and tries to meet the problems of poverty by government-subsidized programs. The Great Society has produced the Great Debt. And these programs are extraordinarily costly and inefficient. But they have all caught the Spirit of Jesus Christ in that they are trying to help the underprivileged, the helpless, and the needy. This is why we call welfare a "Christian heresy."

Many people, rather than wanting to give their own money or sacrifice themselves, are much more willing to have a law passed by the government to take money from other people and use it to meet these needs. Robin Hood is a legend that arose within Christendom. His actions—stealing from the rich to give to the poor—are also a Christian heresy. The Welfare State is like a bloated, inefficient Robin Hood. Most of the welfare money earmarked for the poor never leaves the hands of federal, state, and local bureaucrats who run the welfare programs!

Should we not be concerned for the poor? Absolutely. Local churches, private charities, families being concerned about people, community charities helping people—these have been the ways that America solved this problem for almost 300 years. But now we have tried something else. We have decided to help the poor through the socialistic method of government intervention, which has never worked anywhere else.

When the Bible encourages generosity to the needy, it is always talking about *voluntary* giving within the Church—not forced "contributions" through taxation. One Sunday when I preached on how the Bible does *not* teach socialism, a woman said to me afterward, "I completely disagree with you."

"Wonderful! What do you disagree with?"

She said, "I believe we are our brother's keeper."

I said, "I completely agree with you. I believe we are, too. The difference with you and me is I believe we are our brother's keeper, and you believe that the *government* is our brother's keeper."

Her mouth fell open, and she walked out without saying another word. That concept is the difference between Christianity and socialism.

Furthermore, Paul says something that sounds radical and harsh to our modern welfare state mentality. He writes: "For even when we were with you, we commanded you this: If anyone will not work, neither shall he eat" (2 Thess. 3:10). You would listen a long time before you heard those words today. The apostle knew that people incline toward evil and so we incline toward idleness and laziness. Some will avoid all opportunities to work if they can, but the apostle makes it clear that if one will not work, he or she is not to eat. In a moment, we'll see how taking that verse seriously lifted a whole community from poverty to prosperity.

This verse does not refer to a person who is not *able* to work. The Scripture has a great deal to say about caring for the lame, the blind, the sick, the infirm, the aged, and the young. But if anyone *will not* work, then neither let that one eat.

Because of the prevailing "politics of guilt," most people will feel a twinge of guilt when they hear those words as if they were words without compassion. However, this is one of the most compassionate statements on the subject of economics that has ever been made. Were that not to a large degree followed, wholesale famine and starvation would plague the world. So let it be underscored and proclaimed in bold and capital letters: **IF ANYONE WILL NOT WORK, NEITHER SHALL HE EAT!**

# AN EXPERIMENT IN SOCIALISM

Many people are not aware of the fact that in America, we have seen a perfect, almost laboratory, experiment of socialism. Ironically, America, the land of the free-enterprise system, began with socialism.

Governor William Bradford's account of the story of Plymouth Plantation discusses how the Pilgrims who landed at Plymouth and their leaders initially were obliged to follow a socialistic scheme devised by the merchants who funded the expedition. Although they had benevolent ideas, these ideas were found to be disastrous to the community. They maintained that all things would be held in common, that people would work for the common good, and that this would produce great happiness and satisfaction and prosperity. This was in 1620.

The result was a tremendous crop failure in the first year, a most meager production. Many people were hungry; many people were starving. In spite of the needs of the people and the fact that many had already died from hunger, starvation, and disease, the following year another poor crop developed. By that time half of the population of Plymouth had died.

Therefore, in 1623 Governor Bradford declared that henceforth this experiment in a community of goods, a socialistic experiment, would be abandoned. Every man would receive a parcel of land for his own. He would work it and take care of his own family. Thus, they put 2 Thessalonians 3:10 in practice ("If anyone will not work, neither shall he eat"). The result: People went to work with alacrity. Men who had feigned sickness were now eager to get into the fields. Even the women went out to work eagerly; whereas before, the idea that women should be told to work in the fields was thought to be a great tyranny. They now took their children with them and happily engaged in labor for their own family. The result was that the following harvest was a tremendous, bountiful harvest, and abundant thanksgiving was celebrated in America. Had they not gone into private enterprise, it is likely the Pilgrims would have died off. Note it well: When socialism was abandoned, Thanksgiving was established! When socialism is reinstated in America, thanksgiving will be abolished! That is the history of America—a lesson that we have all too easily forgotten.

# CONCLUSION

Millions today enjoy the incredible wealth we know in the West without a clue as to the ultimate Christian origins of the system that paved the way. Had Jesus never been born, we'd most likely be eking out a modest living.

Wilhelm Roepke has the final word on the positive contributions of Christianity to economics:

"The doctrine of self-reliance and self-denial, which is the foundation of political economy, was written as legibly in the New Testament as in the *Wealth of Nations*" and Lord Acton, the distinguished English historian to whom we owe this bold statement, rightly adds that this was not realized until our age.[18]

# CHAPTER 9

# THE BEAUTY OF SEXUALITY

## Christianity's Impact on Sex and the Family

*Marriage is honorable among all, and the bed undefiled; but fornicators and adulterers God will judge.*

(Heb. 13:4)

In the historical novel *The Last Days of Pompeii*, one character says of another: "Ione has but one vice—she is chaste."[1] This one statement from a fiction character well sums up the attitude toward sex prior to the coming of Jesus Christ. It is also the attitude many have adopted today with the rise of neo-paganism.

The impact of Christianity on sex has been positive or negative depending on who you ask. The hedonist—ancient or modern—will tell you the Christian faith has had a terrible record on the issue of sex. One modern protester's placard sums it up well: "Get your Bible out of my pants!" But from a Christian perspective, sex is holy in the context of marriage. Any deviation from that is wrong. While the Church has had some problems along the way with some anti-sex heresies and even some important leaders who appeared to be against sex (apart from sex for procreation), the overall track record of the Church has been extremely positive.

Christianity has helped to preserve the family as the basic unit of society. It has prevented millions of people from getting sexually transmitted diseases. And it has prevented much unhappiness on the part of those who obey the biblical teaching.

This is still the case today: many Christians (we would wish more) have saved their virginity until marriage and are spared from all manner of diseases and sorrows. Today, in the wake of the Sexual Revolution, with the extensive spread of sexually transmitted diseases, many people are beginning to see that the Bible was right all along.

## OUR "LIBERATED AGE"

Of course, many today do not share this view of sexuality. They feel that as long as "there is love," then virtually anything is permissible. They feel as if, at long last, humankind has emerged into the bright, warm sunshine of sexual freedom; we have been emancipated from the slavery of sexual taboos! It's as new as modern science, as fresh and sparkling as the rocket that carried our astronauts to the moon. It's part of the modern age! Or is it? Well, one writer is not greatly impressed. He said:

> Sexual anarchy assumed extreme forms and spread through a large part of the population. Side by side with an increase of sexual perversions, a shameless sexual promiscuity also greatly increased. They seduced members of the same family. Relations between father and daughter . . . son and mother . . . remained not unknown. The [contemporary] authors especially stress the cases where a man lived sexually with two sisters or with a mother and her daughter. [Adultery, rape, and prostitution greatly increased] . . . homosexual love entered the mores of the population. The contemporary authors seem to sadistically enjoy the enumeration of a variety of turpitudes and sexual perversions. They describe all the aberrations of morbid eroticism with the impudent serenity of the casuist: rape, unnatural sexual relations, flagellations, and sodomy.[2]

Sounds quite familiar, doesn't it? More modern than the thoroughly modern Millie! But it was written by an author at the time of the collapse of the Old Kingdom of Egypt, 4,500 years ago! New? Modern? Hogwash! It's as old as sin and still just as fatal. I remember hearing a television discussion on sexual problems, marriage, divorce, and the like. Several experts were being interviewed, and the question was asked, "Are there no moral standards anymore, concerning sex?" One of the experts said no. That was accepted, without question. All the mores have gone by the board. We live in a new free society where anything goes! In my heart there cried out the words, "What about God?" Is God dead? Does not the One who created us have the right to govern us? What about the moral commandments of God? It matters not how many millions of people conspire together to break the commandments of God. We can only break ourselves against them. God gives us time to repent before the judgment comes, but it will invariably come. There are the same moral standards that have always been.

The Bible presents sex as holy within marriage alone, and even the thought life is to be holy. This ethic, therefore, condemns premarital sex (fornication), adultery, rape, homosexuality, bestiality, incest, and pornography. These standards were given by the Creator of this universe, the Maker of us all. We ignore these standards to our own temporal and eternal peril!

## SATAN'S LIES

Satan has always been saying to mankind, "Do it my way and you're going to find fullness of life, enjoyment, satisfaction, fulfillment and joy." This is the way it always has been from the very beginning. Satan said, in effect, to Eve, "Don't listen to God. He is not with it! Why, He's got a narrow, mean view! He is going to make you miserable and frustrated! If you want to really swing, have a little bite on me and your eyes will be opened." That sounded good, and so she took, she ate, and she found shame, humiliation, guilt, sickness, and death instead. And there was much laughter, as Satan promised there would be, but it was in hell on the part of the demons. They have continually deceived people in the same way down through the ages.

People have always been led to believe that the biblical teaching on sex is really not going to make them happy. For forty years we have been hearing from all sorts of "experts" that if you *don't* spare the rod, you are going to ruin your child; you don't want to have children become inhibited; "let it all hang out"—permissiveness is the name of the game of parenthood. And so, bolstered by quotes from many authorities and, finally, inscriptured in the writings of Dr. Spock, the concept of permissiveness won the day. What happened? We produced a whole generation of permissive little monsters who have succeeded in causing the nation to cringe behind triple-locked doors and locked windows. People are afraid to go out in big cities at night, for there are some people who just can't discipline their urges. They have an urge to rape, so they rape; they have an urge to kill or molest, and they do.

## LESSONS FROM HISTORY

Historians tell us that virtually every great civilization down through history has gone through two phases. First, there is the phase of its ascendancy until it reaches the pinnacle of its power, where it will last for a little while. Then begins a period of descent and finally a plunge into oblivion. This included such kingdoms as the Old Kingdom of Egypt, the Middle Kingdom of Egypt, Babylon, Assyria, the Medo-Persian Empire, the Greek Empire, the Roman Empire, and later the Holy Roman Empire. All went through the same two phases—as, by the way, did the British Empire. Though much bad has been said about the Victorian era, it occurred at the peak of British power and influence in the world.

Historians tell us that during the periods of ascendancy, every one of these nations and kingdoms adhered to a period of moral strictness; there was a societal frown upon sexual promiscuity, even laws that restrained it. Because of the strict moral code of the people, they grew strong and their nations prospered.

After reaching prosperity and success, the moral codes were relaxed, ignored, and finally abrogated. The people began to enter into sexual expression, freedom, immorality, and promiscuity, and the nations plunged into the sea of oblivion. One after another, with no exception, this happened to every nation of antiquity.

The eminent historian Edward Gibbon made it absolutely plain in his monumental work *The Decline and Fall of the Roman Empire* when he said that one of the principal reasons for the dissolution of the Roman Empire was the prior dissolution of the families within it. It is not just a maxim that the family is the building block of the nation. As the Romans were soon to discover, the collapse of families was not just a *private* matter. In fact, when the Goths and Visigoths and all barbarians swept like a tidal wave across the Roman Empire, killing and pillaging, murdering and slaughtering, raping and stealing, the Roman people discovered that marriage was a very public matter after all. As goes the home, so goes the nation.

# EROS IN ANTIQUITY

The ancient, pre-Christian world was rife with sexual immorality and perversion. I was given recently a large picture book entitled *Eros in Antiquity*—Eros, sexual love in antiquity. On every page are pictures of ancient paintings, of marble statuary of every kind, and vases adorned with ancient pictures. They are quite obscene, and the male sexual organ is a constant theme.

Fornication, adultery, group sex, homosexuality, lesbianism, sodomy, bestiality, and every conceivable kind of immorality and perversion was rampant in the ancient world, along with abortion and infanticide.

Long before the Greeks and the Romans, we find cultures in antiquity with all manner of sexual perversions. Biblical archaeologist Joseph Free says that in the temples of the ancient Canaanites—the people whom God told the Israelites to drive out or destroy because of their depravity—practiced "debased sex worship," which resulted in child sacrifice. Their temples were "places of vice."[3] The eminent archaeologist W. F. Albright concurs:

In no country has so relatively great a number of figurines of the naked goddess of fertility, some distinctly obscene, been found. Nowhere does the cult of serpents appear so strongly. The two goddesses Astarte (Ashtaroth) and Anath are called the great goddesses which conceive but do not bear! Sacred courtesans and eunuch priests were excessively common. Human sacrifice was well-known . . . the erotic aspects of their cult must have sunk to extremely sordid depths of social degradation.[4]

The Canaanites were not alone in terms of perversion in antiquity prior to the Greeks. The Syrians and Phoenicians had a goddess whose worship involved "sacred prostitution of both sexes."[5] The ancient Egyptians practiced homosexuality, also as part of their religion:

> As part of their ceremonial worship to the goddess Isis, the Egyptian "priests" (actually they were just male prostitutes) would engage in sex with the men who came to "worship." This debauched form of "worship" was found throughout the Mediterranean region where this goddess was variously known as Ishtar, Mylitta, Aphrodite, and Venus.[6]

The Greeks are well-known for their approval and practice of homosexuality. They, too, had male homosexual prostitutes as part of their religious customs. In Ephesus on a main thoroughfare (Marble Street) a footprint was carved to show the way to the brothel. The Temple of Diana, also in Ephesus, was interestingly one of the Seven Wonders of the World; Diana worship was "a perpetual festival of vice."[7] Likewise consider the temple of Aphrodite at Corinth, which also had temple prostitutes.

Yale history professor John Boswell has written a sympathetic history of homosexuality. On the subject of homosexuality in Ancient Greece he says:

> Many Greeks represented gay love as the only form of eroticism which could be lasting, pure, and truly spiritual. . . . The Attic lawgiver Solon considered homosexual eroticism too lofty for slaves and prohibited it to them. In the idealistic world of the Hellenistic romances, gay people figured prominently as star-crossed lovers whose passions were no less enduring or spiritual than their nongay friends.[8]

Ancient Rome is also known for its rampant sexual sin. Historian Will Durant writes: "Prostitution flourished. Homosexualism was stimulated by contact with Greece and Asia; many rich men paid a talent ($3600) for a male favorite; Cato complained that a pretty boy cost more than a farm."[9]

Durant says that prostitution was so common in ancient Rome

that sometimes the votes of politicians had to be collected through the *collegium lupanariorum*, which was the "guild of brothel-keepers"![10] Durant adds: "Adultery was so common as to attract little attention unless played up for political purposes, and practically every well-to-do woman had at least one divorce."[11] He writes further: "The Roman, like the Greek, readily condoned the resorts of men to prostitutes. The profession was legalized and restricted. . . . The elder Seneca assumed widespread adultery among Roman women."[12]

But of all of the cities of antiquity, there was probably none more vile than Pompeii. In fact, in *Eros in Antiquity*, more pictures are taken of various promiscuous objects from the remains of Pompeii, which was suddenly encased in volcanic ash and preserved for us today, than from any other city. For example, it was common for a phallic symbol to adorn the outside of houses. A most perverse city in a very perverse age, on August 24, A.D. 79, Pompeii was swiftly and suddenly destroyed—like Sodom and Gomorrah before it.

# CHRIST WAS BORN INTO THIS VILE WORLD

Into this defiled world Christ was born, and the apostles went out with the message that was transforming. They came; they declared that God was holy—an absolutely novel idea, for certainly the gods of the heathen were not holy. Not only did they not forbid or restrain vice and wickedness, but they actually encouraged it with the practice of temple prostitution. And now the apostle Paul comes into their Gentile world with the message that God is holy, that He has called us to be holy as He is holy— an absolutely revolutionary message.

The modern hedonists delight to say that Christianity is repressive of sexuality. What they really mean is that it is repressive of immorality and in that they are right.

# THE SANCTITY OF SEX

When God gave the commandment to not commit adultery, He was protecting the sanctity of sex. Immediately after giving the commandment to protect the sacredness and sanctity of life itself, God moved to protect and guard the sanctity of the highest earthly relationship we can know: the relationship of the husband and wife. It was given to purify and protect the procreation of life. Since marriage is the most basic of all human relationships—from it all others, such as the Church or the state, are built up—it is essential that marriage be jealously guarded from every form of attack. In our time, the institution of marriage is under severe siege.

The command is emphatic! It is simple, unqualified, irrevocable, and negative: "Thou shalt not commit adultery." There is no argument annexed; there is no reason given. So destructive and pernicious and damning is the sin involved that none is needed.

When Jesus came, He broadened the scope of this command. Not only was the act of adultery a sin, but now committing adultery in the heart was a sin. He says, "But I say to you that whoever looks at a woman to lust for her has already committed adultery with her in his heart" (Matt. 5:28). The lustful look is condemned—the sin of the heart, for it is out of the heart that proceeds all manner of iniquity, and God calls us to guard our hearts and our minds.

# THE EFFECT OF THE CHRISTIAN ETHIC

What impact did Jesus have on the ancient, perverse world? The early Church generally stood out like a beacon in a dark land. In the midst of the moral chaos described above, Christians were overall pure in an impure world. Latourette writes:

> Sexual intercourse outside of marriage was sternly interdicted and within marriage was permitted only for the procreation of children. Divorce was not allowed, except after the violation of the marriage bond by one of its partners.

Sexual offenses were by no means unknown among Christians, but they were long held to exclude the offender from the Church. Later, as we have noted, restoration was permitted after due repentance and discipline.[13]

In A.D. 125, the Christian Aristides, an Athenian philosopher, wrote a defense of the Christian faith to Emperor Hadrian. Here's what he said related to sexual matters:

They do not commit adultery or immorality . . . Their wives, O king, are as pure as virgins, and their daughters are modest. Their men abstain from all unlawful sexual contact and from impurity, in the hopes of recompense that is to come in another world.[14]

The anonymous "Letter to Diogenes," which is believed to have been written in the second century, gives a lengthy description of the early Christians. Here's what the letter says on sex:

They offer a shared table, but not a shared bed. They are at present "in the flesh" but they do not live "according to the flesh." They are passing their days on earth, but are citizens of heaven. They obey the appointed laws, and go beyond the laws in their own lives.[15]

Will Durant has this to say on the sexual practices of the early Christians:

In general, Christianity continued and exaggerated the moral sternness of the embattled Jews. Celibacy and virginity were recommended as ideal; marriage was tolerated only as a check on promiscuity . . . and homosexual practices were condemned with an earnestness rare in antiquity.[16]

## ANTI-SEX HERESIES

Throughout Christian history, the Church has had to contend with anti-sex heresies. Cults have arisen that condemn sex per se —even within marriage. The Encratites, the Catharites (also known as the Albigensians), and the Manichaeists are a few examples. The early Church definitely had to contend with some anti-sex heresies; these false teachings most likely arose as a reaction to the level of debauchery to which society all around them had sunk. Michael A. Smith comments:

> With sexual excesses all around them, it is likely that some Christians reacted against sex from a fairly early period. However, this was not formally set out or made a matter of special praise. . . . By the third century, celibacy was beginning to be valued as a mark of holiness. Even so, extremes were frowned upon, and Origen earned considerable disapproval because he made himself a eunuch, believing this was commanded in the Gospels.[17]

C. S. Lewis once said, "The devil is always trying to trick us to extremes." That certainly seems to be the case on the history of sex. The pendulum seems to swing, from century to century, from total debauchery to total abstinence (even for the married couple). Neither extreme is biblical.

There certainly have been those—in the Church and out of it—who have looked at sex as something evil. This attitude can still be found today. But they have forgotten that it was God who created sex in the first place, and He said of His creation: It was good. These people look upon sex as something unclean, evil and distasteful, and nice girls or boys never even think about it or talk about it.

Many husbands have told me that their wives have just such an attitude. What they do not realize is that while they think they have adopted a Christian attitude, in truth they have simply exchanged one pagan attitude toward sex—of the deification of sex—for another pagan attitude toward sex—the vilification of sex.

One ancient pagan view of sex, found among the Manichaeans and others, stemmed from the belief that matter was evil. Therefore, the body was evil, and particularly, sex was evil. They looked upon the sexual activity of humankind as contemptible and disgusting. In the early Church, there were some who did not accept the biblical view, either by ignorance or by misunderstanding. And they actually took an ancient pagan view, such as found among the

Platonists, that the body was essentially evil and was basically a tomb for the soul; all sexual functions were looked upon as evil and a source of embarrassment and confusion.

Today people have gone to the other extreme and see the body not as a tomb, but as a tavern for riot of all sorts and anything goes. Actually, the Bible presents the body as neither a tomb nor a tavern but as a temple of the Holy Spirit. Luther very sagaciously observed that the body is evidently not evil, since Jesus Christ, who was the only sinless person ever to live, had a body; and Satan, the most wicked personage ever to exist, has none. The tragedy of those professing Christians who oppose sex per se is that they help the perverters of biblical sexuality—for example, pornographers—by holding such attitudes, and they are producing immeasurable harm to their family.

During the Victorian age in the last century, sex had become something completely hush-hush, something that was not spoken of, something to be ignored and not discussed in polite society. People were supposed to pick up knowledge of it here or there.

In the twentieth century we have seen the pendulum swing to the other extreme. The cry is now for openness and free discussion, and not only discussion but also every sort of picturing in books and magazines and films and television. What is the solution? Some would say that we should go back to the Victorian age. I think not! No, if you read the Bible you will see that the Scriptures are very frank and open about sex. It is interesting to note that God is not the least bit ashamed of what He has created. The sexuality of men and women is part of His creation. God made them male and female, and it was very good. Read the Song of Solomon and see that sex is a holy thing. God's concern is for sex to be holy, for the marriage bed to not be defiled (Heb. 13:4).

## IS THE CHRISTIAN VIEW OF SEX REPRESSIVE?

Today it is stated that biblical teachings lead to frustration and inhibitions, anxieties and mental disturbances; people had better "let it all hang out" and get rid of their frustrations.

It is said that unmarried people who remain continent or chaste will experience all sorts of psychological trauma. People are told to satisfy all of their desires. One man told me that he had never kissed a woman until he kissed his fiancée. Another woman told me that she had frequent sexual liaisons with numerous people. You might readily conclude that the man was someone who had been locked up in a psychopathic ward somewhere, having broken down under the frustration of it all, and that the woman was evidently a prime example of the liberated woman with a healthy mind and body. Actually I met the woman in the psychiatric ward of a hospital, and the man is named Billy Graham.

Dr. Francis Braceland, former president of the American Psychiatric Association and editor of the *American Journal of Psychiatry* (not by any means a Christian organization) wrote: "Premarital sex relations growing out of the so-called new morality have significantly increased the number of young people in mental hospitals."[18] So far from keeping you out of a mental hospital such sexual indulgence is much more likely to put you in! He goes on to say, "A more lenient attitude on campus about premarital sex experience has imposed stresses on some college women severe enough to cause emotional breakdown."[19]

Studies have repeatedly shown that couples cohabitating in so-called trial marriages end up having a much higher incidence of divorce. Furthermore, these individuals have a higher incidence of infidelity during the marriage relationship before it breaks up as well. So much for another lie.

It was said over and over again that people who refrained from premarital sex were not really emotionally well-balanced. A psychologist and her colleagues decided to test that theory, and so they administered a test called the Minnesota Multiphasic Personality Inventory, a standard test used in mental health centers throughout the country, to a group of sexual swingers—young people who were engaged in premarital sex.[20]

They discovered that about half of these people demonstrated unusual degrees of depression, introversion, overactivity, and delusional thinking. The other half scored very low on the truth-telling aspects of the test, showing that they may not even have been telling the truth about their lives. So, indeed, this does not lead to wholeness. We can't say whether or not this is caused by that activity or whether it is emotionally unstable, imbalanced people who get into that lifestyle in the first place. We can't tell which came first, the chicken or the egg, but we see that it is not wholesome, whole, well-rounded people who are engaged in this sort of activity, as so many young people have been told. So much for another lie of the devil.

## ADULTERY IS NOT MERELY A "PRIVATE AFFAIR"

Adultery is a sin against the human spirit and spiritual life which produces traumatic results. It is also a sin against the family, which is the basic unit of society. It is the breaking of our conjugal vows, "Forsaking all others, I choose thee." It is a sin against our children. One of the most flagrant causes of divorce, adultery has produced millions of children who have grown up without a father and a mother in the home, and has created enormous problems in the lives of these children. Adultery and its consequent evils are sins against the nation and society. This country is based on the family unit, and whenever the family is destroyed, the nation becomes weaker.

For a better understanding of the harmful effects of divorce on children see "Divorce and Kids: The Evidence Is In" by Barbara Dafoe Whitehead in *Reader's Digest* for July 1993.

## HOMOSEXUALITY

What can we say about the "gay" revolution? First of all, God says homosexuality is wrong. There are some in our day who twist the Scriptures to try to say it is not. They say that Jesus never condemned homosexuality, but they ignore the fact that He didn't come to destroy God's law—which expressly condemns homosexuality—but to fulfill it (Matt. 5:17).

They also say that the Bible condemns homosexual lust but not homosexual love. But this is not what the Bible states. We read in Romans that the women changed the natural use into that which is against nature; it says nothing about lust. In the next passage in

Romans it talks about the lust of men, burning in their lust one for another (Rom. 1:24–32). We should remember, however, that the Bible condemns both adulterous lust and fornicating lust. Fornication is sexual relations before marriage with someone who is not married.

The Bible says that no adulterer, no fornicator, no homosexual will enter into the kingdom of heaven. In 1 Corinthians 6:9–10, Paul says, "Be not deceived," naming adulterers, fornicators, thieves, murderers, homosexuals, and sodomites. It says nothing about attitude or lust. It condemns the act and those who do it. It expressly says that they shall not inherit the kingdom of God. Be not deceived!

Other passages that prohibit homosexuality can be found in Genesis 19; Leviticus 18:22; and 1 Timothy 1:10. But just as an adulterer can be forgiven and freed from his sin, so also can a homosexual. The gospel of Jesus Christ can effectively change hearts. Thousands living today can attest to this. He has done the same for millions throughout the centuries.

Second, *gay* is a misnomer. If there is one thing that a gay person is not, it is gay—an ill-chosen term. Again the lie of the deceiver, for these people have been found by counselors to be among the most miserable of human beings. Trapped, they feel inescapably condemned by society, desperately reaching out for some fulfillment and yet deep down even hating themselves, but desperately trying to justify their lives as being right.

The two main arguments by which the homosexual endeavors to justify his actions are: first, that he was born this way. Many psychologists, well-familiar with all of the psychological literature on this subject, deny that there is any evidence for this. For instance, Dr. Elizabeth Moberly from Great Britain says: "People are not born that way; they can change. There's a lot of evidence of difficulties in early relationships. The point of therapy is to make good those difficulties."[21]

Psychologist Dr. Joseph Nicolosi of Encino, California, concurs. He says that none of the alleged evidence that a homosexual is born that way is conclusive, but rather the research is flawed. Dr. Nicolosi is hated by the gay community because he has been so successful in helping homosexuals change to become heterosexuals, in what he calls "reparative therapy." (He has written up his findings in the book *Reparative Therapy of Male Homosexuality* (1991).) The success of his practice disproves a couple of their sacred theories—that you're born that way and you can never change—so they hate him. Dr. Nicolosi says that the success of his work and that of other therapists in helping homosexuals change to a heterosexual orientation throws a monkey wrench into the gay agenda, which proclaims, "Once gay, always gay." Even one person who changes in this area dashes their theory on the rocks. Thankfully, there are thousands of homosexuals who have changed in our time![22]

All efforts of the "gay libbers" to form churches in an attempt to find some form of justification and acceptance from God while they continue to practice their sin are vain and futile, for no practicing homosexual will enter the Kingdom of heaven. "Gay churches" are reminiscent of the pagan temples that deified adultery and made pious prostitution the act of the day, and changed the truth of God into a lie. "Be not deceived."

What, then, should be the attitude of Christians? It should be the same as God's. God loves the homosexual. You may hate him, but God loves him, and if you are a Christian you will love him exactly the same way that you love an adulterer or a thief. That does not mean that you love or condone his acts. You accept him, not his deeds. Homosexuals feel desperately trapped; they feel there is no way out; they feel that they are not accepted. We need to accept them and make them know our love and our concern for them. We need to endeavor to lead them to the life-transforming power of Jesus Christ. This inevitably involves repentance, for Jesus said, "Unless you repent you will all likewise perish" (Luke 13:3).

# THE FRUIT OF THE SEXUAL REVOLUTION

What has the sexual revolution, with its acceptance of homosexuality and its promotion of promiscuity, brought us? Beyond the psychological and sociological damage we discussed above, today there are twenty-six sexually transmitted diseases (STD) that are epidemic in this population. In fact, one in five Americans has some type of viral STD! According to a new study by the Alan Guttmacher Institute, 56 million Americans are "infected with a sexually transmitted viral disease like herpes or hepatitis B."[23] The tragedy is that while such viral infections can be controlled, they can't be cured and they often recur.

Worldwide, there are over 100 million cases of gonorrhea alone. In addition, there is syphilis, chlamydia, herpes (millions of people have that), as well as the dreaded AIDS and twenty-one other horrible sexually transmitted diseases.

It has been shown that there are people walking around our streets—who not only have AIDS, but three or four or five other of these diseases as well. A person has got to be insane to do such things as would get them infected in a day like this.

AIDS has devastated much of the homosexual community. Homosexuality reduces the lifespan of men by almost half. Whereas the average married man in America lives to be seventy-four years of age, the average homosexual dies at forty-three. This is the tragic, natural consequence of their unnatural acts, which God has clearly told us to avoid.

So maybe God isn't such an ogre after all. And maybe every good gift and every perfect gift does come down from above, and not up from beneath with a hook in it, and Satan at the other end of the line.

Probably the basic lie of Satan underlying all of his deceptions is that the laws of God will restrict and narrow and diminish one's life. How many people have sadly learned that just the opposite is true, when their bodies have been vitiated by venereal disease, or their minds have been scrambled by various guilt-induced psychoses or neuroses, and found, only too late, that had they followed God's path their life would have been enriched and ennobled?

The problem is that in America today we have confused love with lust, and these are almost antithetically opposed to each other. The essence of lust is a desire to get something from someone else. Love is the opposite. "For God so loved, He gave . . ." This principle of love as it is operative in marriage works out like this: It produces an intense desire to make life for another the finest experience possible. Do you love your husband? Your wife? If so, then your daily conscious desire is to make life for her or him the finest experience possible in every sphere, in every area. Many couples will attest that their best sex comes when they concentrate on pleasing their mate.

# GOD WANTS WHAT'S BEST FOR US

God wants us to have the very best. But as we have seen, the modern enlightened secularist believes that religious people, Christian people, are repressed; they do not have sexual freedom; they do not enjoy the sexual side of their lives; they need to throw off the Lord and His ways.

*Redbook* magazine conducted a survey concerning sex in modern "liberated" America.[24] They listed questions they wanted women to respond to. To their astonishment, 100,000 readers responded! They had never had anything vaguely approaching that before. The largest sexual survey ever taken, and 100,000 American women responded to a secular magazine that told of their sex lives!

What did the survey reveal? Even more astounding than the number of women that replied were the results. They discovered that women who were sexually liberated—the feminists, the free modern women—were the most dissatisfied kind of person sexually. The only person less satisfied was the nymphomaniac (who most men think is just the most sexual kind of woman), who is so sexually frustrated that she runs from here to there and back and forth everywhere trying to find some satisfaction, which, alas, she never finds.

But the more religious women indicated that they had more sexual satisfaction in their lives. The most religious category (women were to judge how much a part religion played in their lives—i.e., whether they were most religious, more religious, least religious), whom the average enlightened American male has been told by the devil are sexually repressed, were the most orgasmic women in the country. And that turns the whole lot right on its head.

Have you believed that lie? Tens of millions have. Who really cares about your happiness? The devil? Oh, the devil would love for you to have chlamydia, herpes, and AIDS all at once, and be pregnant at sixteen. Or God? His banner over us is love. His way is the way of fulfillment, not the way of repression.

Our focus in this chapter has been on the sanctity of the marriage bed, but a lot more could be said about Christianity's other contributions to the family. Above all, applied Christian living does wonders for family living—as millions of happy families can testify. God's principles for a happy home, as stated in the Bible, are the blueprints for a loving family. Take Christ out of these homes, and many of them would fall apart. Many marriages have been healed by a commitment to Christ first and to each other second.

Christian help for the family has taken many forms through the centuries. In our day, psychologist James Dobson has helped untold millions with their everyday family problems in his syndicated radio program, "Focus on the Family." Furthermore, his ministry "responds to as many as 50,000 letters a week, offers professional counseling and referrals in a network of 1,200 therapists."[25] Dr. Dobson is a committed Christian who performs his work for the family as a service to Jesus Christ. Take away Christ and you would have, without opposition or restraint, the accelerated decline of the American family.

## CONCLUSION

Had Jesus not come, far more people would continue to act like the pagans—many of whom have no control over their urges. What would have happened to the human race if sexual diseases had been left unchecked to wipe out a large segment of the population? In short, if Jesus Christ had not been born, you might not have been born either!

# CHAPTER 10

# HEALING

# THE

# SICK

## Christianity's Impact on Health and Medicine

*And great multitudes followed Him, and He healed them all.*

(Matt. 12:15*b*)

In 1931 some North American missionaries started a Christian, shortwave radio station in Quito, Ecuador, that ministered throughout Latin America and beyond. After a while, indigent people from neighboring countries came to the radio station seeking medical help. They somehow assumed that these people who were ministering to their souls would also minister to their bodies. So in the 1950s, this station—HCJB, *Voz Andes* ("The Voice of the Andes")—added a hospital to its mission, and today it is one of the chief hospitals in the whole country. This is one of thousands of examples in the Christian era of believers meeting health needs in the name of Christ—a natural out-working of Christianity in action.

Christianity has made significant contributions in the realm of health. First of all, applied Christian living is healthy. Second, Christianity played an important role in the development of the institution of the hospital, to the point that some historians attribute the creation of the hospital per se to Christianity. The example and teaching of Jesus has inspired ministers, priests, monks, nuns, missionaries, and untold numbers of laymen to bring medical help to the poor in virtually every country of the world. Often, Western medicine has been introduced to a Third World country or to a primitive culture by Christian missionaries. In short, had Jesus not come, medicine would not be as widespread. Nor would it ever have been as compassionate!

## THE ANCIENT JEWS

In ancient times, the Jews were light–years ahead of the pagan world in terms of sanitary codes and customs. God revealed to them a number of health regulations in the ceremonial part of the law. Roberto Margotta, in *The Story of Medicine*, writes:

> The historical importance of ancient Hebrew medicine lies in its fundamental contribution to communal hygiene through concepts contained in the Bible. . . . Principles of bodily cleanliness, nutrition and diet, obstetrics and child welfare were codified in the book Leviticus. Belief in one god denied the use of magical practices.[1]

Margotta points out that when Europeans were facing a big problem with leprosy during the Middle Ages, the Church solved the problem by applying the principles taught in the Hebrew Scriptures.[2] Thus the Christians were able to bridge the gap from what God revealed to the Jews, a relatively small group of people, to the rest of the world. Unfortunately, many of the biblical teachings on hygiene have been ignored for centuries, to our peril.[3]

## THE EXAMPLE OF JESUS CHRIST

In the Gospels we read that Jesus Christ went about healing the sick. He laid hands on people, and they got well. He even was able to heal by "remote control," merely saying the word and someone in a different location was healed (Matt. 8:5–13). Christ's teaching message was made tangible by His healing ministry. Each healing was an eloquent sermon that made the point that He was Lord even over sickness and death. He told us to go and do likewise—to care for the poor and the sick. In 2,000 years, millions of Christians have gone and done likewise.

He touched the blind eyes and the deaf ears, and hospitals sprang into existence all over the world. They had virtually not existed before Christ came. He touched the leper whom no one would come close to, and leprosariums came into existence all over the world because of the example and teaching of Jesus Christ.

# INITIAL REGRESS OF MEDICINE UNDER CHRISTIAN INFLUENCE?

Some scholars argue that Christianity retarded for centuries the medical advances being made by the ancient Greeks and Romans. Margotta writes:

> Some authorities have asserted that Christianity was the cause of the decline of medicine, but this is not entirely true. It may reasonably be maintained that Christianity did nothing to halt the process of decline. . . . Christianity, following the teaching of the Lord, was bound to regard medicine as a work of charity. . . . In practical terms, the Christians did much to relieve suffering.[4]

The early Christians did not allow dissection of corpses, as was true of many other religions. This one fact alone kept back medical advances for centuries during the Christian era, until about the time of the Renaissance. What this meant, then, was that during the Middle Ages, the anatomical work of the Roman doctor Galen was taken as gospel truth—when in fact, he was in error on numerous points.

However, all during this time, advances in compassion and mercy were being made by Christianity that have forever changed how we approach the sick. Furthermore, as we saw earlier, Christianity helped to give birth to modern science; many of those who brought about the great advances in scientific medicine were Christians.

# HOSPITALS

Prior to the influence of Christ, we find that in some cultures there were a few scattered, rudimentary places where the sick were brought. This includes military hospitals for Roman soldiers, and in ancient Greece, temples of Aesculapius, where superstition abounded and where patients were taken advantage of by unscrupulous priests.[5]

Life was cruel prior to the influence of Jesus Christ. So caring for the *nonuseful* sick was not a priority. For example, Plautus, a Roman philosopher of the egoistic school, said, "A man is a wolf to a man whom he does not know."[6] In commenting on private Christian charity, writer John Jefferson Davis points out how cruel the age was, regarding caring for the sick:

> In the pre-Christian Roman Empire, hospitals existed only for soldiers, gladiators, and slaves. Manual laborers and other poor individuals had no place of refuge. Men feared death, and took little interest in the sick, but often drove them out of the house, and left them to their fate.[7]

But hospitals as we know them began through the influence of Christianity. The love and example of Jesus Christ inspired a new attitude toward helping the ill. Even today many of the hospitals reflect their Christian origin in their names—Baptist Hospital, St. Luke's Presbyterian, Holy Cross Hospital, and the like—even, if in some cases, the Christian emphasis may be long gone.

Initially, many of the hospitals were not so much "health factories" as they were hostels. Many of the early hospitals were not devoted exclusively to helping the sick; they were often places of shelter for the poor as well. Colin Jones, who is Senior Lecturer in the Department of History and Archaeology at Exeter University, writes: "To generalize outrageously from highly deficient materials, it does seem probable that only big hospitals in the bigger towns enjoyed the presence of medical men much before

1450 or 1500."[8] We can see this trend even as late as the seventeenth century, at least in France. Richelet's 1680 dictionary definition of a hospital is "A place to retire those poor who do not have the means to live, and where a particular care is taken of their salvation."[9]

Until the nineteenth century, hospitals were utilized by the poor, not by everybody. People of means would be treated in their own homes. The original hospitals were squalid, however well-intentioned they may have been. With nineteenth-century developments in bacteriology by Louis Pasteur, a Christian, and antiseptic surgery by Joseph Lister, also a Christian, hospitals became much more safe and, therefore, became utilized by the general populace. We will have more to say about Pasteur and his faith in a moment; as to Lister's faith, he was a Quaker who wrote: "I am a believer in the fundamental doctrines of Christianity."[10] No matter how squalid the original hospitals may have been, they gave rise to the modern hospital movement. Take away Christ, and we would not have hospitals as we know them.

After Constantine legalized Christianity in the fourth century, Christians built hospitals in numerous locations, sometimes even in "remote and dangerous places" to provide shelter for Christian pilgrims traveling to the Holy Land; some of these pilgrims traveled without money, relying on the generosity of "other accommodating Christians."[11] These hospitals were not exclusively dedicated to providing shelter, nor exclusively dedicated to healing the sick.

In 325, in addition to officially recognizing the trinity as taught in the Scriptures, the Council of Nicaea made a ruling important in the history of hospitals. They decreed that hospitals were to be duly established wherever the Church was established. I. Donald Snook, Jr., writes:

> Many of the great hospitals can be traced to the period directly following the Council of Nicaea in 325 A.D., when the bishops of the church were instructed to go out into every cathedral city in Christendom and start a hospital.[12]

Saint Basil of Caesaria (c.329–379) is credited with founding the first Christian hospital that focused on ministering to the sick. George Grant says that Basil's hospital was the very first "non-ambulatory hospital,"[13] a medical facility with beds; Grant says that prior to Basil all hospitals were essentially "ambulatory clinics." Roberto Margotta writes about Basil's hospital:

It had as many wards as there were diseases to treat, and resembled a little township of its own; it included a leper colony. The rule of love, implying also the care and comfort of the sick, thus embraced even lepers, who previously had always been kept in isolation.[14]

A wealthy Christian woman, Fabiola, a disciple of St. Jerome, is credited with having built the first hospital in the Western world, in Rome, circa A.D. 400.[15]

The oldest hospital still functioning today is the Hotel Dieu (God) in Paris, established by St. Landry around A.D. 600.[16] It was a medical establishment then as well. Snook says: "Even by current standards, this early French hospital could truly be called a medical center, since it embraced many of the varied activities necessary to care for the sick."[17]

The oldest hospital in the New World still in existence today is the Jesus of Nazareth Hospital in Mexico City, established by Cortez in 1524.[18] Indeed, the Christian impact on health, especially in terms of caring for the sick, has been enormous.

## "CHRIST'S POOR"

During the Middle Ages, duty and charity were inseparably linked, so charity was duty. There was the whole idea of "Christ's poor," based on the sheep and goats parable of Matthew 25. Christ's poor were to be the chief beneficiaries of Christian charity. Colin Jones writes:

The whole movement of charitable giving was predicated upon the equation of Christ and the pauper. . . . Although the category of "Christ's poor," the *pauperes Christi* was amorphous and wide-encompassing in the minds of medieval charitable donors, the hospital was a particularly privileged institutional target of testamentary generosity.[19]

In contrast with the Christian-influenced Middle Ages, during the French Revolution of the late eighteenth century—when there was a revolt against the Church—the hospital system essentially broke down. As many as one-third of France's hospitals ceased operating.[20] In fact, during that atheistic reign, "private charity seemed to dry up altogether."[21] Jones adds: "Charitable institutions have always done well in an age of faith."[22]

# HOSPITALS IN THE UNITED STATES

In the United States, the first hospitals were started largely by Christians. Prior to the establishment of the first hospital—the Pennsylvania Hospital (established in Philadelphia in 1751), which received great input from the Quakers—there were almshouses. Started by Christians, these were refuge shelters for the poor and the sick.

Established in the eighteenth century, almshouses were the forerunners of hospitals in America; these helped the urban poor. The first almshouse was founded in Philadelphia in 1713 by William Penn, the great Quaker. Initially it helped only poor Quakers, but it expanded in 1782 to help anyone in need.

Charles E. Rosenberg, a professor of history and sociology of science at the University of Pennsylvania, has written an excellent book documenting the creation of hospitals in America, entitled *The Care of Strangers: The Rise of America's Hospital System.* Rosenberg writes that the early hospitals in the United States were "framed and motivated by the responsibilities of Christian stewardship."[23] The almshouses were unquestionably germ-infested. They would be the last resort, and that for a poor man or woman who had no other alternative. They resembled the hospital of the Middle Ages more closely than the modern hospital of today.[24] Many of the residents of the almshouses would stay there until death.

In contrast, many reformers—mostly Christians—tried to start hospitals, which would help the poor sick, but not the chronically sick, lest it become like another almshouse.[25] A Bostonian advocate of hospitals wrote, "Where Christianity is practiced, it must always be considered the first of duties to visit and heal the sick."[26]

Not only was the physical well-being important in the early American hospitals, but so was the spiritual well-being. For example, in New York Hospital, "Bibles were placed in every ward." "Swearing, cardplaying, drinking, and 'intemperance' were typical grounds for discharge in antebellum hospitals." In the Poor House of Charleston, Sunday services were mandatory.[27] Christian influence in the founding of hospitals in this country is an established fact. As one pastor put it in 1888, when commenting on a local homeopathic hospital, such an organization "in its daily work is simply Christian thought and belief translated into action."[28]

Rosenberg points out that probably *the* most important factor in making hospitals safe and sanitized was the "professionalization of nursing,"[29] As we'll see in a moment, the devout Florence Nightingale had much to do with that. Also critical to this was the work of Pasteur and Lister.

## NURSING SOCIETIES

Nursing has come to be an integral part of health care, and Christianity gave rise to nursing care. Out of love for Christ, women joined convents and became the forerunners of today's nurses. One of the leading groups was the Daughters of Charity, which Colin Jones describes as "the most important community of nursing sisters."[30] Catholic Reformer St. Vincent de Paul (1581–1660) was the co-founder of the Daughters of Charity, along with St. Louise de Marrilac. Saint Vincent de Paul told the Sisters, "You must go and find the sick poor. You do in that what our Lord did. . . . He went from town to town, from village to village and cured all He met."[31] Jones writes about the significance of the Daughters of Charity:

Such women came to take over the running of nearly all hospitals and charitable institutions in France by the end of the Ancien Regime [pre-Revolutionary France], a process which must rank as one of the most remarkable achievements of working women in the early modern period. They contributed in no small measure not only to the better management of hospitals but also to their "medicalization."[32]

These Christian ladies ran the hospital pharmacies. They saw themselves as superior to the apprentice-surgeon. They ran the women's wards. They were knowledgeable about surgery and sometimes had to fill in for the absent surgeon.[33] Even the highly skeptical Voltaire had a good report to give of these committed Christian women:

The religious institutes devoted to succouring the poor and serving the sick are among those most worthy of respect. There is perhaps nothing greater on this earth than the sacrifice that the delicate sex makes of its beauty and its youth in caring within hospitals for the collection of every sort of human wretchedness, the very sight of which is so humiliating for mankind's pride, and so revolting for our niceties.[34]

## FLORENCE NIGHTINGALE

Florence Nightingale (1820–1910), the founder of modern nursing, received much of the inspiration for her work from Jesus Christ. She was an extremely devout woman. Unfortunately, her theology was not entirely orthodox; nonetheless, she would not have accomplished what she did apart from the inspiration of Christ. Take away Christ, and there would have been no Florence Nightingale. She has had a profound, immeasurable impact on the health of humanity.

When she was seventeen, she said that God had called her into His service. But not until her early thirties did she discover what that service was.

Nightingale was influenced by a Lutheran pastor of Germany, Theodor Fliedner (1800–1864), who organized deaconesses within the Lutheran Church. These women were involved in helping ex-convicts, education, and nursing instruction in a type of Christian commune in Kaiserwerth, Germany. Fliedner is credited with founding the first nursing school.[35] Despite the protests of her high-society family, the strong-willed Nightingale went to Kaiserwerth in the early 1850s and for the first time knew happiness.[36] Her first exposure to practical nursing was with these Protestant deaconesses in Kaiserwerth.

Then in 1854, she went to Scutari in the Crimea during the Crimean War, which pitted Britain and France against Russia. So pervasive was the Christian influence on nursing orders that in her attempt to recruit nurses, she had to choose among women of various Christian groups. She called for nurses "with a view to fitness and without reference to religious creed whether Roman Catholic nuns, Dissenting Deaconesses, Protestant Hospital nurses or Anglican sisters."[37] She and the nurses went off to a far-flung battlefield; and thus she began the great and noble profession of nursing. Florence Nightingale became a legend in her time—"the lady with the lamp"—as she went to bind up the wounded and care for the dying. Overnight, she became a national heroine.

When she returned to England, she wrote a most influential volume entitled *Notes on Hospitals*, published in 1859. This book was to have a profound effect on Europe and the United States in improving conditions in hospitals by making them more sanitary. She contributed greatly to "the hospital building's self-consciously hygienic design, its orderly and efficient administration."[38]

In 1860, she opened the Nightingale School for Training Nurses at St. Thomas Hospital in London. This act is said to be the beginning of modern nursing. She personally had influence over thousands of nurses in training, even after she herself had become an invalid.

Again, take away Jesus and there never would have been a Florence Nightingale. She summed up well her practical piety: "The Kingdom of Heaven is within, but we must also make it so without."[39]

# THE RED CROSS

In the mid-nineteenth century, an evangelical started one of history's greatest humanitarian movements, the International Red Cross. Henry Dunant (1828–1910) was a Swiss banker, philanthropist, and a member of "the Church of the Awakening." He helped to establish the Young Men's Christian Association in Geneva in the 1850s, and it was he who first suggested there be an international alliance of YMCAs. In 1855, they held the first world conference in Paris. He wrote most of the YMCA charter, which is still in use today.[40] To a large extent, his international experience with the YMCA—and back then, the "Y" was thoroughly evangelical—helped to pave the way for his work in founding the International Committee of the Red Cross.

In 1859, while on business to see Napoleon III in Solferino, Italy, Dunant witnessed a ghastly battle in Italy's fight for unification. For weeks after the battle, he worked indefatigably as a volunteer, treating the wounded who were housed in churches near the battlefield. He realized that many needless deaths could have been avoided had there only been minimal, advanced preparations to handle the wounded. He wrote down his moving experiences in a book, *Memory of Solferino*, which he published himself in 1862. In it he describes how his calling from God (to help prevent such needless deaths in the future) dawned on him from this experience.

> In this state of pent-up emotion which filled my heart, I was aware of an intuition, vague and yet profound, that my work was an instrument of His Will; it seemed to me that I had to accomplish it as a sacred duty and that it was destined to have fruits of infinite consequence for mankind.[41]

How prophetic! In his book, Dunant speculated about the possibility of an international organization that was neutral yet helped the wounded in battle: "Would it not be possible, in a time of peace and quiet, to form relief societies of zealous, devoted and thoroughly qualified volunteers to bring aid to the wounded in time of war?"[42]

The response to the *Memory of Solferino* was "electric"[43] and galvanized the formation of the Red Cross. He was the driving force behind "the Committee of Five," which founded this international organization in 1864 along with twenty-four delegates from sixteen nations. A truncated red cross was chosen as a symbol allowed by all the nations for neutral assistance. What a milestone in human history! The Red Cross has saved millions of lives since then, and it was founded by an evangelical. The significance of the symbol chosen (although it is essentially the Swiss flag in reverse) should not be lost by anyone. The first Muslim nation (Turkey in 1876) to adopt the idea of the Red Cross felt compelled to change the symbol from a Christian one to a Muslim one; hence, the Red Crescent was born as an outgrowth of the Red Cross. Unlike many in formerly Christian nations today, the Muslims inadvertently recognized the driving force behind one of the greatest humanitarian movements in history—Jesus Christ. In 1919, these two groups united to form the League of Red Cross and Red Crescent Societies; today more than 145 nations subscribe to either society, the vast majority being in the Red Cross.

Unfortunately, Dunant suffered some severe financial setbacks that caused him to go bankrupt and to lose his fortune and good name. Banished from Geneva, he lived for many years in Paris as a virtual vagrant. But near the end of his life, he was able to return to Switzerland with dignity. In 1901, he was awarded the first Nobel Peace Prize ever given (along with F. Passy). Were it not for Christianity, there would be no Red Cross, nor for that matter, any Red Crescent.

## LOUIS PASTEUR

Dr. Louis Pasteur (1822–1895) was a devout Christian. In the realms of medicine and health, we live with the positive effects of his work to this day. His research into bacteriology gave rise to pasteurization, sterilization, and the development of vaccines against many deadly diseases—including rabies, diphtheria, and anthrax. It is interesting that much of Pasteur's developments ran contrary to the Darwinian views that were gaining ground in his day. Henry Morris says this about Pasteur:

He undoubtedly made the greatest contribution of any one man to the saving of human lives, and most scientists today would say he was the greatest biologist of all time. Yet, in his lifetime, he was the object of intense opposition by almost the entire biological establishment, because of his own opposition to spontaneous generation and to Darwinism. It was only his persistence and sound experimental and analytical procedures that finally compelled most biological and medical scientists to give up their ideas of the naturalistic origin of life and their treatment of disease as based on this notion. Pasteur was a strongly religious man, ever more so as he grew older. When asked about his faith, Pasteur would reply: "The more I know, the more does my faith approach that of the Breton peasant. Could I but know all, I would have the faith of a Breton peasant woman."[44]

Pasteur's biographer, Rene Vallery-Radot, writes: "Absolute faith in God and in eternity, and a conviction that the power for good given to us in this world will be continued beyond it, were feelings which pervaded his whole life; the virtues of the Gospel had ever been present to him."[45] When this giant of a scientist died, Pasteur was holding on to his wife with one hand and a crucifix with the other.[46]

# THE MODERN MISSIONS MOVEMENT

The average human lifespan in A.D. 33 was twenty-eight years, whereas in 1990 it was sixty-two.[47] While most of that difference comes primarily from advances in the field of medicine, much of it also comes from the widespread boost to health by medical missionaries spanning the globe in the last century or two. Even this very day, tens of thousands of Christian missionaries are providing basic medical services to millions of people in the Third World, like the Voz Andes Hospital we spoke of at the opening of this chapter. For many of these patients, this is the only health care available.

Because of their love for Christ, Christians have constructed tens of thousands of hospitals all over the world, even in the remotest jungles. These hospitals minister to lepers, to the blind, to the deaf, to the crippled, to the maimed of every sort. Christian doctors, Christian nurses, and Christian missionaries have been working in leprosaria and in hospitals of all kinds, often giving their lives to stem the tide of disease. Who can measure the impact upon human health that has been brought about by such medical missionaries, who have transformed the living standards of innumerable pagans and savage tribes that were living in the most unimaginably unhealthy situations?

Western medicine was introduced to the developing world for the most part by these Christian missionaries. Dr. Martyn Lloyd-Jones, a doctor who became a minister, writes:

In the early days of the developing countries, the building of the hospitals (as, for example, in Africa and parts of Asia), the building of schools, the providing of rules of public health and much else has originally occurred as the result of the concern and the activity of the Christian church.[48]

Ruth Tucker has written a panoramic history of Christian missions, from the beginning of the Church to the early 1980s. She says that medical missions have been a terrific testimony for Jesus Christ: "The ministry of missionary medicine during the twentieth century has been without a doubt the greatest humanitarian effort the world has ever known, and, more than any other force, it has served to disarm the critics of Christian missions."[49] Tucker points out, for example, that as late as 1935, half of the hospitals in China were run by Christian missionaries.[50]

Furthermore, nobody can tell how many people in the United States have gone into the field of medicine motivated by the Christian desire to help people in need. Christ has indeed inspired the greatest humanitarian impulses.

# PREVENTIVE MEDICINE: FAITHFUL CHRISTIAN LIVING IS HEALTHY

It is widely recognized today that the best medicine is preventive medicine. Christianity has helped untold hundreds of millions to not abuse their bodies—e.g., by smoking, drinking, or promiscuous sex. Applied Christianity is healthy. The Scripture teaches that our body is the temple of the Holy Spirit (1 Cor. 6:19). This Christian teaching implies that our body should be dealt with reverentially; if you have a view of your body as being the temple of the Holy Spirit, it's going to have a different impact upon your lifestyle than if you viewed it as being a garbage can.

The greatest preventable cause of death in America today is smoking, which is responsible for taking about 400,000 lives prematurely in America each year. These deaths are caused by "cancers, strokes, pneumonia, influenza, tuberculosis, emphysema, asthma, ulcers, stillbirths, and coronary heart trouble."[51] Thus smoking kills more than 1,000 people a day, and it kills eight times the number of those killed in traffic accidents in America each year. There are millions and millions of Christians in America who do not smoke because of their Christian convictions. I have personally seen and read about thousands of Christians who were converted to Christ and gave up smoking—one of the many changes in their lifestyle that was effected by Christ.

Being spiritually committed is good for your health, physically and mentally. That's not just a preacher's opinion; that was the conclusion after a review of numerous scientific studies. Recently, psychiatrist David Larson, "a senior governmental researcher who worked nearly 10 years at the National Institute of Mental Health (NIMH),"[52] compiled empirical data, and this was his conclusion: Going to church is good for your health! Mark Hartwig, Ph.D., writing in *Focus on the Family Citizen* magazine, sums up Larson's findings:

Scientific studies suggest that religious commitment offers some major health benefits. . . . In reviewing his own research and that of others, Larson has found that religious commitment seems to have an overwhelming positive effect on people's lives.

Indeed, when he tallied up the findings, the results were remarkable. In the area of psychiatry, 92 percent of the findings showed that religious commitment produced some kind of beneficial effect. In the area of family medicine, 83 percent of the findings demonstrated a beneficial effect. And in the health literature, 81 percent of the findings were also positive. . . .

In addition to lengthening your life, religion can also help lower your chances of getting sick. . . .

"It seems clear that frequent attendance [of church] is a protective factor against a wide range of illness outcomes," the researchers said.[53]

Appropriately, the title of Dr. Hartwig's article, from which this quote comes, is "For Good Health, Go to Church."

# CONCLUSION

Following the example of Jesus Christ, the Great Physician, Christians have fueled some of the greatest humanitarian advances in medicine. Every once in a while, a skeptic will admit the positive effect of Christian faith in terms of helping people. W. O. Saunders said this in *American Magazine*:

Your agnostic is tremendously impressed by the power of your faith. He has seen drunkards and libertines and moral degenerates transfigured by it. He has seen the sick, the aged, the friendless comforted and sustained by it. And he is impressed by your wonderful charities, your asylums, your hospitals, your nurseries, your schools; he must shamefacedly admit that agnostics, as such, have built few hospitals and few homes for the orphans.[54]

I think that Mr. Saunders was flattering himself by even using the word "few." To my knowledge, they have built none at all. They are but "Christian thought and belief translated into action."[55]

# CHAPTER 11

# THE CIVILIZING OF THE UNCIVILIZED

## Christianity's Impact on Morality

*Let your conduct be worthy of the gospel of Christ.*
                                        The apostle Paul (Phil. 1:27)

In the last century, there was a great attack on foreign missionaries in the *London Times*. An experienced traveler wrote a letter to the editor in which he criticized this attitude. The letter writer said that such an attitude on the part of a voyager was particularly inexcusable—for should he happen to be cast ashore on some uncharted island, he would devoutly pray that the lesson of the missionary had preceded him! The writer of the letter was no less than Charles Darwin, later an enemy of the Christian faith. Nonetheless, he recognized the *utilitarian* value of the faith.

Nothing in the annals of history compares to what Christianity has done, and can still do, to civilize barbaric people. Nothing! Much of the "civilized" attitudes we have in society ultimately come from our Judeo-Christian heritage.

The Western world in particular owes a great debt of gratitude to the Christian faith for the way it has changed the uncivilized tribes, peoples, and nations into a much more humane lot. This includes the Franks, from whom comes the name France, the Anglo-Saxons, and the notorious Vikings. Even today, when we do not act humane, it is by a *Christian criterion* that our behavior is deemed inhumane. Like no other force in history, Christianity has elevated the standard of morality worldwide.

# THE JEWISH BASE

In many ways it would be fair to say that Christianity did not invent a view of morality; rather, it elevated the Old Testament view. (See the Sermon on the Mount, Matt. 5–7). The moral code of Christianity is based on Judaism and the Ten Commandments, which gave us the standard of right and wrong for centuries. As Abraham Lincoln once said, the Bible is the greatest gift God gave to man; apart from it, we would not know right from wrong.[1] Judaism gave to the world a much higher view of morality than what it had known before. Jesus Christ took that Jewish base, expanded it, and then sent it out into the whole world. Had Jesus never come, we would live at an unbelievably low scale of morality. Our sense of right and wrong would be no better than the heathen we encounter today in certain parts of the Third World, for we ourselves would still be heathens.

Christ did more than bring a higher standard of right and wrong into the world; He caused it to spread, and changed many cultures for the better. Throughout history, many barbaric and cruel tribes and cultures have been civilized by the positive influence of Jesus Christ. Had Christ never come, we might well be drinking out of human skulls as many of our ancestors did!

# THE MORAL BACKDROP

The ancient Jews were surrounded by pagan societies that worshiped the gods Moloch, Baal, Astoreth (Baal's wife), Anath, and others. The god Moloch was exceptionally cruel; his worshipers offered their own children in sacrifices of fire. Baal was a god of sexuality; temple prostitutes of both sexes were employed in his worship. Henry Halley says of the ancient Canaanites that "their temples were centers of vice."[2] In contrast, the Ten Commandments revealed to the Hebrews were light–years ahead of the moral standards of the pagan cultures of antiquity. In fact, the Decalogue is still relevant today, some 3,400 years later.

The God of ancient Israel, who is the God of the Christians, stands in stark contrast to the ancient pagan gods. He is holy, and He judges people's sins, but not until first mercifully extending them the opportunity to repent. In great contrast, we read this description of Anath, Baal's consort and sister, who was one of the goddesses of the Canaanites:

> As a patroness of war Anath appears in a fragment of the Baal Epic in an incredibly bloody orgy of destruction. For some unknown reason she fiendishly butchers mankind, young and old, in a most horrible and wholesale fashion, wading delightedly in human gore up to her knees—yea, up to her throat, all the while exulting sadistically.[3]

The moral standards of the ancient pagans were abysmal. While the Canaanites' standards of morality may well have been the lowest, other cultures were also bad. But, you say, all that changed with the Greeks. No, it didn't. The Greeks have contributed many positive things to mankind, but a higher view of morality is not one of them!

The gods of the Greeks and then later of the Romans were neither infinite nor almighty. They knew no such concept as an Almighty God. They were all finite gods. Furthermore, they were not gods that could be loved. The idea of loving a god was absolutely and totally foreign to the ancient pagan mind. The gods were to be feared. The gods were to be placated. But they were not to be loved.

Even more, we should understand the chaos that heathenism produced in people's thinking. The idea that we should live by the will and law of God was utterly incomprehensible to the pagan mind because the gods operated by no law. If the gods had a law, they would certainly not have revealed it to man. The gods operated by purely arbitrary decrees and acts. The pagan gods would wake up one morning in an irascible mood and begin to cast about their thunderbolts and wreak havoc in people's lives. No, laws were the accomplishment of men and not of gods. That is why Socrates could conceive of no higher morality for any person than to simply live according to the laws of the city of Athens. Many people today have progressed not one inch higher than supposing that the height of morality is simply living by the laws of men.

Philosophy, too, degraded from the golden age of Greek philosophy. By the time of Christ it had sunk to an all-time low. Epicureanism, the philosophy of the time, was simply a measured sensate culture, the fullest enjoyment of the senses that one could experience. Skepticism and agnosticism were the twin results of religion and philosophy in the pagan world, and the moral consequences were grim indeed.

Not only did the gods require a moral code and not act morally themselves, but the philosophers, moralists, and ethical teachers taught a system of morals that many would find repulsive today. We've already seen in previous chapters the sexual perversions, the rampant abortion and infanticide, and widespread practice of slavery in the ancient world.

## THE CRUELTY OF ROME

It was a cruel age, typified by barbaric tyrannies and cruel despotisms. Take Emperor Nero as an example. He had received the finest of pagan philosophical educations, and yet he degenerated into one of the worst conceivable men. He visited brothels, frequently in disguise. He practiced, as one historian says, "lewdness on boys . . . striking, wounding, murdering." He took a mistress. He wanted to have an affair with her, and his wife objected. What do you do in a case like that? Well, it should be obvious to any and all: you simply kill your wife!—which is what he did. But his mother objected. So he killed his mother. But he wasn't completely without feeling. In fact, when he looked down on her corpse at her funeral, he said, "I did not know I had so beautiful a mother."

And so he married his mistress. Then one day she made the sad mistake of nagging him because he came home late from the races. She was in the latter stages of pregnancy. Nero kicked her in the stomach, killing both her and the child. Keep in mind, this was the ruler of the world at that time! It was indeed a cruel age.[4]

# THEN JESUS CAME

Into this cruel, lewd, licentious, and immoral world, the spotless Son of God was born. The impact of Christianity on the morality of the early Christians was profound. First of all, the people who joined their ranks were quite sincere, knowing that they could be killed for following Christ. From the days of Nero, the law existed on the books that to become a Christian was a capital offense. Some emperors enforced the law; others winked at it. In any event, those who joined the early Church were for the most part very committed. There was virtually nothing in it for them except eternal life. According to Hippolytis of Rome, a presbyter and Christian teacher who lived in the third century, the livelihood and personal relations of a new convert were examined, while undergoing three years of pre-baptismal instructions.[5] Three years! No "easy believism" here. The results were a higher standard of morality for the Christians of that time.

Will Durant points out that Roman morals had declined from the time they had overcome the Greeks—thus the conquered overcame the conquerors! Not until Christian influence was felt did there begin to be a turn around in morals. "Moral disintegration had begun with the Roman conquest of Greece, and had culminated under Nero; thereafter Roman morals improved, and the ethical influence of Christianity upon Roman life was largely a wholesome one."[6] This is astounding when you consider that even by the time of Constantine in the early part of the fourth century, the percentage of Christians was relatively small, approximately 5 percent. Durant says, "The little Christian communities were troubling the pleasure-mad pagan world with their piety and their decency."[7] Durant adds: "The morals of the early Christians were a reproving example to the pagan world."[8]

The Christian code of morality was a much higher standard than any the pagans had. In fact, it is still today higher than any other in the world. No one lives by it perfectly; only Christ did that so He could become the perfect sacrifice for our sins. Nonetheless, millions strive to live to please Christ, and by His Spirit they find change in their lives. This reminds me of the gospel song that says, to the effect, "I'm not all I ought to be; I'm not what I'm going to be; but thank God I'm not what I used to be." Durant says of the moral character of the early Church:

> The general picture of Christian morals in this period is one of piety, mutual loyalty, marital fidelity, and a quiet happiness in the possession of a confident faith. The young Pliny [a pagan] was compelled to report to Trajan [another pagan, the emperor] that the Christians led peaceful and exemplary lives. Galen [yet another pagan] described them as "so far advanced in self-discipline and . . . intense desire to attain moral excellence that they are in no way inferior to true philosophers."[9]

In the early Church there were many martyrs who faced a terrible dilemma. Their Roman conquerors knew believers would not deny Christ to save their lives. And so they would bring their spouse, or their child or father or mother, and they would ask them to deny Christ or their loved one would die horribly. And we read in the ancient writings of the Church of the pleadings that went forth from these people, begging their Christian relatives not to deny Christ to save their lives, and many thus died. The Bible would not teach that we should damn our souls, said Augustine, in order to save the bodily life of another. For the Scripture does not see this fleeting temporal life, which is but as the smoke that rises up and blows away, or the grass that grows up and is cut down, as the greatest and highest good that must be preserved at all costs. And so the moral convictions of the early church were so strong that Christians were even willing to die for Christ rather than lie.

# THE CIVILIZING OF
# THE BARBARIANS

Christianity spread to the Greeks and the Romans. And it spread to the barbarian cultures, even those that were attacking Rome. The first Romans to have an active part in civilizing these barbarians were Christian missionaries.[10] Many of the barbarians were Germanic tribes, including the Goths, the Franks, and the Saxons.

These barbarian tribes were fierce and warlike. Prior to Rome's fall, they were constantly pressing the limits of the empire by attacking the outposts of Rome. Often when these barbarians conquered, they killed everyone—men, women, and children. They even destroyed their enemies' weapons and possessions. There was "wholesale sacrifice both of living creatures and material things to the god of war."[11] This practice of total slaughter and destruction perplexed a Christian writer of the eighth century, Paul the Deacon. He said this in his history of the Lombards:

See how many people there are on both sides! What need is there that so great a multitude perish? Let us join, he and I, in single combat, and may that one of us to whom God may have willed to give the victory have and possess all this people safe and entire.[12]

Furthermore, the law of the barbarian tribes of Europe did not judge individuals alone for their own crimes, but it would also demand vengeance on the individual's relatives. Cornell University professor Brian Tierney writes: "If a man was murdered, his kin had the right and duty of inflicting vengeance on the murderer and his kin."[13] But Christianity slowly began to penetrate these cultures and tribes.

A lot of these tribes, especially the Teutons, were very superstitious—prior to Christianity. The magic arts were important to the Teutons, "for in no race, probably," writes historian Henry Charles Lea, "has the supernatural formed a larger portion of daily life, or claimed greater power over both the natural and the spiritual worlds."[14]

Over time, though, these cruel tribes—ancestors of most of us —were changed by the gospel of Christ. One of those who brought the gospel to the barbaric Anglo-Saxons in England was Augustine (not to be confused with St. Augustine, Bishop of Hippo). Augustine hesitated in Rome, prior to his great work of evangelizing the Anglo-Saxons "apparently discouraged by the stories he heard about the savagery of the English."[15] But his mission was successful, and over time these cruel savages were transformed by Christ. Although it was a gradual process that did not happen overnight, the civilizing of the barbarian people was a marvelous feat and a glorious victory for Christianity and Christ.

# THE VIKINGS

Perhaps the greatest example of the transforming power of the gospel is the Vikings, who were particularly fierce. These ancestors of the Scandinavian peoples stopped their plundering raids only when the gospel of Christ took hold in their hearts. Had Jesus never come, there is no guarantee these people would ever have stopped their brutality.

In the ninth and tenth centuries the Vikings, who were marauding adventurers, terrorized much of the coastline of Europe in their quest for plunder. They would plant their crops in the spring, then go raiding, and then return for the harvest. The Christians in the pillaged lands would pray, "God, save us from the Norsemen [Vikings]." Religious institutions (e.g., monasteries) were a particularly favorite target of the Vikings because they often housed treasures and were often poorly defended. The Vikings pillaged, raped, and killed men, women, and even children! They would systematically put to the torch what was left. Their fighting men, *berserkers*, were so fierce in battle that our word *berserk* comes from them. What changed this horrible scourge of humanity? Jesus Christ did. The gospel managed to penetrate even the Vikings—not without some resistance—and not even without some violence on the part of the new converts who didn't know better! Nonetheless, over time, many of the Scandinavians became true Christians, and so the Vikings stopped their terrible raids. Virtually every Norwegian, Dane, Swede, and even many British are descendants of these formerly fierce and warlike people.

In A.D. 1020, the Norwegians had the first national assembly in their history. At this gathering, presided over by King Olav, Christianity became law. "At the same time," writes Norwegian historian Sverre Steen, "old practices became illegal, such as blood sacrifice, black magic, the 'setting out' of infants, slavery and polygamy."[16]

Christianity has made a great contribution to world civilization by raising morality in various nations, cultures, and tribes to a much higher level. And while no one has ever achieved Christian perfection—with the exception of Jesus Christ Himself—this higher standard has elevated morality everywhere the gospel has penetrated. In the 1940s a history professor at New York University, Dr. Joseph Reither, wrote a book on world history in one volume, entitled *World History at a Glance.* Here is what he says about Christianity and the civilizing of all the barbarian tribes in which it had come into contact by the ninth century:

> When we contemplate the violence and chaos which attended the disruption of Charlemagne's great empire, and when we recall that distracted and disunited Europe was beset upon all sides by enemies—Vikings to the north, Saracens to the south, Magyars and Slavs to the east—we marvel that out of this confusion there arose a great civilization. Throughout these early centuries of turmoil one institution above all others patiently and persistently labored to combat the forces of disintegration and decay. During the era that has long been known as the Dark Ages, it was the Latin Christian Church which succeeded little by little in restraining violence and in restoring order, justice, and decency. A distinguished and critical student of the Latin church has acknowledged that in all the history of mankind no other institution "has exercised so vast an influence on human destinies."[17]

# INTERMITTENT PERIODS OF MORALITY AND IMMORALITY

There have been times of mighty outpourings of the Spirit of God that have changed whole nations. The Reformation of the sixteenth century changed the whole face of Europe.

A few centuries later England had sunk low into deism. God

was gone from the landscape, and the people were overwhelmed in their iniquity. It is said that iniquity flowed in the streets and filled the gutters. Then God raised up John Wesley and George Whitefield. They began to pray and to preach, and God poured out His Spirit on England. There was a great reformation again in that country, and the people were brought back to God.

Many years later the same thing happened in the Irish revival. There was also a revival in Wales in which first one man began to pray, then a few others, and then God poured out His Spirit in the same way that He did in the great Hebrides revival. After the Church of God began to get right, God so moved in each of these places, by His Holy Spirit, that multitudes of people began to be converted. People thronged into the churches where there was standing room only.

During the time of the Hebrides revival, the Spirit of God fell on one town, then moved out into other towns. Hundreds of thousands of people were swept into the Kingdom of God. In many towns the bars were closed; the saloons were closed; the jails were emptied. Can you imagine that? People didn't need to lock their doors! They didn't need jailers watching prisoners. God so changed the hearts of people that the jails were empty! The Great Awakening in America did the same thing.

# THE MODERN
# MISSIONS MOVEMENT

What happened in the latter part of the first millennium of the Christian era with many of our ancestors turning away from barbarianism and turning to Christ, has taken place in parts of Asia, Africa, and Latin America in the last two hundred years. Churches and mission agencies have been sending Christians out into the far corners of the world to spread the gospel. They have gone out with their wives and children among cannibals and barbarians and savages who had the cruelest habits. These missionaries have accomplished incredible things!

Unfortunately, there has often been much apathy (even presently) on the part of many so-called Christians, who cannot even be bothered to come out and hear about missions. The Christian missionary movement has operated with just the offscourings of money the Christian Church has raised. Eighty-eight percent of the workers in the Christian world work in English-speaking countries. But with a handful of workers and a modicum of money, the Christian missionary movement has, in my opinion, accomplished the most astonishing results ever witnessed on this planet. I believe the Christian missionary movement is the most remarkable and successful movement in the entire history of the human race.

It is amazing to see a brutal people in New Guinea—who would ferociously kill their neighbor for merely a slight violation of superstitious customs[18]—fall before the spell of the gospel of Jesus Christ and come to the place where virtually the entire tribe is converted and worshiping the living Savior. It is amazing to see the vicious Aucas even become missionaries to other tribes farther downstream. The Auca Indians of Ecuador had previously never allowed anyone who entered their domain to live; in 1956, they killed five Christian missionaries, an event that was written up in *Life* magazine. To see that whole tribe converted to Christ was, as Darwin would have worded it, "the work of the enchanter's wand"—and is a marvelous thing to behold. I am sure Christianity is a supernatural work when one considers the results it has produced in the lives of people.

# MARY SLESSOR OF CALABAR

The work of William Carey is well-known, as is that of David Livingstone and Hudson Taylor. But for every one of these famous missionaries of the last two centuries, there are thousands of lesser-known lights who carried the gospel to those who previously lived in darkness. Literally hundreds of stories from the modern missionary movement could be told at this point; stories that underscore the fact that the gospel of Jesus Christ changes the morality of people by transforming their hearts. I will tell of only one, Mary Slessor of Calabar (1848–1915), who was from Scotland. She was converted in her teens, and after doing mission work in the slums of Dundee, she felt the call of God to serve as a missionary to Africa. In 1876, she left for Nigeria.

She learned that beyond Okoyong, deeper in the heart of Africa, around Calabar, was an area in which lived four million savages so ferocious, so fierce, that even the government soldiers feared to penetrate the land. These four million cannibals were so degraded, their customs so vile, that it stretches the imagination to consider the types of things they did.

Witchcraft and drunkenness were rampant. The savages worshiped fetishes; they murdered twins; they turned the mother of twins out into the jungle to be devoured by beasts because they believed twins were brought about by a conjunction with a demon. Almost half of the population was slaves. When a man died, they would eat fifty slaves; twenty-five more would have their hands tied behind them and their heads would be whacked off. Unmarried women were chattel. They could be raped, tortured, or murdered at will. It was an incredible degradation, especially for women. Children were considered no better than animals, often simply left to die.

Mary's heart was touched by the plight of twins always left to die or ground to pieces in a pot. She would snatch them up and take them in. At first the people were astonished because they believed that anybody who touched a twin would die, but Mary didn't die. So she gathered around her over the years many of these young "bairns," as she called them, to nurture them.

In incredible ways, by her faith in God, in her prayer, her winning countenance, the love she demonstrated, she was accepted. People milled around her and looked. They had never seen a white person before. They touched her skin.

She began to teach them about the Son of God who had loved them enough to die for their sins. Astonishingly, God opened up their hearts. They became very willing to hear. One after another the chiefs of the various villages yielded their lives to Christ. One after another the tremendously horrible customs plaguing these people for years were abolished; the murder of twins, infanticide, the slaughter of wives and slaves, the trial by poison and boiling oil, and all other terrible customs.

Perpetual warfare among the different tribes had continued for innumerable centuries, but when she would hear of a tribe of warriors going out to attack another tribe, she would run barefoot through the jungle, where there were poisonous snakes and plants. She would head them off, standing in front of a whole host of armed cannibals with outstretched arms to demand that they stop. They did! Through her ministry, thousands from the Ibo tribe became Christians and abandoned their degrading ways. Indeed, the moral standards of many parts of the world have risen dramatically because of Christianity. Without Jesus Christ, there would never have been a Mary Slessor of Calabar.

# MODERN REJECTION OF CHRISTIANITY

But today as the Christian influence—particularly in the West —is pushed back, we see more and more what it was like *before* Christ. The riots in Los Angeles in 1992 are only a taste of what could come, unless we return to God.

"Ours is a cut-flower civilization," said Dr. Elton Trueblood many years ago. A cut-flower civilization may for the moment have some beauty—its technological advances are stirring—but it has been cut off from the source of its life and is inevitably decaying. Already we see the wilting petals and the drooping of the leaves. Our nation is already in a state of advanced degeneration.

What is wrong with ethics in America? A few years ago an edition of *Time* magazine featured this cover story: "What Ever Happened to Ethics?"[19] That same kind of story has been found in virtually every news magazine in America.[20]

Does that make any difference to you? Well, let me point out that the U.S. Chamber of Commerce declares that because of widespread employee theft in America today, across-the-board consumer goods cost as much as 15 percent more than they would otherwise. We talk about a 1 percent increase in sales tax and get alarmed, yet we have a 15 percent sin-tax on all consumer goods in America today!

We have created a morals-free, values-free society and now we are reaping the whirlwind. All of the scandals we've seen in America—in government, on Wall Street, in banking institutions, even in the Church—are simply the pimples on the surface that are arising from the moral corruption within.

## CANNOT GET AN "OUGHT" FROM AN "IS"

As soon as you get rid of God you have nothing left but to look around and examine the experience of people. The *Humanist Manifesto* says that human ethics are experiential; they are based on human experience. What they don't realize is something that every intelligent, ethical teacher knows: "You cannot get an ought from an is." George Gallup may survey the entire population of America and decide that 99.9 percent of the people are doing such and such. That does not mean the people *ought* to do such and such. You could conduct a survey and determine that 100 percent of the American people are sinning. That doesn't mean we *ought* to sin. We saw recently that 91 percent of Americans confessed to lying. That doesn't mean we *ought* to lie. You can never obtain an "ought" from an "is." So once you get rid of the divine revelation of God and religion, there is no way that you can ever establish what people ought to do simply by some rational means. But there is a God, and He has shown us what is right and what is wrong. And He gives those who believe in His Son the Holy Spirit, so that we may be empowered to obey His law.

## CONCLUSION

The religion of Jesus Christ has done more to elevate moral standards than any other force in history. Had Jesus never come, it's unlikely the Ten Commandments would be known beyond the Jews. Had Jesus never come, many of us—those who are of Anglo-Saxon stock—might still be drinking out of human skulls as they used to. Had Jesus never come, the Scandinavians might still be out plundering and terrorizing their neighbors as their ancestors, the Vikings, used to, until the gospel of Christ took hold. Had Jesus never come, many of the formerly cannibalistic tribes of Africa, Asia, or the Americas would no doubt still be gorging on human flesh. But Jesus *did* come, and He elevated morality and life on earth to a much higher level than ever before. As many in the West continue to reject Him and His standards of right and wrong, we seem to be regressing to the vile and unspeakable sins that besmirched the ancient pagan world.

# CHAPTER 12

# INSPIRING THE WORLD'S GREATEST ART

## Christianity's Impact on the Arts and Music

*Then Moses called Bezaleel and Aholiab, and every gifted artisan in whose heart the LORD had put wisdom.*

(Exod. 36:2*a*)

**Y**ou've probably seen them repeatedly throughout your life. You've seen them reproduced in books, magazines, wall plaques, and in embroidery. What we're talking about is "the praying hands," which are based on a 500-year old woodcut by Christian artist Albrecht Dürer (1471–1528) from Germany. But do you know the touching story behind that woodcut? Dürer and an older friend were aspiring artists. But they were both so poor that they lived together to cut down on their expenses. They entered into an agreement that one would work so the other could study and paint; and then after a few years, the other would reciprocate. Dürer volunteered to work first, but his friend, seeing greater potential in Dürer's abilities, insisted that his younger friend study and paint first.

After several years of hard work, when it was time to trade places, the friend of Dürer could no longer paint; his hands were too worn and stiff. He had missed his chance to paint so that the world would be made richer by Albrecht Dürer's God-given talent! But being a man of prayer, he wasn't embittered. One day, when Dürer found his friend in prayer, his "work-worn" hands inspired him to make the wood-cut. And now you know the significance of those praying hands that you've seen countless times.[1]

Jesus Christ has given art its loftiest themes. As one writer put it, the idea that God spared not His Son but delivered Him up for us all has "inspired the highest flights that pictorial art has reached."[2] Many of the greatest masterpieces in the world have had a Christian theme or base. Often the Church, particularly the Roman Catholic Church, has been a major patron of the arts. The great cathedrals of Europe are among the finest architectural masterpieces known, and their inspiration comes from Jesus. It was a servant of Christ, Bach (a man who dedicated every note he wrote to the glory of Jesus Christ), who changed Western music for all time. Had Jesus never been born, art would depict only the finite. The attempt to capture the Infinite on canvas or in stone would never have been introduced. In short, had Jesus never come, the world would be poorer, even in the realms of art and music.

Unfortunately, many Christians today don't seem to put much emphasis on the fine arts. They are, as Franky Schaeffer once put it, "addicted to mediocrity." But we believe that in all areas, our lives must be explicitly offered to God and to His glory. All the world is to be subdued for Jesus Christ. We are called to be conquerors in the name of the King. We are, as it were, the co-partners of God in the conquest of this world. We need to go and conquer in the name of Christ and bring His Word to bear on all things and then offer them to His glory. This is as true in the arts as in any other field.

Both the Old and the New Testaments have provided art with some of its greatest subjects. Prior to Christianity, Jews interpreted the second commandment so strictly that visual art was rare. Richard Muhlberger, an art museum curator and author of *The Bible in Art: Old Testament* and *The Bible in Art: New Testament* writes: "The advent of Christianity brought forth a desire to match words with images, and since then the texts of the Old Testament have held a place in art equal to those of the

Gospels and Epistles."[3] If Jesus had never been born, there would be no art from the Old Testament as well as the New.

# JESUS, THE INSPIRATION OF GREAT ART

Earlier this century, author Cynthia Pearl Maus compiled an anthology of some of the greatest pictures, poetry, music, and stories about Jesus. Here is what she writes in the Introduction of that book, which is entitled *Christ and the Fine Arts*:

More poems have been written, more stories told, more pictures painted, and more songs sung about Christ than any other person in human history, because through such avenues as these the deepest appreciation of the human heart can be more adequately expressed.[4]

The Christian revelation of God stands in great contrast with any other religion. The awe-inspiring God of the Jews becomes human in Jesus Christ. The Infinite becomes temporarily finite and observable to the human eye! Wonder of wonders. And art has never been the same since.

# ART IN THE FIRST MILLENNIUM OF THE CHRISTIAN ERA

In the first three centuries of its existence, the Church produced little art that survives to this day. Indeed, the Church was fighting for its very life as it endured wave upon wave of hostile persecution. The little Christian art that survives from this period is mostly what has been found in the catacombs.

After Constantine legalized Christianity and moved his capitol to Byzantium—which was later to be known as Constantinople (today it is Istanbul, in present-day Turkey)—the Byzantine style of art eventually began to flourish. In architecture, there was "an almost overnight blossoming of church architecture."[5] Many of these great basilicas went beyond the Greek temple. The Greek temple was believed to contain the finite god or goddess to whom the temple was dedicated. But the Christian church building contained only the worshipers of the Infinite God, whom heaven and earth cannot contain!

After Christianity became legal, many great basilicas were built, although the most glorious buildings to the glory of God were built in our millennium. The craftsmen who skillfully built these early church buildings were able to create, in the words of art historian H. W. Janson, "a shimmering realm of light, where precious marble and glittering mosaics evoke the unearthly splendor of the Kingdom of God."[6] Some of the churches that survive from this period are most impressive, such as Haggai Sophia in modern-day Istanbul.[7]

## THE GREAT CATHEDRALS

The great cathedrals, pre-Gothic, Gothic, and post-Gothic, of the Middle Ages are among the greatest works of art ever produced. They were marvelous achievements in stone and glass. And they are still marvels today. Around A.D. 1000, cathedrals began to be built. The period roughly between 1000 and 1200 is known as "Romanesque." All over the Christian world of the West—"from northern Spain to the Rhineland, from the Scottish-English border to central Italy"[8] great, impressive cathedrals were constructed to the glory of God. These churches had vaulted ceilings made of stone, no longer wood. These were extremely elaborate buildings, many of which survive to this day, despite two world wars.

During the next two centuries, from roughly 1200 to 1400 comes the Gothic period. Then the elaborate cathedrals got even more beautiful! In France, Abbé Suger of the Abbey Church of St. Denis was a chief adviser to King Louis VI. He wanted to make the Abbey the "spiritual center of France, a pilgrimage church to outshine the splendour of all the others."[9] He had the Abbey rebuilt from 1137 to 1144 in a stunning new way, and visitors from all over Europe came and marveled at what they saw, and so the new Gothic style was born. Immediately it began to be imitated and diffused throughout the Western Christian world.

The most important aspects of the new style were directly reflected in the Cathedral of Notre Dame in Paris, which began construction in 1163. Many centuries later, people still marvel at this and other great cathedrals of Europe. Every day they point upward to God. They delight the eyes and senses; they communicate visually the splendor and grandeur of God.

# THE RENAISSANCE

The Renaissance was a golden age of art, and biblical themes were among the most predominant motifs. Some historians superficially evaluate the Renaissance as if all these innovators were "neo-pagans." But that's not accurate. In fact, they "went to great lengths to reconcile classical philosophy with Christianity; and architects continued to build churches, not pagan temples."[10]

Look at the great work of Michelangelo (1475–1564). His great statues are of biblical characters, such as David, Moses, and the Pieta—the crucified Christ in the arms of His grieving mother. His masterpiece is his work on the ceiling and walls of the Sistene Chapel, which is also biblical in nature.

Not only did Michelangelo paint and sculpt great Christian works, but he himself was a devout Christian. A talented genius in every way, he even wrote poetry late in life. The Christian religion was a major theme of his poetry. He also supervised some architectural projects, including the building of the awe-inspiring dome of St. Peter's Church in Rome. Michelangelo brought forth great works to the glory of God, and to this day his work inspires millions.

Other great artists of the Renaissance—whether they were Christian or not—painted on Christian themes. Raphael's (1483–1520) greatest work, like Michelangelo's, was Christian. Although he lived to be only thirty-seven, he painted hundreds of beautiful paintings, including some three hundred of the Madonna. Reportedly, our image of the way Mary looked comes from Raphael's hands! Leonardo da Vinci (1452–1519), one of the most versatile human beings that ever lived, pioneered in a variety of fields. He too has left the world with great works of art inspired by Christianity, such as *The Last Supper* (which is now *the* definitive Last Supper), *St. John the Baptist*, *Annunciation*, *Madonna and Child*, *St. Jerome*, and *Adoration of the Magi*.

There are numerous other examples we could list of great painters who produced great art based on Christian themes, from the Van Eyck brothers to Rembrandt van Rijn. All one has to do is glance through a book on the history of art or visit an art museum to see that indeed the Christian religion has provided the greatest themes for the greatest art.

# MODERN ART: IN REBELLION AGAINST CHRISTIANITY

It's interesting how modern art reflects the modern irrationality of modern man. Living in a post-Christian culture, we see the effects of man's rejection of God even in art. Much art started to become irrational as the West began to move away from God and His divine revelation.

Art reflects life, and if life to the artist is meaningless, so will art be meaningless. To the laity, much of modern art is a joke. This point was brought home on an episode of the TV sitcom "Get Smart," when Maxwell Smart was explaining the meaning of a modern painting and in particular a black dot that seemed to be the focus of the painting. His theory made sense until that black dot, a fly, flew away! Writer Thomas Howard says that modern art *purposefully* rejects Christian influence in art:

Christianity and art were causally linked between the fourth and the twentieth centuries. Even the "post-Christian" art and literature of the last two hundred years in the West emerges from Christian roots—and often involves a more or less conscious repudiation of Christian categories, and an attempt to forge new forms, free of Christian influence.[11]

## CHRIST AND LITERATURE

Jesus has also had a very positive impact on literature, providing us with some of the greatest themes and ideas. As one writer put it, "Literature and the gospel are bosom friends."[12] From Dante to Chaucer, from John Donne to Fyodor Dostoevsky, the Christian faith has influenced literature, and literature has helped to spread the gospel.[13] Author Joseph Nelson Greene writes:

English literature owes a large debt to Christianity. Much of the subject matter and many of the themes of our best literature have their origin and inspiration in the gospel of Christ . . . the debt of literature to the gospel is large, for the spirit and teachings of the gospel color the pages of all our literature. . . . Take out of all secular literature the truth that had its birth in the gospel of Jesus, and you have made a wound in the literature of the nations from which the lifeblood will speedily ebb away.[14]

William Shakespeare (1564–1616), one of the world's greatest writers, was heavily influenced by Christianity. In his book on the bard from Stratford-upon-Avon, Victor Hugo wrote, "England has two books: one which she made; the other which made her—Shakespeare and the Bible."[15] The Christian influence on Shakespeare is demonstrated in Ernest Marshall Howse's *Spiritual Values in Shakespeare* and in Dr. George Morrison's *Christ in Shakespeare*. It is clear that Shakespeare knew the Bible and knew it well, for there are numerous passages where we can "trace its phraseology, and beyond its phraseology we can detect its thought."[16] Shakespeare clearly reflects his Christian faith in his last will and testament: "I commend my soul into the hands of God my Creator, hoping and assuredly believing through the only merits of Jesus Christ my Saviour, to be made partaker of life everlasting; and my body to the earth, whereof it is made."[17]

John Bunyan (1628–1688) gave the world one of the greatest novels ever written, *Pilgrim's Progress*. This parable of the Christian life is one of the all-time most published and widely read books in the history of the world. In the simplest of languages, our native English comes forth with its greatest power. Bunyan has enriched our lives with vivid images, each of which preaches a practical sermon. In so doing he coined phrases that permeate our culture, such as "Vanity Fair," the "Celestial City" or the "Slough of Despond."

Another towering literary giant who was inspired by the Christian faith is John Milton (1608–1674), author of *Paradise Lost* and *Paradise Regained*. These two masterpieces deal with the first Adam, who brought sin into the world, and Jesus Christ, the second Adam, who was the beginning of a whole new creation. Milton's inspired thought has lifted and enriched the lives of millions. Though he became physically blind, he had great spiritual sight that he was able to impart to his readers. Here's a short clip from this great writer, from *Paradise Regained*.

> Then in the realm of Death's unbroken shade
> Appeared the Conqueror in light arrayed.
> It was as tho' in crimson and in gold
> The splendour of a thousand suns had tolled
> Their mingled glory in one matchless beam,
> And lit up Death Shade with the lustrous gleam.

Charles Dickens (1812–1870), yet another magnificent writer of English literature, once wrote that the greatest story in *all* of literature was Christ's parable of the prodigal son. Dickens's *A Christmas Carol*—on the transformation of the miserly Scrooge —is believed by many to be a parable of Christian conversion. The last published book of Dickens was *The Life of Our Lord*, which he wrote to teach his children about Jesus Christ. He opens the book with these words:

> My dear children, I am very anxious that you should know something about the History of Jesus Christ. For everybody ought to know about Him. No one ever lived, who was so good, so kind, so gentle, and so sorry for all people who did wrong, or were in any way ill or miserable, as he was.[18]

Music was judged by its ability to lift the soul toward God. Music was a servant of the Word.

# MUSIC DURING THE MIDDLE AGES: THE BIRTH OF MUSICAL NOTATION

The work of the eleventh century monk Guido of Arezzo (c. 995–c.1050) was critical in the development of Western music. This Benedictine monk was the father of the modern musical notation. He wanted his students to memorize the notes *c-d-e-f-g-a*. So he took the words of a familiar hymn "Ut Queant Laxis," which was a Christian song centered on St. John, and he created a mnemonic device:

UT queant laxis REsonare fibris
MIre gestorum FAmuli tuorum
SOLve pollutis LAbiis reatum
Sancte Iohannes[21]

The initial syllables of the words of the six phrases became the names of the notes: "ut," "re," "mi," "fa," "sol," "la." We still learn them this way today, except we say "doh" for "ut" and have added a "ti" after "la." Guido of Arezzo also developed more accurate notation of the pitch of a note, and so Western music was freed from depending on oral traditions. This was as crucial to the development of music as written language is to literature!

Even though some music existed at that time outside the Church, it is predominantly the Church music that has been preserved. In Church music we have the foundation of all Western music. Therefore, we can say that music as we know it in the Western world is largely a product of the Church.

Because of Guido of Arezzo, the eleventh century was the crucial turning point that made Western music different from all other music of the world. We want to underscore three main developments:

1. With the notation of music it became possible to compose, and music could exist in itself outside of the performance! It could be written down and taught from a score.
2. Order, rules, and logic—i.e., music theory—followed from notations.
3. Polyphony (more than one melody playing at the same time) developed. So also did harmony.

These changes were gradual, but they originated during this time. They developed so rapidly into new discoveries that by the sixteenth century new expressions and new techniques had opened a new world of musical language. So much so that the period of music history in which we now live is still part of that period, although to some music critics, this period is ending.

The Church continued to lead the development through the Middle Ages with the choirmasters at Notre Dame in Paris. Notations became accurate in rhythm as well as in pitch. From the School of Notre Dame came the motet. The motet was the beginning of four-part harmony—soprano, alto, tenor, and bass. The motet spread through Europe in the thirteenth century with two- and three- and up to four-part arrangements.

In the beginning, all polyphonic, or multi-part, music was Church music. But as it developed, both sacred and secular texts were used. The next centuries saw an enormous development of musical styles and functions. After the thirteenth century, secular music began to flourish and had its outlets at the courts and castles of Europe. New forms of music, such as the madrigal and the rondeau (rondo) developed. These in turn developed into more complex forms.

# THE RENAISSANCE AND THE REFORMATION

Although handwritten scores and books were common before the printing press, Gutenberg's invention made musical scores accessible to more people, but not yet the masses. During the Renaissance, music became more and more independent of words. Widespread use of instruments, secular music, and the beginning of national styles developed. At this time music and the Church were no longer tied to each other, but the foundation for our musical system had already been born in the Church. And during this time, many of the compositions (e.g., those of Palestrina), were Christian in theme.

With the Reformation, more music came into the Church. Martin Luther loved songs and music. He composed and played the lute, which was the forerunner of the guitar, and he wanted the congregation to participate in the music of the Church. The German chorale became very important. Luther himself wrote some, most notably "A Mighty Fortress Is Our God." Luther even brought some secular songs into the Church and gave them sacred lyrics. For example, a love song by Hans Leo Hassler was changed into the hymn "O Sacred Head Now Wounded." The musical heritage from the Reformation era is enormous. Luther made music for the congregation to sing; by using chorales and hymns, he sought to teach the masses—many of whom were illiterate—basic Christian doctrines through music.

# THE BAROQUE PERIOD

The Baroque period reached its height with Johann Sebastian Bach (1685–1750) and George Friedric Handel (1685–1759). Both of these men were Christians, whose greatest works were composed to the glory of Jesus Christ. Handel has ministered to millions with his sacred oratorios, most notably the *Messiah* (written in 1741, first performed in 1742). Handel composed this fantastic work in less than twenty-five days, and he felt that he was under divine inspiration. We will have more to say about Bach in just a moment. The major-minor system that was hammered in stone during the Baroque era—especially by Bach's "Well Tempered Clavier"—completed the foundation for all Western music to come.

A Catholic priest, Antonio Vivaldi (c.1680–1741), was the Master of the Italian Baroque. Known as "the Red Priest" (because of the color of his hair), Vivaldi was excused from priestly service because of bad asthma. So he devoted himself to music. As a conductor, composer, and teacher, Vivaldi's influence was enormous. His writings for string orchestra were revolutionary. His work was pivotal in the development of the concerto with a soloist or solo group. Vivaldi's clarity of form, rhythm, logic, and musical ideas were a direct influence on J. S. Bach, who copied Vivaldi's concertos, arranging them for different instruments. Through Vivaldi's concertos, his style is found throughout the following centuries.

# THE GREAT CONTRIBUTIONS OF J. S. BACH

Many music critics declare that Bach is the greatest musician that ever lived. His genius is unsurpassed. He not only begat twenty-three children, but he also is famous for a paternity of another sort: He is the father of modern music. That is, the father of all modern music of the last few centuries. He left no musical form as he found it, says one critic. On the other hand, with every form he touched he said the last word. Bach's development of the fugue—and, therefore, contrapuntal music—is the foundation of what we call today "classical music." Growing from this base, concertos, sonatas, quartets, and even symphonies were able to develop. Bach's teaching notebooks and violin books have been the basis for music theory and practice ever since his day. Four of Bach's sons, including C. P. E. and W. F., helped in this process.

There can be no doubt that Johann Sebastian Bach was a Christian. He was a Christian to the very core of his life. He was, in fact, an orthodox Lutheran. When he died there were found in his library eighty-three volumes of entirely religious works. Included were all of Luther's works and many of the other German divines. Bach believed in the great doctrines of the Christian faith. In fact, several have noted that in his music and in his writings you can see an almost eager desire to depart this world to be with Christ, which, as Paul said, was far better. An example of this is Cantata #140, "Wachet Auf" (or "Sleepers, Awake"). Co-author Jerry Newcombe remembers being told by one of his professors of music at Tulane University that every single note Bach wrote was dedicated to the glory of Jesus Christ!

Bach knew what it meant to be a real Christian. In fact, it has been noted by many historians that over all of his manuscripts you find different things, different letters, such as "S.D.G." Do you know what that means? *Soli Deo Gloria*: "Solely to the glory of God." At the beginning you would find the letters "J. J.," standing for *Jesu Juban*, "Help me, Jesus." He would dedicate many of his books and cantatas "I.N.J.," *In Nomine Jesu*, "In the name of Jesus"; "To the most high God." Such Latin phrases as these are found everywhere throughout his manuscripts. He told his pupils that unless they committed their talents to the Lord Jesus Christ, they would never be great musicians, for music, according to Bach, was an act of worship.

So pervasive was his influence that Beethoven studied greatly and in-depth the works of Bach. He was tremendously influenced, as was Haydn, Mendelssohn, Mozart, Chopin, Wagner, Brahms, and many others.

Bach was the culmination and climax of the Baroque era of music, which laid the foundation for all music that followed. He was the first man to play keyboard instruments with five fingers. Can you imagine that before that time everyone played with just three? But Bach used the thumb and the little finger as well.

Not only that, Bach created the "well-tempered" scale, so that from any point on the piano or organ—from any note—one could begin a scale, which was impossible before that time. As one critic said, "Bach is to music what Shakespeare is to literature. They are both the greatest." Interestingly enough, they were both Christians.

Even though Bach's influence was enormous, his own music was actually out of use for almost a century. It was not until Felix Mendelssohn (1809–1847), another devout Christian, performed Bach's *St. Matthew Passion* in Berlin in 1829 that Bach's music started to grow in popularity again all over the world.

## WESTERN MUSIC AFTER BACH

Some of the great masters of the years to follow through the Classic and Romantic periods were Christians; most were not. But it is not crucial for music history, for the critical point is that the foundation for Western music, and its subsequent development, was laid by the Christian Church. Because of the Church, we have today an enormous treasure of classical music—from simple songs to complex symphonies—all based on their scales and musical principles.

In the twentieth century, we have seen a partial breakdown of our tonal system with the twelve-tone scale. With Stravinsky, Schönberg, and Bartok, a new music has been introduced, and a millennium of Christian music is possibly at an end. Subjectively speaking, some of Stravinsky can be stomached, but listening to the other two, in our opinions, is about as pleasant as a visit to the dentist. A lot of this new music is built upon pagan and primitive rhythms and atonal ideas. Most of these changes away from the musical foundations of the Church are virtually unknown to the laity. They may be reflected in some noisy rock songs, but they are not reflected in most pop music (easy listening, country, light contemporary, etc.). They are most often heard in some strands of "classical music" of the twentieth century. Musical changes happen slowly—sometimes over centuries —but the Church of Jesus Christ has given the world a rich heritage of great music.

Had Jesus never been born, music would sound very different from what we're used to. If He had never been born, music today would probably sound somewhat similar to what we hear in the Middle East or Far East. There never would have developed the cantata, the concerto, or the symphony.

# EVEN HOLLYWOOD SOMETIMES PRAISES HIM!

Even the motion picture, which is generally a very secular genre, has on occasion—directly or indirectly—glorified Him who has inspired the world's greatest art. Some of the finest films ever made have had strong Christian themes or characters—depicted in a positive way. This would include such films as *Ben-Hur* (which won more Oscars than any film in history), *It's a Wonderful Life, On the Waterfront, The Sound of Music, A Man for All Seasons*, and *Chariots of Fire*.[22] *Ben-Hur* has one of the main plot lines—the leprosy of Ben-Hur's mother and sister—resolved by Jesus Christ; they are healed of the dreaded disease because of Christ's death on the cross.

Film critic Michael Medvid, who co-hosts PBS's "Sneak Previews," points out in his book *Hollywood vs. America* that Hollywood makes numerous films that are anti-religious, yet invariably these flop in the box office. On the other hand, when they make films dealing with religion in a positive way, they are often surprise box office hits.[23]

# CONCLUSION

Whether made by a Christian or a non-Christian, the greatest theme of art has been inspired by the life of Christ. We close with a thought on Christ's impact on literature, which applies equally as well to Christ's impact on art in general. Here's an observation written eighty years ago by author Joseph Nelson Greene:

There is a strange legend of a world that grew colorless in a single night. The color faded from the sky; the sea became pale and motionless; the green vanished from the grass and the color from the flowers; the fire died from the diamond, and the pearl lost its light. Nature put on her robes of mourning, and the people who lived there became sad and afraid. A world had lost its life and light. If to-night, with one sweep of the arm you brush from literature the Christ, the scenes and suggestions from His life, the spirit which He exhibited, the principles for which He stood, you would have a world made colorless in a night. It would be the world of letters, for Christ is the color thereof.[24]

# CHAPTER 13

# AMAZING
# GRACE

## Lives Changed by Jesus Christ

*Therefore, if anyone is in Christ, he is a new creation; old things have passed away; behold, all things have become new.*

The apostle Paul (2 Cor. 5:17)

In the nineteenth century, Charles Bradlaugh, a prominent atheist challenged a Christian man to a debate on the validity of the claims of Christianity. The Christian, Hugh Price Hughes, was an active soul-winner working among the poor in the slums of London. Hughes told Bradlaugh he would agree to the debate on one condition.

Hughes said, "I propose to you that we each bring some concrete evidences of the validity of our beliefs in the form of men and women who have been redeemed from the lives of sin and shame by the influence of our teaching. I will bring 100 such men and women, and I challenge you to do the same."

Hughes then said that if Bradlaugh couldn't bring 100, then he could bring 50; if he couldn't bring 50, then he could bring 20. He finally whittled the number down to one. All Bradlaugh had to do was to find one person whose life was improved by atheism and Hughes—who would bring 100 people improved by Christ—would agree to debate him. Bradlaugh withdrew![1] If such a debate challenge and counterchallenge were offered today, the response would be comparable. People are not improved by atheism, unless they so define that as abandoning a twisted form of Christianity that isn't Christianity at all! But people *are* improved by the gospel of Christ.

In this chapter, we'll meet:

- a Parisian playboy
- a fourth-century skeptic who lived according to the flesh
- a twentieth-century skeptic who lived according to the flesh
- a prostitute
- a cheat who lived high off the hog on his neighbors
- an accomplice to murder
- a ruthless politician who used dirty tricks to advance his politics
- a drunk
- a slave-trader
- a headhunter
- a prisoner of war consumed by hatred of his captors
- the Japanese captain who led the raid on Pearl Harbor

See if you can recognize them as you read along. All of these people have one thing in common: They were changed from what they were to a new creation in Jesus Christ. This change was from "the inside out."

Jesus Christ is in the business of changing people's lives. From the first century to the present, He has been active in the miracle of transforming human hearts. In His own day, there was a dishonest and greedy tax collector named Zacchaeus, whom Christ changed into a generous man (Luke 19:1–9). As a tax collector at that time and in that context, he was living well by extortion of his neighbors—until he met Jesus.[2] On the occasion of Zacchaeus's conversion, Jesus said: "For the Son of Man has come to seek and to save that which was lost" (Luke 19:10).

There was a woman of ill repute—Mary Magdalene—whom Jesus changed from being a prostitute to being a part of His mission. In God's providence, He allowed Mary Magdalene to be the first person to see Christ after His resurrection. He took a life that was meaningless and menacing to society and changed that life into one that had meaning and was contributory to society.

Jesus transformed the life of an accomplice to murder into one of those who would have the greatest impact on the world, and particularly Western civilization—the apostle Paul! In a special issue of *U.S. News & World Report* magazine, historian Daniel J. Boorstin wrote an article entitled, "History's Hidden Turning Points," and subtitled, "The true watersheds in human affairs are seldom spotted quickly amid the tumult of headlines broadcast on the hour."[3] The *first* major watershed he wrote about was "The Momentous Mission of the apostle Paul." Boorstin observes:

> Contemporary historians did not deem him worthy of a single mention, having no inkling of how great a tent maker Paul of Tarsus was. They could not know that he was erecting the theological tent of Christianity, making it broad enough to accommodate all manner of humankind, to girdle the globe and to survive two millenniums as a major force in history.[4]

This achievement is even more significant when we realize that Paul initially persecuted the Christians, and was a willing accessory to the murder of Stephen, the first recorded Christian martyr (Acts 7:58; 8:1,3). But the Saul who had been active in serious persecution of Christians became a totally new man thanks to Jesus Christ. As Paul (formerly Saul) himself wrote, under inspiration of the Holy Spirit: "If any man be in Christ, he is a new creature: old things are passed away; behold, all things are become new" (2 Cor. 5:17).

But this story, written on human hearts, is no mere quaint tale that happened long ago and far away and is no longer seen in our day—like the miracle of the parting of the Red Sea. The story of Christ changing the human heart is found throughout the centuries and is happening today. Even many of you reading this book can testify that Jesus has changed you for the better. Had Jesus not come, these lives would yet be in their sins; many of them might be dead because of drugs or alcohol or suicide or gang membership.

In accounting terms, Jesus takes liabilities to society and transforms them into assets! He did it in His day; He has done it through the centuries; He does it in our day; He can do it for *you*. The liability becomes an asset, when Christ is part of the equation. In this chapter, we will explore a few prominent conversions through the centuries and conclude by showing how Christ can change your life, too, if you don't know Him.[5]

# AUGUSTINE OF HIPPO

Augustine of Hippo (354–430) was "the greatest of the Latin Fathers."[6] He was "the last major thinker of the ancient world and the first philosopher and theologian of the middle ages."[7] Augustine has written up his pre-Christian and post-Christian experience in his classic work *Confessions*. Writing from a post-conversion perspective, he bravely spells out the sins and debauchery of his former life.

> I will now call to mind my past foulness, and the carnal corruptions of my soul; not because I love them, but that I may love Thee, O my God.[8]

Theologian Ronald Nash sums up well Augustine's pre-Christian life in a sentence by saying that from the time "when he was about sixteen, Augustine seldom lost an opportunity to pursue one sin or another."[9] He had sex out of wedlock and fathered a son prior to his twentieth birthday.

But over time, his various arguments against Christianity were refuted, and he became a Christian in 386, "in a villa outside Rome."[10] When he heard a little child's voice repeat "take up and read," he noticed a portion of Scripture nearby and he read from it. In particular, he came across Romans 13:14, which states, "But put on the Lord Jesus Christ, and make no provision for the flesh, to fulfill its lusts." This cut him to the quick, and thus Augustine experienced "one of the more dramatic conversions in the history of the Christian church."[11] For more details, see Book 8 of his *Confessions*. Augustine went on to become one of the most important thinkers, writers, philosophers and theologians in history. His work had great impact on the centuries to come—and all this from a former hedonist.

# FRANCIS XAVIER

Another hedonist to become a strong Christian leader was Francis Xavier (1506–1552). Xavier was born in Xavier Castle and was the youngest of five children born to Basque aristocrats. Robert Linder writes:

> Apparently intended for a career in the church by his parents, Xavier soon rebelled against their wishes and became a Parisian playboy. Charming, witty, urbane, athletic, musical, good-looking, successful with women, and somewhat vain, he was a complete worldling—until one day he met a devoted Christian and fellow-Basque named Ignatius Loyola.[12]

Linder writes that over time, Xavier became disappointed and bored with his worldly lifestyle. He was converted late one night when he was talking with Loyola, who mentioned in passing the quote from Jesus: "For what shall it profit a man if he shall gain the whole world, and lose his own soul?" (Matt. 16:26, KJV). Linder writes that these words "seared his heart" and Francis Xavier gave his life to Christ at that time. He went on to become one of the greatest missionaries in the history of the Church. He adopted the customs of the locals among whom he lived, in order to try to get them to listen. He is viewed as "the inspiration of modern Catholic missions."[13]

# JOHN NEWTON

The man who wrote the hymn "Amazing Grace" knew firsthand what God's amazing grace was all about. He knew firsthand what it meant for Christ to take a shriveled heart and implant, instead, a new heart with a new vision. John Newton (1725–1807) knew what it meant for Christ to forgive even the most wretched and basest of sins. For Newton actually worked in the slave trade prior to his Christian conversion. His livelihood was earned on a ship that traded in human cargo!

During a violent storm at sea in 1747, he called upon God for protection and was spared. This marked the beginning of his

Christian conversion. He did not immediately give up the slave trade, but he did within a few years because of his Christian convictions.

John Newton eventually became a pastor and served as pastor to William Wilberforce, the evangelical who couragiously led the prolonged fight in Parliament against the slave trade. Rev. Newton was a great friend and inspiration in Wilberforce's long struggle. In fact, at one point feelings of restrictive pietism made Wilberforce consider abandoning politics for the ministry; Newton talked him out of it by convincing him he could do more for God where he was. This is no minor point of history, for as we saw in chapter 2, Wilberforce played a critical role in the abolition of modern slavery.

A recent *USA Today* poll showed Newton's testimony in song, "Amazing Grace," to be America's favorite hymn.

> Amazing grace! how sweet the sound
> That saved a wretch like me!
> I once was lost, but now am found,
> Was blind, but now I see!

This hymn in reality reflects every true Christian's story—no matter how depraved or how "innocent" he or she may be at the time of conversion. Only God's amazing grace saves any of us.

## MEL TROTTER

Mel Trotter gave a whole new meaning to the terms "no good." He was so "no good" it was almost written on his forehead. He was the very scum of the scum. He abused his family. He neglected his children. He was fired from his jobs. He was a drunkard in the gutter and would do anything for a drink. In fact, one day he came home and found his little daughter very seriously ill. He was so "concerned" that he took off her shoes and went out and sold them for a drink! When he returned, he found that his little girl was dead. He was so overwhelmed by remorse that he said he was going to end his life. He made his way across one of the worst parts of Chicago, to throw himself into Lake

Michigan. But as he passed down the street, he could hear some-one preaching over a loudspeaker. He stepped into the building's doorway and heard a man talking about Jesus Christ, who loved sinners. He said to himself, "Can it be that there is anyone who could love someone like me?" He stood transfixed by that mes-sage of love that he heard. All of the grasp of that addiction suddenly was loosened. Mel Trotter was set free!

He later established a great mission for the down-and-outers in downtown Grand Rapids, and ultimately established fifty more missions around the nation. Tens of thousands of drunks and ne'er-do-wells had their lives transformed by Christ through Trotter. Take Christ out of the picture, and all you end up with is a drunken suicide!

"Ah," you say, "Christianity is only for the down-and-outers and feeble-minded. It is only for those who need a crutch." First of all, we all need a crutch when it comes to our sin. In fact, we need more than a crutch; we need new life to be breathed into us. Every one of us is in need of a Savior—only, some of us recognize the need; others are blinded to their need by their pride. Second, numerous people have come to Christ who had brilliant minds. One of them was C. S. Lewis.

## C. S. LEWIS

One of this century's greatest writers was C. S. Lewis (1898–1963), who was a professor at Oxford and, later, Cambridge. Lewis was born in Belfast, Ireland, and was raised in a nominal Protestant family. When he was still a child, his mother died. This experience, combined with a skeptical tutor who taught him to think critically, led Lewis to become an atheist early in life, or at the very least, he questioned whether there was a God. He was wounded in World War I, which led him to conclude "there was nothing worth pursuing besides things of the mind and pleasures of the flesh."[14]

However, some of his favorite writers—including G. K. Ches-terton and George MacDonald—were decidedly Christian. Their writings and some Christian friends played an important part in Lewis's reluctant conversion, which took place when he was in his early thirties.[15] He became probably *the* greatest Christian writer of this century, and certainly one of the greatest Christian writers in all of Christian history. Interestingly, *Time* magazine thought enough of his writings to do a cover story on him.[16]

To this day, his books still sell well and are used by God to bring people to Himself. One such person is Chuck Colson, whom we'll discuss in a moment; Colson readily acknowledges that Lewis's classic book *Mere Christianity* was pivotal in his conversion. Lewis was a "master communicator. He knew his audiences, and he pointed them to the theme of themes, Christ."[17] C. E. M. Joad said that he had the "rare gift of making righteousness readable."[18] Christianity did not necessarily make C. S. Lewis a brilliant writer. But the Christian faith gave his writings an eternal significance and most of his lofty themes.

## SERGEANT JACOB DE SHAZER AND CAPTAIN MITSUO FUCHIDA

Even the most inveterate hatred can be removed by Christ. Sergeant Jacob DeShazer was a bombardier in General Doolittle's squadron. While bombing Japan in World War II, DeShazer's plane was crippled by anti-aircraft fire. He and his crew bailed out and were captured. DeShazer was placed in a five-foot-wide cell in a prison camp. He was treated with the most horrrible forms of cruelty. He developed an intense hatred for his Japanese guards. All he wanted was to get his hands on one of their throats to squeeze the life out of him. But they continued to torture him. Day by day his hatred grew until it became a veritable mountain. He lived for only one reason, and that was to seek revenge on his torturers.

One day a Bible was brought into the prison. It was passed around and finally came to DeShazer. He read it. He devoured it eagerly! And he came across the words of Jesus, who said, "Father, forgive them, for they do not know what they do" (Luke 23:34a). The love of Christ melted that mountain of hatred inside of Jacob DeShazer and filled him with the joy of Jesus Christ. He said, "My heart was full of joy. I wouldn't have traded places with anyone." Soon after that a guard slammed the cell door on

DeShazer's bare foot and began kicking at the foot with hob-nailed boots. DeShazer said nothing but thought of Jesus' words, "Love your enemies." That guard's attitude changed substantially.

When the war was over, DeShazer returned home. He determined that God wanted him to go back to Japan, not to seek revenge, but, rather, as a missionary to bring the love of Christ. This he did.

The story of Jacob DeShazer's conversion and return to Japan was printed in a tract. One day a Japanese man who was disheartened, broken, dejected, and hopeless was given that tract by an American stranger. He read that tract, and his heart was touched. He sought out Christian missionaries and the Bible. He too was converted. His name was Captain Mitsuo Fuchida. He was the Japanese officer who spearheaded the 1941 attack on Pearl Harbor on December 7. The very man who had declared, "Tora! Tora! Tora!" gave his heart and life over to Jesus Christ. He, too, began to preach the gospel of Jesus Christ to people all over Japan and America. He even came back to Pearl Harbor on the twenty-fifth anniversary of the attack with a gift in hand for the survivors: a Bible with Luke 23:34a inscribed in it ("Father, forgive them, for they do not know what they do"). Fuchida asked for forgiveness, for he had acted a quarter century earlier in moral ignorance. Fuchida's story is well-told in the book *God's Samurai*, written by the same team that wrote the book *At Dawn We Slept*.[19]

## CHIEF TARIRI

Some thirty years ago we celebrated the New York World's Fair, highlighted by the lighting of the Tower of Light. Never in history had there been such a collection of lights in one place. When those lights went on there was an illumination of brightness never before seen. It could be seen for hundreds of miles. The switch that lighted the Tower of Light had been thrown by a dignitary from South America (though not exactly what we might normally think of as a dignitary). Actually, he was a Peruvian headhunter. In fact he was the chief of a whole tribe of headhunters. His name was Chief Tariri.[20] He was so fearsome that he had personally killed and decapitated ten other chieftains, plus an uncounted number of common jungle Indians. And the heads of those ten chieftains decorated poles in front of his hut. The Peruvian army was terrified of him and would not enter into his territory at all.

But two young Wycliffe Bible translators, Lorretta Anderson and Doris Cos, armed with nothing more than the weapons of a translator—pens, pencils, and Bibles—pierced into the Peruvian jungle and headed for the camp of Chief Tariri and to what would seem certain death. But in the inscrutable providence of God, for some reason, the chief looked upon them with favor. Apparently, they appeared no threat whatsoever to him. They showed him a strange and unknown form of love that piqued his curiosity. They learned his language and began to speak to him about One who had loved the world with a love that had never been seen before; a love that took Him all the way to the stake and all the way into the very pit of hell for us.

Finally, the heart of this hardened headhunter was softened by the power of the gospel of Christ, and he yielded his life to the Lord. He himself ultimately led about two hundred of his tribesmen to Christ. It was this Peruvian headhunter, Chief Tariri, that pulled the switch at the New York World's Fair in 1964 that illuminated the Tower of Light! Jesus Christ, the Light of the world, had come into the darkness and blackness of Tariri's heart and had produced a light and a joy that had transformed his life.

## CHUCK COLSON

Chuck Colson is a marvelous example of a life changed for the better, thanks to the gospel of Jesus Christ. Known as Nixon's "hatchet man," Colson was a high-powered attorney who joined the Nixon team as special counsel to the president. Colson had access to a man who made himself accessible to very few. Colson will be the first to tell you that he was no saint in those days and that his creed was anything and everything for the president no matter who it might hurt. He was an active participant in the many dirty tricks of the only U.S. president who had to resign because of dirty tricks. If you haven't read his "tell-all" classic,

*Born Again*, you are missing out on a terrific book. In other books on Watergate, Colson consistently comes off as somewhat of a heel—prior to his conversion.

Listen to what a colleague of Colson said about Chuck in those pre-conversion days. This comment comes from Jeb Stuart Magruder, interestingly another life changed by Christ.[21] Magruder served Nixon as the Deputy Director of the Committee to Re-Elect the President (so-called CREEP). Here's what he said about Colson in 1974:

> I came to regard Colson as an evil genius. His brilliance was undeniable, but it was too often applied to encouraging Richard Nixon's darker side, his desire to lash out at his enemies, his instinct for the jugular. I would have to say— granting always Nixon's central responsibility for what happened in his administration—Colson was one of the men among his advisers most responsible for creating the climate that made Watergate possible, perhaps inevitable.[22]

Today, this very same Colson heads up a ministry he started that preaches the gospel to tens of thousands of inmates. Prison Fellowship, which grew out of Colson's own jailhouse experience, is now a worldwide outreach, located in northern Virginia, that helped more than 100,000 prisoners last year. It ministers to them in prison and helps them get readjusted out of prison and back into society. Prison Fellowship even provides Christmas gifts for the families of inmates.

Many people today know Colson also for his magnificent books and his inspiring talks and daily radio commentary, "BreakPoint with Chuck Colson." Colson's genius refreshes people every day worldwide; take Christ out of the equation, and all we're left with is an *evil* genius!

## _____ (YOUR NAME GOES HERE!)

What Jesus has done in all these different lives, He can do in your life—if you will but let Him. If Jesus had never come, all of the lives mentioned above would never have been changed, nor would the countless millions you don't hear or read about—the

shall be rendered perfect. And throughout the unending ages of eternity, I shall live with Him in paradise.

# BEGINNING AGAIN

Have you ever wished you could start your life over again? Have you ever felt like you made some wrong turn somewhere, but you're not sure where, nor are you sure how to correct it? As the poem says:

> I wish that there were some wonderful place
> Called the Land of Beginning Again,
> Where all our mistakes and all our heartaches
> And all of our poor selfish grief
> Could be dropped like a shabby old coat at the door,
> And never be put on again.

You can find that wonderful place of Beginning Again by coming into a personal relationship with Jesus Christ. Like Augustine, Fuchida, or Colson, you too can begin your life afresh through Christ.

My friend, He loved you even unto the cross. He took upon Himself your guilt, your sin, and the punishment that it deserves. He paid the price entirely. He offers you forgiveness. By His grace, unmerited and free, He offers you the gift of life abundant and eternal, freely bestowed to those that will place their trust in Him. Those who will cease to trust in any supposed goodness of their own and rest their hopes upon Christ and His atoning work may know now the blessings of His heaven. What a difference that will be to you because He came.

It is a sad fact that I have met hundreds of people who suppose that they can earn their way into heaven by becoming church members or by living a moral life, rather than having a personal relationship with Christ. These things are certainly commendable, but they can in no way obtain eternal life in heaven with God.

The Bible tells us in Romans 6:23, "For the wages of sin is death, but the gift of God is eternal life in Jesus Christ our

Lord." Heaven is a free gift! We need only reach out and take Jesus as our personal Savior and Lord, and heaven is ours.

Because heaven is a free gift, it can't be earned or deserved. No one can work his or her way to heaven, for no one can be good enough! God's standard for heaven is perfection, yet no one has ever lived a perfect life, except Jesus Christ. Sin separates us from God. The good deeds we may do can never overcome this gap or earn for us God's blessing. Left on our own, we are lost and without any hope of eternal life in heaven.

However, God solved this dilemma for us through Jesus Christ. Jesus, who is God in the flesh (John 1:1, 14), loved us so much that He left His glorious home to live in our sin-sick world. He took abuse, suffering, and death in our place, paying God's penalty for sin on the cross. As someone once put it: "He paid a debt He didn't owe, so we could be released from a debt we couldn't pay."

They placed His body in a tomb and sealed it. Yet, He rose from the dead three days later. He is now in heaven preparing a place for all those who trust in Him alone for their salvation.

Jesus is the only way to heaven. The Scriptures teach: "Believe on the Lord Jesus Christ, and you will be saved" (Acts 16:31). It is made clear in the New Testament that we must welcome Jesus into our lives as Lord and Savior, to accept Him as the Ruler and King of our lives. To receive Him as Savior is to depend solely on His death on the cross to pay for our sins.

To truly believe means we must repent of our sins and trust in Jesus to save us from the punishment of hell. God has promised that all who do this will be granted the joy of heaven (John 3:16; 14:6). Jesus promises that when we accept Him into our lives He will be with us now and forever.

If you have never repented from your sins and accepted Jesus into your life to be your Lord and Savior, I entreat you to stop reading right now and invite Him in. If you don't know what words to pray, you could pray something along these lines:

Lord Jesus Christ, I come to You right now. I come seeking You. I want to find You. Lord, Son of God, Savior of men, come into my heart right now. There is room in my heart for You. I turn from my sins and ask that You take Your rightful place on the throne of my heart. Thank You that You have paid for my sin. Take me and make me Your own. Please, cleanse me from the sin in my life and make me new again. In Jesus' name. Amen.

If you prayed that prayer in all sincerity, you have begun the greatest adventure on which you could ever embark. And I would strongly urge you to begin to read the Bible every day and to pray. If you've never read the Bible before, start with the Gospel of John (the fourth book of the New Testament).

I also would urge you to get involved with a Bible-based, Bible-believing church. If you would like a free book to help you become established in the Christian faith, write to me: D. James Kennedy, Box 40, Ft. Lauderdale, FL 33308, and ask for *Beginning Again.*

Once we know Jesus as our personal Lord and Savior, our "thank you" to Him for His gift of salvation will be to serve Him in every area of our life. Good works will naturally flow from our lives, as good apples grow naturally on a good apple tree.

## CONCLUSION

Had Jesus not been born, all the lives mentioned above—and the tens of millions we didn't discuss—would not have changed. They would have been awash in their own vices, and faced the consequences of their sins, and society would not be spared the public scourge of their private immorality. In fact, all of the benefits of Christianity outlined in this book would be missed, because here is where it all starts: the human heart. But the fact is Christ *did* come and we *can* know Him personally and be transformed by His love.

Jesus Christ is still working in this world through the transformation of the human heart. This is an ongoing project, and it is exciting to be a part of it. If you know Him and are making Him known to others, then you are a part of the most exciting phenomenon on Planet Earth: the advancement of the Kingdom of God!

# CHAPTER 14

# THE SINS OF
# THE CHURCH

## Negative Aspects of Christianity
## in History

*The name of God is blasphemed among the Gentiles because of you.*

(Rom. 2:24)

**D**espite all the good done in the name of Christ that we've explored in the preceding chapters, we would be remiss not to address the issue of the negative aspect of the Church's record in history. To some people the Church's credibility has been forever ruined by these "sins of the Church." But that is as fair as saying that Judas Iscariot is representative of the twelve apostles!

The Church has never been perfect. Far from it. But the *total* record should be examined. In doing so, the good far, far outweighs the bad. Besides, Christian belief is in Christ, not in Christians. Despite all the good the Church has done and continues to do, we're reminded *ad nauseum* about the Crusades, the Inquisition, and the witch hunts—as if they are the sum total of the Christian record in history!

I heard a man recently talk about evangelical Christianity, saying that the endeavors of religion trying to affect the life of mankind have only led to incidents like the Inquisition, or to men like the Ayatollah Khomeini. I thought how ignorant this person must be. There are so many who do not even know enough about history to be aware that evangelical Christians were receiving the tortures of the Inquisition and not giving them. To compare evangelical Christianity to the fanatical Muslim faith of the Ayatollah Khomeini, for whom Christianity has long been one of the most despised of faiths, is like saying, "Rulers and governors have been a great scourge upon earth. Think about the terrible rulers of the world and what a mixed curse they have been. There have been Genghis Kahn, Attila the Hun, Abraham Lincoln, Adolf Hitler, George Washington, and Joseph Stalin." Anyone who would offer such a mixture is simply saying that he knows absolutely nothing about history, government, or politics.

Genuine Christianity must be distinguished from nominal Christianity. Some people have called themselves "Christians" who have lived in total opposition to the principles and teachings of the Master from Nazareth. But when we distinguish between name and reality, we see that genuine Christianity has been an unmixed blessing on the world.

One last introductory observation: While Jesus told us to love our neighbor and even our enemies, He did predict that Christianity would prove divisive per se. Jesus said:

> Do you suppose that I came to give peace on earth? I tell you, not at all, but rather division. For from now on five in one house will be divided: three against two, and two against three. Father will be divided against son and son against father, mother against daughter and daughter against mother, mother-in-law against her daughter-in-law and daughter-in-law against her mother-in-law (Luke 12:51–53).

Now, the Scripture teaches we are to be at peace with all, inasmuch as it is up to us (Rom. 12:18). But we are to put Christ first in our lives, even if that goes against the wishes of family members. True faith can elicit a hostile reaction, even when practiced with a gentle and humble spirit. The division that Christ talked about here is the natural outworking of unbelief reacting against godliness, or belief reacting against ungodliness. Now, let's examine some of the most prominent, dark moments in Church history.

# THE CRUSADES

The Crusades began as a reaction to Islam. The religion of Mohammed had spread by the sword in the seventh century, and millions of Christians were forced to convert or be killed. In fact, the forces of Mohammed even tried to conquer Europe, but they were checked in 732 on French soil by Charles Martel (the Hammer) in one of history's most important conflicts, The Battle of Tours.[1]

Initially, when the Muslims took over Jerusalem in the seventh century, they let Christian pilgrims still come to the Holy City for worship and to visit what was believed to be Christ's Holy Sepulchre. But in the eleventh century, reports filtered back from Jerusalem that Christian pilgrims were being molested by the Seljuk Turks, a very crude brand of Muslims.

Furthermore, the Turks had a fortress at Nicaea, right across from Constantinople. Alexius, the emperor of Byzantium, part of Christendom, tried to expel the Turks from the area and was unable to do so. He then requested help from the pope, the head of Christendom. In one of history's most moving speeches at Clermont, France, in 1095, Urban II was able to mobilize an army of thousands of warriors and knights to expel the infidels from the Holy City.[2]

Some frustrated Crusaders actually made it to Jerusalem four years later, after innumerable hardships, in which many of their own number had died along the way. So when they finally arrived in Jerusalem, these aggravated "soldiers of the cross" massacred thousands of the inhabitants, in accord with the barbaric type of warfare generally practiced at those times. They are reported to have mercilessly slaughtered all of the Muslims, and even many of the Jews. The chief goal was achieved: The Holy City was back in "Christian" hands. In the history of the Crusades, which spanned about two centuries, this was the only successful one, in terms of securing Jerusalem.

Fifty years later, Edessa, one of the key outposts Crusaders had created to protect the region, fell to the Muslims. The fall of Edessa ignited the Second Crusade. The call for this crusade came from the otherwise-godly St. Bernard of Clairveaux. Bernard gave a very unflattering description of the "Soldiers of

Christ." It is helpful to get an idea of exactly who these Crusaders were, as evaluated by a godly man.

> In that countless multitude you will find few except the utterly wicked and impious, the sacrilegious, homicides, and perjurers, whose departure is a double gain. Europe rejoices to lose them and Palestine to gain them; they are useful in both ways, in their absence from here and their presence there.[3]

Thus he recognized them as essentially unregenerate reprobates, and everyone could rejoice that they were gone! This indicates the general caliber of the Crusaders and the fact that they were Christians in name only.

Later Crusades were even worse. There was one in which the Venetians sneakily used the Crusaders to destroy one of their main competitors, the city of Constantinople, which was also part of Christendom! This attack helped to weaken Constantinople, paving the way for its eventual fall in 1453 at the hands of the Ottoman Turks. The sacking of Constantinople by the Crusaders brought the whole enterprise to a new low and laid the foundation for the waning popularity of the Crusades.

Probably the most tragic of these military expeditions was the Children's Crusade, wherein a number of children—misguidedly stirred up to "fight for Christ," which is an oxymoron—went to their doom, or were taken into captivity and sold as slaves!

While the warring Muslims were being consistent with the Koran which sanctions the use of force to win converts (Koran chapter 9, verse 29)[4] the Christians were not being consistent with Christianity by this kind of fighting. In the early Church, many of the Christians would not take up arms for expansionist Rome. They would not serve as soldiers in the Imperial Army, and they were encouraged not to by many of their leaders.[5] About a millennium later, professing Christians were taking up arms and even slaughtering innocent people (e.g., Jews in Jerusalem or Muslim civilians, or even their fellow Christians in Constantinople). How low could Christendom sink?

# CHRISTENDOM VS. CHRISTIANITY

How are we to understand the excesses and the un-Christian nature that characterized much of the Crusades? These military campaigns underscore the necessity of distinguishing between *Christendom* and *Christianity*. Christianity is comprised of those who have repented of their sins and truly believe in Jesus Christ as their Savior and their Lord. In times past Christendom was comprised of those people living in "Christian" territories. Today, Christendom is comprised of true Christians and those professing Christians who have never experienced the saving grace of Christ. Many members of Christendom have lived lives that were totally unworthy of the name Christian.

When people are unregenerate—that is, if their hearts are not changed by Christ—they are prone to do all sorts of ungodly and inhuman things. It doesn't matter whether they're atheistic Communists or clerics in the Church. And in the case of unregenerate Church leaders, their evil actions have brought the blame of history upon Christianity.

There is a Church visible (Christendom) and there is a Church invisible (true Christianity). The church building in which we worship is a part of the visible Church of Christ. It may be seen by any passerby or any person who would come in to look at it. Its membership consists of all who have made a profession of faith in Jesus Christ. However, the Bible points out that the visible Church is not the real Church of Christ. The real Church of Christ is invisible, and it consists of all who truly belong to God as His elect—all those who will ever be regenerated by the Holy Spirit. Judas Iscariot was a member of the visible Church of Christ, but not the invisible.

Jesus told a parable that helps us to see the mix of believer and nonbeliever together that we find in the visible Church. He said:

> The kingdom of heaven is like a man who sowed good seed in his field; but while men slept, his enemy came and sowed tares among the wheat and went his way. But when the grain had sprouted and produced a crop, then the tares also ap-

peared. So the servants of the owner came and said to him, "Sir, did you not sow good seed in your field? How then does it have tares?" He said to them, "An enemy has done this." The servants said to him, "Do you want us then to go and gather them up?" But he said, "No, lest while you gather up the tares you also uproot the wheat with them. Let both grow together until the harvest, and at the time of harvest I will say to the reapers, "First gather together the tares and bind them in bundles to burn them, but gather the wheat into my barn." . . . He who sows the good seed is the Son of Man. The field is the world, the good seeds are the sons of the kingdom, but the tares are the sons of the wicked one. The enemy who sowed them is the devil, the harvest is the end of the age (Matt. 13:24–30, 37–39).

Although this parable applies to the state of the world in general, it could also easily apply to the state of the Church. We have seen its fulfillment throughout Church history. The devil has been able to infiltrate the Church. Thus, as Jesus forewarned, the Church contains believers *and nonbelievers* alike.

During the Middle Ages, everyone in Europe, except the Jews in their ghettos and the Moors in Spain (who were Muslims), was a part of Christendom. Thus they were allegedly Christian. But from a biblical point of view, that's absurd! Only those who have come to put their faith in Christ alone for their salvation and who trust in His atoning death for them are saved.

Individuals need to put their faith in Jesus. When whole territories became "Christian," then there were countless people who didn't know the Lord, whose behavior was immoral, who suddenly became "Christians." The Roman Emperor Theodosius (A.D. 378–398) made the empire officially Christian and thus many non-believers became "Christians" overnight.[6] Clovis (d. 511), who was the first king to organize the Franks into what is today France, reportedly converted to Christianity.[7] Clovis ordered his soldiers to march into the rivers for wholesale baptism. Those were grave mistakes. Christianity doesn't work that way. Individuals need to individually repent of their sins and trust in Him for salvation. Mass baptisms, like those of Clovis's soldiers, only admit unsaved people into the visible Church. In short,

Christianity degenerated for many centuries (all over Europe) into Christendom. And Christendom does indeed have much from which to repent!

# THE SINS OF CHRISTIANITY

But what about the bad things done at the hands of those who *truly* believe in Jesus? We mentioned earlier St. Bernard of Clairveaux having preached the Second Crusade. He was a true Christian, who helped found monasteries that spread the Christian faith, preserved the Scriptures, and fed the poor. So how could he be involved in launching a Crusade? Primarily because he was a product of his time, and we feel—with perfect 20/20 hindsight—that he was grossly mistaken for doing so. But how will future generations judge today's American Christians? Surely, we have so many blind spots and open sins that in comparison we do well to call Bernard a saint!

Furthermore, we are *all* products of our own age and our own time to some degree. For example, take America's Founding Fathers who wrote the Constitution. Overall, they wrote what was perhaps the greatest governmental document in history; nonetheless, slavery is implicitly enshrined in Article 1, Section 3a, which was superseded by the 14th Amendment. It states that the whole number of "free persons" shall be added up to determine the number of representatives, but only "three-fifths of all other persons" shall be counted. In other words, black slaves were less deserving of full representation than their white counterparts; they were deemed worthy of only three-fifths representation. And this inequity has been inscriptured in our founding document for all time, even though it no longer applies.

So what are we to do? View the Founding Fathers as hopeless racists and scrap the Constitution as hopelessly flawed?[8] Not at all. The Constitution contained within it the seeds that would one day destroy the inequity of Article 1, Section 3a; this took place within a century of its being ratified. In the same way that it does not make sense to write off American constitutionalism because of Article 1, Section 3a, it is irrational to throw out Christianity because of the sins of the Church in ages past, such as the

Middle Ages, it was the "Christians" who persecuted the Jews and forced them into ghettos. When power was in the hands of the Christians, many so-called Christians often used it in an un-Christ-like way.

On the issue of Deicide (killing God, i.e., the crucifixion of Christ), it is historically true that the Jews were responsible for delivering Jesus up to the Romans for execution; but in a very real sense it is the *Christian* who is responsible for the death of Christ! It was God's will that His Son be put to death for our sins. Jesus voluntarily gave up His life, so that we who trust in Him may have eternal life. So *who* is ultimately guilty of killing Christ? I am, and you are—if indeed you know Him.

Earlier this century, Count Heinrich Coudenhove-Kalergi wrote an important book on this subject, entitled *Anti-Semitism Throughout the Ages*. Here is what the Count said at that time:

> Anti-Semitism is absolutely un-Christian and diametrically opposed to the Will of Christ who had loved His people so much. . . . It is one of the many successes of Christian teaching that gladiatorial contests, slavery, polygamy, torture, and in some countries also capital punishment, the slaughtering of prisoners of war, dueling and Harakiri, have disappeared from the surface of the earth. Anti-Semitism, too, is doomed, and its days are numbered.[12]

The Count's vision has not yet been fulfilled, but it will be. Interestingly, a Gallup poll in the 1980s revealed that for the most part fundamentalist and evangelical Christians are not anti-Semitic. In fact, they are, next to the Jews, the most pro-Israel group in America.

## THE INQUISITION

The Inquisition represents undoubtedly one of the darkest moments in Church history. Set up to root out heresy, it used force to ensure orthodoxy. Historian Joseph Reither writes:

> The Inquisition, set up in 1233, was a court. Its purpose was to determine whether a Christian accused of heresy was in

fact guilty of holding heretical beliefs. If he were, the purpose of the court was to persuade him to abandon his false beliefs and repent. If he remained obdurate the court turned him over to the secular authority. Death by burning at the stake was usually the punishment meted out to condemned heretics.[13]

Dr. Henry Charles Lea wrote a three-volume set on *A History of the Inquisition of the Middle Ages* in 1888. He says that the key to understanding the Inquisition lay in the corruption of the Church at that time. Simony was rampant. Bishoprics, priesthoods, and sometimes even papal seats were bought and sold. In short, there were many ungodly men throughout various levels of leadership of the Church at the time.[14] Dr. Lea points out:

Wealth and power have charms even for bishop and priest, and in the Church, as it grew through the centuries, wealth and power depended upon the obedience of the flock. A hardy disputant who questioned the dogmatic accuracy of his ecclesiastical superior was a mutineer of the worst kind; and if he succeeded in attracting followers they became the nucleus of a rebellion which threatened revolution, and every motive, good or evil, prompted the suppression of such sedition at all hazards and by every available means.[15]

In this context, some religious movements arose among the laity, movements that said that the Church was not necessary for salvation. One of them, that of the Waldensians, was a precursor to modern evangelicals. But another one, that of the Albigensians (also known as the Catharists), rejected the historic Christian faith. These heresies were not easily contained. So another crusade was called in order to wipe out these new religions.[16] Although many were killed, these heresies were not stamped out. What the Crusade was unable to accomplish, the Inquisition was set up to complete.

We don't know for certain how many thousands were killed in the Inquisition, but we have some reasonable approximations. Dr. David Barrett, one of the greatest authorities on Church-related statistics alive today, says that the Spanish Inquisition generations will judge our performance as a Church! We have such a large percentage of Americans professing to be born again, but our morality continues to plummet.

We could go on and on about the sins of the Church both in history and in the present. We could talk about how Southern Christians used the Bible to justify slavery. We could talk about the Christians who joined up with the Nazis and initially looked at Hitler as a good political leader. We could talk about the system of apartheid in South Africa, justified for a long time by the state church in that country. We could talk about the many evils done by "fringe groups"—that may appear to the outside observer as being Christian groups but in reality are far from the gospel, such as Jim Jones or David Koresh. We could talk about the many priests and ministers who have had sexual relations with parishioners, worse yet with children! We could talk about the numerous churches that have split to the detriment of the congregation; sometimes the splitting is literally over such trivial matters as the carpeting for the building!

# CONCLUSION

The Church has never been perfect, but its track record in history should be remembered for the good as well as the bad. Its sins should not be taken out of their context, blown out of proportion and remembered forevermore, as if this has been the only activity of the Church. It's not accurate to do so.

Furthermore, the Church has seemed to learn from many of its past sins and then it moves on. We no longer engage in crusades, except the Billy Graham type! We no longer torture alleged heretics on the rack to get them to change to more orthodox doctrine. We no longer burn or hang alleged witches.

One of the greatest historians alive today is Paul Johnson of England, author of *Modern Times*, *A History of the Jews* and *The History of Christianity*. When he was researching and writing his book on the history of the Church, his own faith as a Christian was reinforced, despite the numerous sins of the Church in history:

Such a history is marked by the folly and wickedness of leading Christians on almost every page, but I came to realize, in studying the account, that men have done evil not because of their Christianity but despite it—that Christianity has been not the source of, but the supreme (often the sole) restraining factor, on mankind's capacity for wrong-doing. The record of the human race *with* Christianity is daunting enough. But without its restraints, how much more horrific the history of these last 2,000 years must have been![25]

# CHAPTER 15

# A CRUEL WORLD

## What Happens when Christian Restraints Are Removed

*The fool has said in his heart, "There is no God." They are corrupt, they have done abominable works.*

(Ps. 14:1)

During one of the darkest periods of World War II, after the collapse of France and before American involvement, Churchill wrote that the question in the minds of friends and foes was: "Will Britain surrender too?"[1] At the time, he made a speech that contained this sentence: "What General Weygand called the Battle of France is over. I expect that the Battle of Britain is about to begin. *Upon this battle depends the survival of Christian civilisation.*"[2] The great statesman—probably the finest in this century—recognized the link between Christianity and civility, in contrast with neo-paganism and tyranny. Providentially, Christian civilization won. But where it has lost, all manner of terrors have been unleashed.

In the preceding chapter, we looked at the sins of the Church. In this chapter, we want to look at the sins of atheism, particularly in this century.

# THE ATROCITIES OF THE TWENTIETH CENTURY

No century has been like ours in terms of man killing his fellow man. Easily more than 170 million people have been killed by other human beings in this century. And that is a "conservative estimate."[3] About 130 million of these died because of atheistic ideology—whether it was Hitler's racism that viewed Jews as human bacteria or Mao's attempt to liquidate Christianity in the Great Proletarian Cultural Revolution (1966–1976).[4] While modern technology has helped make all these deaths possible, for the most part the atrocities of the twentieth century happened because modern man rejected God. As one wag put it: "In the 18th century, the Bible was killed; in the 19th century, God was killed; in the 20th century, man was killed."

Faith in the Bible began to be undermined in the so-called Enlightenment two centuries ago. Then, one century later, faith in God was undermined; for example, Nietzsche was the first to say "God is dead." In the twentieth century, this wrong thinking came to full fruition and the bitter harvest saw more people killed than ever before. Interestingly, someone spotted graffiti that declared: "God is dead" and was signed "Nietzsche." Under it were the words "Nietzsche is dead" and was signed "God"!

The frightening thing about a humanist and atheistic state is that there is nothing beyond man to which one can make an appeal. The founders of this country said that men have been created equal and have been endowed by their Creator with certain inalienable rights. Therefore, our rights are not given to us by the State, which can extend or withhold them as it pleases, but rather they have been inalienably given to us by God. We have an appeal beyond man, beyond the State, to God Himself, whereas in the humanist state there is nothing but man. The humanist state inevitably leads to tyranny and despotism. As Dostoevsky said, "If God is dead, then all things are permissible."[5]

# THE STRANGLEHOLD
# OF ATHEISM

There are consequences that flow as inevitably and as irresistibly from what we think, as water irresistibly flows through a broken dam. The Bible says that "as he thinks in his heart, so is he" (Prov. 23:7). As a people think in their hearts so will the world be in which they live. There are results that come from our thinking; and above all else, the greatest results flow from what we think about God.

The consequences that flow from unbelief are very real and very tragic. No concept makes known all of its implications and results instantly. Even as the dam breaks, the entire valley may be sleeping peacefully below as the water creeps into every nook and cranny, fills every hollow, and finally leaves behind a black pool of death where once there were green and fertile plains and hills. So it is with unbelief and atheism. It has slowly seeped into every area of thought and knowledge, philosophy and culture, and has brought with it inevitable death.

When a person denies the existence of God, he finds himself suddenly in a materialistic universe. The atheist has dichotomized the universe, gotten rid of the spiritual half, and has been left with the material universe, which is nothing but matter in motion.

# NIETZSCHE

In the middle of the last century, Friedrich Nietzsche, the German philosopher, gave atheism its greatest impetus when he described his mad man running into the town square with his lantern, looking under tables, under the benches, crying out, "Where is God? Where is God? God is dead and we have killed him." It was a great event. Yet, he said its time is not yet, but it is coming. The atheists say Nietzsche was a great prophet, but the time was not quite ripe in the nineteenth century; but his prophecies have unfolded in the twentieth.

Paul Johnson, the eminent historian, has written a monumental history of the twentieth century entitled *Modern Times*. He comments on the watershed issue of nineteenth century atheism:

[Nietzsche] wrote in 1886: "The greatest event of recent times—that 'God is Dead,' that the belief in the Christian God is no longer tenable—is beginning to cast its first shadows over Europe." Among the advanced races, the decline and ultimately the collapse of the religious impulse would leave a huge vacuum. The history of modern times is in great part the history of how that vacuum had been filled.[6]

That vacuum has been filled with the totalitarian state, the loss of freedom for millions, the concentration camp and the gulag, the rise of abortion, infanticide, euthanasia, and suicide, crime out of all proportions, and the most savage wars in the history of the world.

Johnson writes that the period of "Modern Times" began in 1919 when scientists confirmed the Einsteinian doctrine of relativity (the theory of relativity) through an eclipse.[7] When that was confirmed, suddenly we were ushered into an entire new universe of relativity.

The response of the public, which began under the tutelage of first one and then another leader and writer, was to take the concept of relativity out of the astronomical and physical realms and to introduce it into art, the humanities, and morality. Thus we have found ourselves in "an unguided world adrift in a relativistic universe," which proved to be a "summons" for "gangster-statesmen [Lenin, Stalin, Hitler, etc.] to emerge."[8] Einstein himself strongly protested the intrusion of relativity into the moral affairs of men; he said that relativity applied to physics not ethics. Johnson says that, despite Einstein's protest, the response of the public to the theory of relativity is simply the history of the twentieth century.

# MORAL RELATIVISM

With atheism there are no objective moral standards. Evolutionary humanism and all forms of various atheistic concepts have been trying for years to establish some sort of moral standard, and they have failed miserably. The Scripture says, "The fool has said in his heart, 'There is no God' " (Ps. 14:1) and goes on to say that they have "done abominably."

This is not to say that all atheists are immoral people. In reality, there are many nice people who are atheists, but their niceness is borrowed capital from Christianity; it is not *because* of their atheism, but *despite* it. The Christian who is a boor, and there are many, is unloving *despite* his professed Christianity, not *because* of it. As C. S. Lewis points out, the nice, young man down the street who's not a believer would be that much nicer if he were a Christian. And heaven help us if that cantankerous lady down the street who professes to be a Christian had no Christian influence on her life!

Each of us could create his or her own moral code and write down six or eight or ten rules for living. You may draw up a moral code, but you can't get people to follow it. This is what the humanists seem to forget.

James Michener, recently featured on the cover of *Parade* magazine, says in the accompanying article: "I am a humanist." He later says:

If you want to charge me with being the most virulent kind —a secular humanist—I accept the accusation. . . . I am a humanist, because I think humanity can, with constant moral guidance, create reasonably decent societies.[9]

That is very interesting, isn't it? Where is that constant moral guidance going to come from, Mr. Michener? Surely not from your books. Where shall we find it? You will notice he gives no examples of any of these "reasonably decent societies" that humankind has created without religion. More knowledgeable or honest is the historian Will Durant, who was also a humanist. In the February 1977 issue of the *Humanist Magazine*, Durant, one of our leading historians of the twentieth century, said:

Moreover, we shall find it no easy task to mold a natural ethic strong enough to maintain moral restraint and social order without the support of supernatural consolations, hopes and fears. . . . There is no significant example in history, before our time, of a society successfully maintaining moral life without the aid of religion.[10]

Napoleon said that he saw men without God. He saw them in the French Revolution. He said, "One does not govern such men; he shoots them down [they have descended to the level of the beasts]."

The existentialist writer Jean-Paul Sartre saw very clearly what would happen if we got rid of God—as he had done. He said, "[Without God] all activities are equivalent. . . . Thus it amounts to the same thing whether one gets drunk alone, or is a leader of nations."[11] In other words, it doesn't matter if, when you see an old woman trying to cross the street, you stop your car and help her across, or whether you simply run over her. It doesn't matter whether you are Florence Nightingale or Al Capone—all activities are equivalent without God.

Would that some of our modern thinkers realize the truth of Sartre's statement. One of them certainly has. Ludwig Wittgenstein, one of the founders and leaders of the modern analytical philosophy, said that if there are any ethical absolutes, they would have to come to man from *outside* the human situation. He writes, "If a man could write a book on ethics which really was a book on ethics, this book would, with an explosion, destroy all the other books in the world."[12]

Wittgenstein did not believe there was such a book because, like Sartre, he had rejected God and His Word. But these people, unlike many today, knew what the result would be. For the last few decades in this country, God has been banished from the public sphere as much as has been possible for the humanists to accomplish. What have been the results? Have we maintained morality in the absence of religion as President Washington said we should be very careful to consider doing? Pollster George M. Gallup, Jr., who has appraised the situation better than most, says, "The United States is facing a 'moral and ethical crisis of the first dimension' and needs to find spiritual answers to deal with the situation."[13] At least he knows where the solution is to be found.

## TRAGIC RESULTS

For a few decades now, children in our schools have been taught that there are no moral absolutes; no one can tell them what to do. They are simply to choose their own values, their own ethics. In the last verse of the book of Judges, we read: "Every man did that which was right in his own eyes" (Judg. 21:25). That is exactly what we have today in our country.

Just about every day, we hear in the news the consequences of these views. We hear about one youth killing another, often over the most trivial matter. Boston College professor William Kilpatrick, who has written a helpful book on this subject, *Why Johnny Can't Tell Right from Wrong* (1992), says that our children are "moral illiterates." He writes:

> Youngsters are forced to question values and virtues they've never acquired in the first place or upon which they have only a tenuous hold . . . a recent national study of 1,700 sixth- to ninth-graders revealed that a majority of boys considered rape to be acceptable under certain conditions. Astoundingly, many of the girls agreed.[14]

Thus, when atheism takes hold of a society, moral relativism quickly follows. When moral relativism takes hold, then nothing is sacred and human life becomes cheap—as it was before Jesus Christ entered our world. Obviously, some societies have gone down this path much farther than others. The growing menace of youth crime in America is still a Sunday school picnic when compared with Nazi Germany or Stalin's Russia.

## THE DEVALUING OF HUMAN LIFE

When you devalue God, you devalue human life. How could Hitler ruthlessly exterminate six million Jews and millions of others? How could the Communists kill and torture over a hundred million people? How could they do that to other human beings? Would you have difficulty killing a rat? Some of you might be a little squeamish about that. How about a roach? Could you step on a roach? But a human being is made in the image of God! He is a rational creature. Nonsense! Image of whom? What? God? Why, don't you know we got rid of God with Nietzsche! Rational? Where have you been? Haven't you had your eyes opened to anything? Haven't you looked at a picture, listened to music, looked at some sculpture, read a poem, gone to the theater? There is no reason! Everything is absurd. Step on a roach. Kill a man. Millions, it makes no difference. Remember Stalin's observation that one person being killed was a "tragedy," but 10,000 killed was merely a "statistic"?

# THE UNDERLYING VIEW OF MAN

What is a human being? "God created man male and female, after His own image, in knowledge, righteousness and holiness, with dominion over the creatures" (answer ten to question ten, Shorter Catechism of the Westminster Confession of Faith, 1647). He is a child of the Almighty; he has a God-ordained purpose for his life and a mission to fulfill; he is destined to be with the Creator forever in Paradise. That is one answer to the question. A second, quite diverse answer is that a human being is a complex animal, related to the anthropoids, which has emerged from the primordial ooze, entering existence through the chance concatenation of molecules and amino acids, squirming out of the ancient sea, climbing up into the trees from which it descended again and voilá!—here we are! First cousins of the chimpanzee, distantly related to guinea pigs and mice.

The answer you give to the question "What is a human being?" will determine precisely what you can do to one. Need I remind you of what we do to mice and guinea pigs in this country? Should we come to think of human beings in the same terms, we will begin to do the same things to them that we do to mice and guinea pigs—the same things Hitler and the Communists, who held such a view, did to human beings.

The evolutionary view of humans, which gained circulation in the nineteenth century and came to full fruition in the twentieth century, has greatly cheapened the value of human life on earth.

Ernst Mayr, professor at Harvard and one of our country's leading evolutionists, has written: "Man's world view today is dominated by the knowledge that the universe, the stars, the earth and all living things have evolved through a long history that was not foreordained or programmed."[15]

What kind of a view of man is given to us by evolutionary atheists? Is man a noble creature with a noble origin and a noble destiny? Here is what the evolutionists say:

"A mere insect, an ant . . ." (Church)
"A fungus on the surface of one of the minor planets." (Du Maurier)
"A rope stretched over an abyss." (Nietzsche)
"Small potatoes and few . . ." (Kipling)
"A jest, a dream, a show, bubble, air . . ." (Thornbury)
"A hairless ape." (Schoenberg)
"An accidental twig" (Gould)

This is what man is to them. Next to nothing at all! Yet, this is what students are being indoctrinated with from kindergarten all the way through graduate school.

One of our Supreme Court justices (and by no means the only one), Oliver Wendell Holmes, highly regarded, said: "I see no reason for attributing to man a significant difference in kind from that which belongs to a grain of sand."[16] The fungus just got demoted.

## CRIMES AGAINST HUMANITY

Once the evolutionary view of man was applied, appalling crimes against humanity began to be committed. The worst crimes were committed by the Communists, who felt they could build heaven on earth. Marx predicted that when the workers had their revolution, then government would wither away, since it was no longer necessary; the Proletariat would essentially be living in harmony. But as Paul Johnson says, "The experience of the twentieth century shows emphatically that Utopianism is never far from gangsterism."[17]

Since the beginning of Communism, human life has been cheap. Like the Jews in Nazi Germany, tens of millions of farmers were taken and shipped all over Russia, thousands of miles, on long trains of boxcars jammed full of people without food, and without the opportunity to get out of the boxcars for as long as five, fifteen, twenty days. Many of them died; the rest were spread all over the country. They separated them, changed them, did everything to them. Ten million people were killed to bring about collectivization in the Soviet Union.

When we list the statistics of those killed, we too can be hardened; they're just numbers. But these were real people that the Communists killed, much less maimed. I am thinking about a boy, ten or eleven years old, who was guilty of stealing a potato—a potato!—because he and his family were starving. He was caught, and what did the Communists do to him? They broke his right leg below the knee, and they broke his left leg below the knee, then they broke both his legs above the knees, and finally they broke both his hips. They left him alone to heal.

The problem was that the boy's legs did not heal straight. They healed outward like a crab's, with his pelvis a few inches from the floor and his face turned always to the ground. He was sent to Siberia, to the hard labor camps of the Gulag, but he could not work because he could not stand. They would throw him a little piece of garbage now and then. He could only walk sideways like a crab. He was about fourteen then. It didn't bother them that he was helpless, defenseless, and a child. You can treat someone like this only when you view human life as worthless, as the mere product of time and chance.

Thus, when the restraining influence of Christianity is removed from a country or culture, unmitigated disaster will naturally follow. This has been a repeated pattern of the 20th century.

## THE REFUTATION OF A COMMON MYTH

And yet we sometimes hear the statement that "more people have been killed in the name of Christ than in any other name." We hear it so often that some people take it as gospel truth. It's like Hitler's Big Lie: If you tell a big lie often enough and loudly enough, sooner or later, many people will take it for the truth. But what are the facts? Indeed, have more people been killed in the name of Christ than in any other? No. Far more have been killed in the name of atheism than in the name of Christianity. For example, far more have been killed by Marxists or Communists than were ever killed by professing Christians.

The numbers killed by atheists totally dwarf the number of those killed by professing Christians. Part of the point of those who make the obnoxious statement "that more have been killed in the name of Christ" is that included in the deceased are all Christian martyrs. But even with that inclusion taken into consideration, it is still a gross distortion of history.[18]

To disprove this myth, we don't need to bother going any earlier than this century, because the twentieth century has seen the worst atrocities ever committed. After all, it wasn't until this century that the term *genocide* was coined!

## STALIN SLAUGHTERED MORE THAN FORTY MILLION PEOPLE

As horrible and as inexcusable as the Inquisition was, it was rather like a tea party when compared with the purges of Stalin. The entire Inquisition is reported to have killed thirty thousand, and it treated death as the last resort, trying to get the alleged heretic to recant.[19] In contrast, the purges of Stalin showed no mercy and no chance for repentance. It is generally agreed that the number of people Stalin killed was 40 million.[20] Someone once tried to blame the Church for Stalin, since at one point he studied in a seminary in Tiflis. However, this was essentially the only avenue of higher education open to him. The school was a hotbed of anti-government subversion; it produced virtually as many radicals as it did priests. Stalin persecuted the Church, sometimes ruthlessly. Dr. Barrett says that in 1934, Stalin "widely regarded as the Antichrist, attempt[ed] liquidation of [the] entire Christian church."[21]

# HITLER'S BLOODY RECORD

Hitler, who hated God as much as Stalin did, had learned well from their mentor, Lenin, the father of the modern totalitarian state. Hitler was a total racist who wanted to remove from the world those he viewed as human bacillus. He killed Jews, Gypsies (most of whom were professing Christians),[22] Slavs, Poles, and others deemed racially inferior.

The Nazis worked out a system where Jews and others were to be worked until they died. Once they were no longer able to work, then they were to be exterminated. The Nazis didn't even want to waste money on bullets in killing the Jews and others in the concentration camps, so poison gas was used to exterminate many at once. Even the gas was sometimes used in lesser amounts to economize; so often the victims were still alive when the gas ovens were opened!

The first victims of the Holocaust were 70,000 insane and "incurable" people. The only courageous public voice against this came from two Christian leaders.[23] Thus the Holocaust actually began with euthanasia. By the end, 6 million Jews and 9–10 million others (mostly Christians) were liquidated.[24]

# HITLER HAS SLAIN HIS MILLIONS, MAO HIS TENS OF MILLIONS

It is estimated that Mao alone killed more than 70 million Chinese. In the first ten years after Mao's takeover in 1948, 24.7 million were killed in "purges, famines, deaths in slave labor camps."[25] From 1959–1962, about 25 million were killed or were starved to death in the collectivization effort and its failure.[26] Finally, from 1969–1976 in the "Great Proletariat Cultural Revolution" of China, an estimated 22 million were killed. Dr. Barrett calls this "history's most systematic attempt ever, by a single nation, to eradicate and destroy Christianity and religion; in this it fail[ed]."[27] Thus Mao was responsible for killing about 72 million human beings.

It is estimated that the Communist takeover of Cambodia (a

nation of 7 million) resulted in the death of two or three million innocent people. This was due to the political elimination of possible opponents and the insane attempt to create a consistent Marxist agrarian economy, in which everyone was forced to leave the cities and work in the fields. The Communists were not concerned about the number of dead, but about the creation of an ideal state. Such acts of complete devotion to the doctrines and cause of Communism, regardless of the cost in human suffering and lives, is common in Communist history.

There is really no way to count all the number of people slaughtered in other Communist revolutions and Communist-sponsored wars. The ground is screaming with the spilled blood of untold millions in Korea, Vietnam, Laos, Thailand, Cuba, Czechoslovakia, Hungary, Angola, Mozambique, Ethiopia, Afghanistan, the Philippines, and numerous other nations around the world.

## ADDING UP THE NUMBERS

Now let's add up these figures: Mao killed about 72 million human beings from 1948 to 1976. When we add the 40 million Stalin is responsible for, we come to a number of 112 million. Throw in Hitler's 15 million (not counting the devastating war he started!), and we come to about 127 million. Add other killings by other atheistic and totalitarian states—as a result of their atheistic ideology—you come up with a number of more than 130 million.[28]

If we were to add those dead from the wars of this century, the number would easily jump to 170 million; but in order to compare apples with apples, we'll stick with the 130 million figure.[29]

Using the most exaggerated criteria and numbers, one could come up with no more than 17 million people killed by professing Christians "in the name of Christ" in twenty centuries of Christian history.[30] So when compared with the top estimate of 17 million allegedly killed in the name of Christ, we see a *huge* difference with the estimated 130 million killed by atheists. Thus, the number of those killed in the name of the secular state *in this century alone* is about eight times more than our estimate of the number of those killed in the name of Christ in all centuries of the Christian era!

An interesting point about our comparison is that we're only talking about those born. The unborn are not even taken into consideration. It's no secret the Church has always been opposed to abortion. There are *millions* alive today who would have been aborted were it not for the Christian stance on this issue. World-wide, the present number of abortions is estimated to be a staggering 65 million per year![31] This means that approximately one billion people (or 1,000 million!) have been killed by abortion alone just within the last twenty years. Thus, if we added up the aborted unborn to the total picture, the number of those killed by professing Christian perpetrators "in the name of Christ" would appear microscopic compared to those killed by the ideas and practices of atheism.

The next time someone tries to say that old lie that more people have been killed in the name of Christ, correct them with the facts. As Paul Johnson—the great historian—says, the twentieth-century State has "proved itself the great killer of all time."[32] Columnist Joseph Sobran writes about the secularist who repeatedly looks to the crimes of the past committed in the name of religion, ignoring the crimes committed in this century in the name of "irreligion":

> They will keep their eyes fixed in horror on wrongs committed centuries ago, because, as a friend of mine puts it, they haven't noticed the twentieth century. But that century is one of mass murder, genocide, and institutionalized terrorism, the fruits of that phantom faith in the secular state that persists in promising 'liberation' even as it attacks the most fundamental human attachments.[33]

## CONCLUSION

More than a century ago, James Russell Lowell, the great literary man who was Minister of State for the United States to England, was once at a banquet where the Christian religion (the mission enterprise, in particular) was being attacked by scoffers. He spoke up and said:

> I challenge any skeptic to find a ten square mile spot on this planet where they can live their lives in peace and safety and decency, where womanhood is honored, where infancy and old age are revered, where they can educate their children, where the Gospel of Jesus Christ has not gone first to prepare the way. If they find such a place, then I would encourage them to emigrate thither and there proclaim their unbelief.[34]

# CHAPTER 16

# WHERE DO WE GO FROM HERE?

## Fulfilling Our Purpose

*"By this all will know that you are My disciples, if you have love for one another."*

Jesus Christ (John 13:35)

There are countless blessings that the Christian faith has helped bring about that are not mentioned in this book because of space limitations or because the authors weren't even aware of them. We have clearly geared this book to a North American audience; similar books could be written to audiences of other continents. We pray that God would use this book to spawn similar studies for His glory.

"Religion begat prosperity, but the daughter hath consumed the mother," so wrote Cotton Mather, the great Puritan divine. As we have seen on page after page of this book, many of the good things we enjoy today grew out of the religion of Jesus Christ, but He is often denied the credit.

## OUR PURPOSE ON THIS EARTH

As organizations and individuals will sometimes sit down and write out a "mission statement," so should we remind ourselves why we're here. What is God's purpose for our lives? There are two great mandates God has given to the world: The first one (the Cultural Mandate), which He gave at the very beginning of the Old Testament and the second one (the Great Commission), which He gave at the beginning of the Christian era after the death and resurrection of Christ; the first one at the dawn of creation and the second one at the dawn of the new creation. The first one, which is found in Genesis 1:26–28, was God's initial instructions to the human race. The second one, which is found in Matthew 28:19,20, contains the instructions of Christ for us to go and spread the gospel and make disciples, teaching them everything Jesus has commanded.

Most Christians give lip-service to the command to spread the gospel. Gratefully, a minority has been very active and obedient in evangelism.

But in this century, many Christians seem to be clueless concerning God's first command—the Cultural Mandate. We are to take all the potentialities of this world, all of its spheres and institutions, and bring them all to the glory of God. We are to use this world to the glory of God. We are to bring it and surrender it at the foot of the cross. In every aspect of the world, we are to bring glory to God and this means in all of the institutions of the world. For example, in the institution of marriage and the home; in the institution of the school; in the institution of the Church (which has not always brought glory to God); in the institution of the state (which most certainly has not always brought glory to God); in the various spheres of life, whether they be music, literature, art, commerce, business, architecture, government, education, or whatever—in every sphere of life the potentialities, the treasures which God has placed in this world, are to be brought out, fashioned, and offered to His glory.

Providentially, many Christians throughout the ages have taken the cultural mandate seriously; they have provided much of the material for this book. Unfortunately, the Church in the last seventy-five to a hundred years has often ignored the cultural mandate, and we wonder why we have so little impact on the world. In fact, a recent survey showed that most people feel the Church is irrelevant to modern society. Granted, the skewed picture the media present of Christianity probably played a key role in causing that survey result; nonetheless, there is a truth there. We have allowed ourselves to be irrelevant, and we're reaping the consequences.

The Church has withdrawn to a large extent into a pietistic ghetto with the hopes that the world might go away. We have turned our educational system, which was founded by Christians, over to unbelievers. We have turned science, which was founded by believers in the living God, over to unbelievers in many cases. We have turned much of the media over to the rankest of unbelievers, so that we are continuously bombarded by their godless thoughts and ideas. We have handed over the reins of government, to a large extent, to unbelievers who have been busily engaged in legislating the devil's agenda for the world. We have been in retreat and have not sought to fulfill the Cultural Mandate.

## IS THE TRIUMPH OF SECULARISM INEVITABLE?

Is secularism inevitable? From Harvard University to the YMCA, so many of the institutions we discussed in this book were started by Christians for Christian purposes, often at great sacrifice and expense; and then eventually they drifted away from their original *raison d'etre*. Is this trend unavoidable?

"Religion begat prosperity, but the daughter hath consumed the mother." Cotton Mather made this observation toward the end of the seventeenth century after the Christianity of the Pilgrims and Puritans had begun to wane. They had only been in the New World for three or four generations, and they were already beginning to allow the prosperity they enjoyed to crowd out the cause of that prosperity: Christianity. This is an ever-present danger for God's people. It was true for the Puritans. It is true for us today, and it was true for ancient Israel. God warned them through Moses:

Beware that you do not forget the LORD your God by not keeping His commandments, His judgments, and His statutes which I command you today, lest—when you have eaten and are full and have built beautiful houses and dwell in them; and when your herds and your flocks multiply, and your silver and your gold are multiplied, and all that you have is multiplied; when your heart is lifted up, and you forget the LORD your God who brought you out of the land of Egypt, from the house of bondage; . . . then you say in your heart, "My power and the might of my hand have gained me this wealth." And you shall remember the LORD your God, for it is He who gives you power to get wealth, that He may establish His covenant which He swore to your fathers, as it is this day. (Deut. 8:11–14, 17–18)

These words were prophetic, for indeed Israel did fall away from God after they prospered, and they were judged for their apostasy. Although apostasy does not inevitably flow from prosperity, it can. We have been forewarned, and, therefore, we must be on our guard.

As the price of liberty is eternal vigilance, so also, the price of orthodoxy is eternal vigilance. For those of us who have started institutions, we have no guarantee that they're going to continue along the lines that we started them. In fact, they may end up opposing the very thing they were created to do. A perfect example of that is Harvard University. Established by the generosity of Rev. John Harvard to train ministers of the gospel of Christ, today this prestigious institution is for the most part squarely opposed to the furtherance of Christ's Kingdom. Certainly, we need to put checks and balances into place in our institutions to try to prevent that kind of apostasy.

Perhaps, the very example of all of these institutions that we have before us can teach us what to avoid. Hopefully, we will be forewarned by their negative example not to follow down that path. Perhaps, some fresh studies could be written up on how Christian institutions fall away from their original purpose and what steps can be taken to try to prevent that.

In the spiritual realm, there is a factor similar to what we know in the physical realm as entropy, or the Second Law of Thermodynamics. This law says that everything is running down, running out and going from order to chaos. The great law of physical decay applies to microbes, men, stars, constellations, and galaxies. In the spiritual realm, there is also that tendency downward —away from God, in response to the work of Satan, who is continually trying to pull us down and is fighting against us. If we are aware of the inevitability of that attack, we may be able to effect defenses that will at least hold off for longer and longer periods, the threat of spiritual entropy. We can certainly take precautionary steps to avoid apostasy in our lifetime, but to my knowledge there's nothing that we can do to absolutely safeguard a Christian institution from falling away from Christ. But we must do all that we can to keep them on the straight path.

Our prayers for these ministries is critical. With God, all things are possible. It behooves us to pray now for their continued faithfulness even when we may be long gone.

Personally, I don't believe in tenure for professors in Christian colleges, universities, or seminaries. Tenure has been the cloak under which so much damage has been done to the Christian faith. Once they have tenure, you can't fire these professors, except for very grievous crimes or sins that are difficult to prove. Therefore, as long as I'm Chancellor of Knox Theological Seminary, we won't have tenure.

Other professions generally don't have tenure. It is something that exists almost entirely in the academic world. And it's in the academic world—both sacred and secular—that we've had some of the greatest apostasy from either biblical truth or American traditions. I don't think tenure has much to say in its own defense. That's certainly one thing we can do to help prevent the secularizing of our Christian institutions.

## THE GREATEST THING IN THE WORLD: LOVE

But not only do we need to be orthodox in our beliefs; we need to be orthodox in our actions. The Bible says that if we don't have love, then we become a noisy gong or a clanging cymbal (1 Cor. 13:1). We must abide in faith, hope, and love, and the greatest of these is love.

We may well be the only Bible many non-Christians ever get to see. That being the case, many of us surely need revision! The world is indeed watching, waiting to see if we really do have the answers or if ours is just another man-made religion. If you truly know Jesus Christ, it's imperative that your lifestyle reflects your love for Him. Your love for Him is evidenced in large part by your love for His people. Our actions in this life have profound ripple-effects on the people all around us—for good or for bad. How will future historians judge you or me? Will we be remembered like Tomas de Torquemada, the infamous Spanish Inquisitor—at one extreme—or will we be remembered like St. Francis of Assisi—at the other? What we say is not half as important as what we do.

The great secret of life is not to get but to give. In the final analysis, when you look back over all your life, it will be in those moments of self-less giving, in humble bestowal upon others, that you will see that life has taken on its true significance. Compared with all other things, love stands out as the greatest.

A shameful aspect of Christian history has been the lack of love exhibited by those who profess to know Jesus Christ. He said, "By this all will know that you are My disciples, if you have love for one another" (John 13:35). How short we all seem to fall from His standard. I'm not promoting a unity of institution—like another World Council of Churches, which is essentially apostate. But I am promoting a fellowship of love that allows believers to transcend their denominational ties and work together "for the glory of God and the advancement of the Christian faith" (to quote the Pilgrims in their Mayflower Compact).

Believe it or not, there are reported to be 23,500 separate and distinct Christian denominations in the world today.[1] There are many Christian groups trying to reinvent the wheel, rather than pooling resources and working together. Thankfully, there are good brothers like Billy Graham, Bill Bright, and many others who often work together with other ministries for the common good. Thankfully, the major international Christian shortwave broadcasters—HCJB, TransWorld Radio, and Far Eastern Broadcasting—are working together to not duplicate their efforts. In the mid-1980s, they all agreed to try to have a Christian broadcast in every language for which there are a million or more people who speak it. Such an ambitious goal can be reached only by cooperation. We need more of that in the body of Christ.

# WHERE IS HISTORY GOING?

During this day, when the Christian Church seems to be in retreat, we can rest assured that truth and history are on our side. How are we to interpret history? As my friend, Bill Bright, founder and director of Campus Crusade, once put it: History is His-Story (talking about Jesus). The time of history we are now in is the time between Christ's first coming and His second. Where is history going? Psalm 110:1, written by David a millennium before Christ, tells us:

> The LORD said to my Lord,
> "Sit at My right hand,
> Till I make Your enemies Your footstool."

So what is God doing in the world today? He's making the enemies of Jesus Christ a footstool for His feet! If you're an enemy of Christ, you're on the wrong side of history. You can either join Christ's side or become His footstool. Jesus is the King of kings and Lord of lords. We're not advocating Christians taking up the sword to try to force Christ's kingdom on the earth—as has been attempted and has failed miserably in history. But God is accomplishing this in His own special time and He will complete it one day.

Is there a pattern to history? Yes, God is at work making His enemies a footstool for Christ's feet. Whether it's Marx, Lenin, Stalin, Hitler, Mussolini, or Mao, God is at work making His enemies a footstool for His feet. Even if they prosper for a while, they will be brought down unless they repent. This includes all of the enemies of the cross today, and there are seemingly millions of them as seen in our pop culture of today! If you're one of them, consider your options: Repent and believe or become a footstool. If you're a sincere seeker, there are numerous resources I can direct you to if you would like to write to me.[2]

History is always being written. And God has given us the great privilege of serving Him. In doing so with all our hearts, we can have great impact in our own little sphere of influence for His glory. If more and more Christians took up such a challenge, imagine the impact on our society and our world! May God raise up more Christians, like those featured in this book and the countless millions not mentioned, to change our world for the better and for the glory of Christ! Amen.

*Soli Deo Gloria!*

# NOTES

## Chapter 1

1. Dionysius Exiguus, a Scythian monk, created "the Christian era" in A.D. 525. He began time with the birth of Christ at A.D. 1. He was later proven to be off by 4 years, which means that Christ was born four years Before Christ! No matter, for the coming of the Son of God into our world demarcates the history of our world. It has never been the same since.

2. David Barrett and Todd Johnson, *Our Globe and How to Reach It: Seeing the World Evangelized by AD 2000 and Beyond* (Birmingham, AL: New Hope, 1990), p. 7.

3. Philip Schaff, *Person of Christ: The Miracle of History* (Boston: The American Tract Society, undated), pp. 323, 328.

4. Friedrich Nietzsche, *The Birth of Tragedy and the Genealogy of Morals*, (Garden City, NY: Doubleday Anchor Books, 1956), p. 170.

5. Quoted in Will Durant, *The Story of Philosophy* (New York: Simon and Schuster, 1953), p. 332.

6. Nietzsche, *The Birth of Tragedy and the Genealogy of Morals*, p. 185.

7. Ibid., pp. 168–68.

8. F. W. Nietzsche, *The AntiChrist*, trans. by H. L. Mencken (Torrance, CA: The Noontide Press, 1980), p. 180.

9. Quoted in Durant, *The Story of Philosophy*, p. 322.

10. Ibid.

11. *Information Please Almanac, Atlas & Yearbook 1993*, 46th Ed. (Boston: Houghton Mifflin Company, 1993), p. 112.

12. Armin Robinson, ed., *The Ten Commandments: Ten Short Novels of Hitler's War Against the Moral Code*, with a Preface by Herman Rauschning (New York: Simon and Schuster, 1943), p. ix.

13. Ibid., pp. xi, xii.

14. Charles Lam Markmann, *The Noblest Cry* (New York: St. Martin's Press, 1965), p. 67.

15. David B. Barrett, *Cosmos, Chaos, and Gospel: A Chronology of World Evangelization from Creation to New Creation* (Birmingham, AL: New Hope, 1987), p. 52 on Stalin (listed under year 1934), p. 60 on Mao (listed under year 1966).

16. James Allan Francis, *The Real Jesus And Other Sermons* (Philadelphia et al.: The Judson Press, 1926), p. 123. Note: this version of "One Solitary Life" is slightly modified from the original.

# Chapter 2

1. Sherwood Eliot Wirt, *The Social Conscience of the Evangelical* (New York: Harper and Row, 1968), p. 37.

2. Henry Halley, *Halley's Bible Handbook* (Grand Rapids: Zondervan Publishing House, 1927, 1962), p. 141.

3. Ibid.

4. Robin Lane Fox, *Pagans and Christians* (San Francisco: Perennial Library, Harper and Row Publishers, 1986, 1988), p. 47.

5. Ibid.

6. George Grant, *Third Time Around: A History of the Pro-Life Movement from the First Century to the Present* (Franklin, TN: Legacy, 1991, 1994), p. 20.

7. Fox, *Pagans and Christians*, p. 343.

8. Help is only a phone call away. If you know someone who may need help like this, call 1-800-Bethany to reach someone who cares anywhere in the country.

9. Wirt, *The Social Conscience of the Evangelical*, p. 31.

10. Ibid., p. 30.

11. Grant, *Third Time Around*, p. 38.

12. Ibid, p. 39.

13. Ibid., pp. 46–47.

14. Fox, *Pagans and Christians*, p. 48, emphasis mine.

15. Harald Stene Dehlin, *Pionerer i skjort* [*Pioneers in Skirts*], Passage translated by Kirsti Saebo Newcombe (Oslo: Norsk Luthersk Forlag A/S, 1985), p. 67.

16. Adam Smith, *An Inquiry Into the Nature and Causes of the Wealth of Nations*, (Chicago: William Benton, Publisher, 1956), p. 30.

17. Jo McGowan, "In India, They Abort Females," *Newsweek*, January 30, 1989, p. 12.

18. See Michael Breen, "Daughters Unwanted: Asian Quest for Boys Backed by Sex Tests, Abortions," *Washington Times*, February 13, 1993.

19. C. H. Spurgeon, *My Sermon Notes* (Grand Rapids: Christian Classics, 1884), p. 292.

20. Chuck Colson, *Breakpoint with Chuck Colson* (Washington, D.C.: Prison Fellowship, May 16, 1992).

21. Wirt, *The Social Conscience of the Evangelical*, p. 10.

22. Isaac Asimov, *Asimov's Guide to the Bible, Vol. 2, The New Testament* (New York: Equinox Books, 1971), p. 489.

23. Fox, *Pagans and Christians*, p. 296.

24. Ibid., pp. 297–98, emphasis mine.

25. Ibid., p. 299.

26. Kenneth Scott Latourette, *A History of Christianity*, Vol. 1 (New York: Harper and Row, 1953, 1975), p. 246.

27. Wirt, *The Social Conscience of the Evangelical*, p. 39.

28. *Liberty* (Sept./Oct. 1984).

29. Ferdinand S. Schenck, *Christian Evidences and Ethics* (New York: Young Men's Christian Association Press, 1910), p. 100.

30. Dinesh D'Souza, *The Catholic Classics II* (Huntington, IN: Our Sunday Visitor, Inc., 1989), p. 16.

31. Tacitus, *Annals* 15.44. Quoted in Tim Dowley, ed., *A Lion Handbook: The History of Christianity* (Oxford: Lion Publishing 1977, rev. 1990), p. 85.

32. Latourette, *A History of Christianity*, p. 245.

33. Will Durant, *Caesar and Christ: A History of Roman Civilization and of Christianity from Their Beginnings to A.D. 325* (New York: Simon and Schuster, 1944; renewed 1972), p. 652.

34. James C. Hefley, *What's So Great About the Bible?* (Elgin, IL: David C. Cook, 1969), p. 76.

35. Ted Baehr and Bonnie Harvey, Critique of *Alive, Ted Baehr's Movieguide: A Family Guide to Movies and Entertainment* (Atlanta, GA: The Christian Film and Television Commission, January 11, 1993), pp. 8–9.

36. *Compton's Pictured Encyclopedia*, vol. 5 (Chicago: F.E. Compton Co., Division of Encyclopaedia Britannica, Inc., 1965), p. 109.

37. See Durant, *Caesar and Christ*, pp. 203, 207–8, 296, 306, 386, 422 for everyone listed except Pontius Pilate.

38. David B. Barrett, *Cosmos, Chaos and Gospel*, p. 21.

39. Durant, *Caesar and Christ*, p. 300.

40. *National Review*, June 8, 1992, p. 26.

41. Quoted in Paul English, "Animal Rights vs. Human Rights," *Christian American*, March 1993, p. 21.

# Chapter 3

1. J. D. Douglas, gen. ed., *The New International Dictionary of the Christian Church*, rev. ed., (Grand Rapids: Regency Reference Library of Zondervan, 1974, 1978), p. 586.

2. Durant, *Caesar and Christ*, p. 71.

3. Latourette, *A History of Christianity*, p. 247.

4. Ibid.

5. Ibid., p. 248.

6. Dowley, *A Lion Handbook: The History of Christianity*, p. 191.

7. Quoted in ibid., p. 147.

8. Durant, *Caesar and Christ*, p. 667.

9. Fox, *Pagans and Christians*, p. 324.

10. Ibid., p. 668.

11. Ibid., p. 17.

12. Ibid.

13. See Joseph Reither, *World History at a Glance* (New York: The New Home Library, 1942), p. 146.

14. Will Durant, *The Story of Civilization: Part IV. The Age of Faith: A History of Medieval Civilization—Christian, Islamic, and Jewish—from Constantine to Dante: A.D. 325–1300*, (New York: Simon and Schuster, 1950), p. 831.

15. Quoted in John Jefferson Davis, *Your Wealth in God's World: Does the Bible Support the Free Market?* (Phillipsburg, NJ: Presbyterian and Reformed Publishing Company, 1984), p. 66.

16. Leland Ryken, *Worldly Saints: The Puritans As They Really Were* (Grand Rapids: Academie Books, Zondervan, 1986), p. 177.

17. Wirt, *The Social Conscience of the Evangelical*, p. 36.

18. Douglas, *The New International Dictionary of the Christian Church*, p. 875, emphasis mine.

19. The widow's mite refers to an incident in the Gospels where Jesus observed the wealthy hypocrites giving much money out of their abundance and He saw a poor widow give only a few coins (a few mites). He extolled her generosity for "this poor widow has put in more than all" (Luke 21:1–4).

20. *The Washington Times*, March 30, 1990.

21. "Religious Faith: Firm Foundation for Charity," *Christianity Today*, November 19, 1990, p. 63.

22. Ibid.

23. Mother Teresa, Francis Schaeffer, et al., *Who Is for Life?* (Westchester, IL: Crossway Books, 1984), p. 30.

24. Douglas, *The New International Dictionary of the Christian Church*, p. 710.

25. Quoted in Davis, *Your Wealth in God's World*, p. 68.

26. Jean-Paul Sartre, *Being and Nothingness,* trans. Hazel E. Barnes (New York: Washington Square, 1965) p. 627.

# Chapter 4

1. Douglas, *The New International Dictionary of the Christian Church*, pp. 330–31.

2. Hyatt Moore, ed., *The Alphabet Makers: A Presentation from the Museum of the Alphabet, Waxhaw, North Carolina* (Huntington Beach, CA: Summer Institute of Linguistics, 1990), p. 13.

3. Ruth Tucker, *From Jerusalem to Irian Jaya: A Biographical History of Christian Missions* (Grand Rapids: Academie Books, Zondervan, 1983), p. 37.

4. The Arians rejected the Trinitarian view of the Godhead, and believed Jesus was divine, but inferior to the Father, having been created by Him. "There was a time when he [Jesus] was not," held the Arians. The Council of Nicaea (A.D. 325) and later the Council of Constantinople (381) wisely rejected Arianism as heretical.

5. Moore, *The Alphabet Makers*, p. 21.

6. Tucker, *From Jerusalem to Irian Jaya*, p. 37.

7. Kenneth Scott Latourette, *A History of the Expansion of Christianity, vol. 1: First Five Centuries* (Grand Rapids: Zondervan, 1970), p. 214.

8. Douglas, *The New International Dictionary of the Christian Church*, p. 278.

9. Moore, *The Alphabet Makers*, p. 32.

10. Ibid., p. 30.

11. Ibid., p. 27.

12. Philip Schaff, *History of the Christian Church*, vol. 7 (Grand Rapids: Wm. B. Eerdmans, 1910/1980), p. 560.

13. Samuel L. Blumenfeld, *Is Public Education Necessary?* (Boise: The Paradigm Co., 1985), p. 10.

14. Loraine Boettner, *The Reformed Doctrine of Predestination* (Philadelphia: The Presbyterian and Reformed Publishing Company, 1975), p. 396.

15. John Calvin, *Institutes of the Christian Religion*, vol. 2, Henry Beveridge, ed. (Grand Rapids: Wm. B. Eerdmans, 1962), p. 677.

16. Robert Skolrood, "Invocations and Benedictions at Public School Graduation Ceremonies" (Virginia Beach, VA: The National Legal Foundation, 1990), pp. 16–17.

17. Quoted in Blumenfeld, *Is Public Education Necessary?*, p. 17.

18. Quoted in Gary de Mar, *God and Government*, vol. 1 (Atlanta: American Vision Press, 1983), p. 19.

19. Quoted in Skolrood, "Invocations and Benedictions, . . ." p. 18.

20. John H. Westerhoff III, *McGuffey and His Readers* (Milford, MI: Mott Media, 1982), pp. 103–4.

21. Ibid., p. 19.

22. Ibid.

23. Ibid., p. 15.

24. Quoted in ibid.

25. Joseph Reither, *World History at a Glance*, p. 180.

26. Thomas Bender, ed., *The University and the City: From Medieval Origins to the Present* (New York: Oxford University Press, 1988), p. 13.

27. H. Rashdall, *The Universities of Europe in the Middle Ages*, vol. 1, part 3, 1895, p. 82.

28. Quoted in Bender, *The Universities and the City*, p. 13.

29. Paul Lee Tan, *Encyclopedia of 7700 Illustrations: Signs of the Times* (Rockville, MD: Assurance Publishers, 1984), p. 157.

30. Quoted in ibid., p. 158. Note that the words presented here are in modern English, but the words on the wall at Harvard's entrance are in seventeenth-century English.

31. Quoted in ibid., p. 159.

32. Quoted in ibid., p. 158.

33. Quoted in ibid. Princeton was originally the College of New Jersey.

34. Ibid.

35. A. A. Hodge, *Popular Lectures on Theological Themes* (Philadelphia: Presbyterian Board of Publications, 1887), p. 283.

36. *A Nation at Risk: The Imperative for Educational Reform, A Report to the Nation and the Secretary of Education, United States Department of Education by The National Commission on Excellence in Education* (Washington, D.C.: U.S. Department of Education, 1983), p. 5.

37. For example, see Georgie Anne Geyer, "Vital Role of Modern Missionaries," *Washington Times*, November 5, 1992, p. G3.

38. Frank C. Laubach, Elizabeth Mooney Kirk, Robert S. Laubach, *Teacher's Manual for Skill Book 1: Sounds and Names of Letters* (Syracuse, NY: New Readers Press, Publishing Division of Laubach Literacy International, 1981), p. 5.

# Chapter 5

1. *The Washington Times*, November 23, 1992.

2. *Time*, February 15, 1954, p. 49.

3. Quoted in Boettner, *The Reformed Doctrine of Predestination*, p. 389.

4. Quoted in ibid., p. 385.

5. Quoted in ibid., p. 389.

6. Quoted in ibid., 390.

7. Quoted in ibid., p. 383.

8. Quoted in ibid.

9. Paul Carlson, *Our Presbyterian Heritage* (Elgin, IL: David C. Cook, 1973), p. 13.

10. Boettner, *The Reformed Doctrine of Predestination*, p. 384.

11. Quoted in Carlson, *Our Presbyterian Heritage*, p. 73.

12. See John Eidsmoe, *Christianity and the Constitution: The Faith of Our Founding Fathers* (Grand Rapids: Baker Book House, 1987), pp. 17–26.

13. Boettner, *The Reformed Doctrine of Predestination*, p. 391.

14. Transcript from a Coral Ridge Ministries TV interview with Dr. Charles Wolfe (Ft. Lauderdale: CRM, July 1992).

15. *The World Almanac and Book of Facts* (New York: World Almanac, 1991), p. 472.

16. Ibid.

17. Robert Merrill Bartlett, *The Pilgrim Way* (Philadelphia: Pilgrim Press, 1971), p. 235.

18. Ibid., p. 54.

19. Eidsmoe, *Christianity and the Constitution*, p. 28.

20. Quoted in David Barton, *The Myth of Separation: What Is the Correct Relationship Between Church and State? A Revealing Look at What the Founders and Early Courts Really Said* (Aledo, TX: WallBuilder Press, 1992), p. 88. (Used by permission, WallBuilders, Inc., Aledo, TX 76008.)

21. Transcript from a Coral Ridge Ministries TV interview with Dr. Charles Wolfe (Ft. Lauderdale: CRM, July 1992).

22. Ellis Sandoz, *A Government of Laws: Political Theory, Religion, and the American Founding* (Baton Rouge: Louisiana State University Press, 1990), p. 147.

23. Ibid., p. 129.

24. Eidsmoe, *Christianity and the Constitution*, p. 247.

25. Barton, *The Myth of Separation*, p. 93.

26. Quoted in Eidsmoe, *Christianity and the Constitution*, p. 247.

27. Quoted in Selim H. Peabody, ed., *American Patriotism: Speeches, Letters, and Other Papers Which Illustrate the Foundation, the Development, the Preservation of the United States of America* (New York: American Book Exchange, 1880), p. 34.

28. Quoted in William V. Wells, *The Life and Public Services of Samuel Adams*, vol. 3 (Boston: Little, Brown & Co., 1865), p. 408.

29. Barton, *The Myth of Separation*, p. 97. Sources: Cushing Strout, *The New Heavens and the New Earth* (New York: Harper and Row, 1974), p. 59; Clifford K. Shipton, *Sibley's Harvard Graduates*, vol. 13 (Boston: Massachusetts Historical Society, 1965), pp. 475–476 quoting from *Election Sermon by Peter Powers, Jesus Christ the King; Newburyport, 1778*.

30. Quoted in Barton, *The Myth of Separation*, p. 25.

31. Eidsmoe, *Christianity and the Constitution*, p. 101.

32. Ibid., p. 81.

33. Ibid., p. 130.

34. Ibid., pp. 130–31.

35. John C. Fitzpatrick, ed., *The Writings of Washington*, vol. 12, (Washington, D.C.: U.S. Government Printing Office, 1932), p. 343.

36. "Washington's Farewell Address," reproduced in *Compton's Pictured Encyclopedia and Fact-Index*, vol. 15 (Chicago: F.E. Compton Co., 1965), p. 26.

37. Transcript from a Coral Ridge Ministries TV interview conducted on location in Dallas (Ft. Lauderdale: CRM, June 17, 1992).

38. Eidsmoe, *Christianity and the Constitution*, pp. 51–52.

39. See ibid., pp. 54–62.

40. Sandoz, *A Government of Laws*, p. 126.

41. Lynn R. Buzzard and Samuel Ericsson, *The Battle for Religious Liberty* (Elgin, IL: David C. Cook, 1982), p. 30.

42. See M. E. Bradford, *A Worthy Company* (Marlborough, NH: Plymouth Rock Foundation, 1982).

43. Alexis de Tocqueville, *Democracy in America,* in two volumes, Henry Reeve text, as revised by Francis Bowen; further corrected and edited by Phillips Bradley (New York, NY: Vintage Classics, Vintage Books, 1990), p. 307.

44. Quoted in Eidsmoe, *Christianity and the Church*, p. 102.

45. Barton, *The Myth of Separation*, p. 97.

46. Quoted in Buzzard and Ericsson, *The Battle for Religious Liberty*, p. 81.

47. *Church of the Holy Trinity v. U.S.*; 143 U.S. 457, 465, 470–471 (1892).

48. Robert Cord, *Separation of Church and State: Historical Fact and Current Fiction* (New York: Lambeth Press, 1982), p. 18.

49. Quoted in ibid., p. 13.

50. Christopher Columbus, *The Book of Prophecies,* quoted in John Eidsmoe, *Columbus and Cortez, Conquerors for Christ: The Controversy, The Conquest, The Mission, The Visions* (Green Forest, AR: New Leaf Press, 1992).

51. Abraham Lincoln, *Proclamation of a National Fast-Day,* March 30, 1863. Quoted in Marion Mills Miller, ed., *Life and Works of Abraham Lincoln, Centenary Edition,* In Nine Volumes: Volume VI (New York: The Current Literature Publishing Co., 1907), p. 156.

# Chapter 6

1. See Haim Shapiro, "Messianic Jews Being Expelled for Beliefs,'" *The Jerusalem Post, International Edition*, February 6, 1993.

2. Transcript from a Coral Ridge Ministries TV interview conducted on location at Reston, VA (Ft. Lauderdale: CRM, December 12, 1990).

3. Transcript from a Coral Ridge Ministries TV interview (Ft. Lauderdale: CRM, July 1992).

4. Ibid.

5. Ibid.

6. Quoted in Verna M. Hall, *The Christian History of the Constitution of the*

*United States* (San Francisco: Foundation for American Christian Education, 1966), p. 372. From J. Wingate Thornton, "The Pulpit of the American Revolution" (Gould & Lincoln, 1860).

7. Ellis Sandoz, ed., *Political Sermons of the American Founding Era, 1730–1805* (Indianapolis: Liberty Press, 1991), pp. xiii, xiv.

8. Franklin Cole, *They Preached Liberty*, "An Anthology of timely quotations from New England ministers of the American Revolution on the subject of Liberty: Its source nature, obligations, types, and blessings" (Ft. Lauderdale, FL: Coral Ridge Ministries, undated), p. 38.

9. Ibid.

10. Douglas, ed., *The New International Dictionary of the Christian Church*, p. 1052.

11. Ferm, *Pictorial History of Protestantism*, p. 184.

12. Rosalie J. Slater, *Teaching and Learning America's Christian History* (San Francisco: Foundation for American Christian Education, 1965, 1989), p. 202.

13. Transcript from a Coral Ridge Ministries TV interview with Dr. M. E. Bradford on location at the University of Dallas (Dallas, TX; CRM, June 17, 1992).

14. Cord, *Separation of Church and State: Historical Fact and Current Fiction*, p. 13.

15. John Quincy Adams, *An Oration Delivered Before the Inhabitants of the Town of Newburyport at their Request on the Sixty-First Anniversary of the Declaration of Independence* (Newburyport: Charles Whipple, 1837), pp. 5–6.

16. Quoted in Barton, *The Myth of Separation*, p. 32. From Alexis de Tocqueville, *The Republic of the United States of America and Its Political Institutions, Reviewed and Examined*, trans. Paul Reeves Vol. I, (Garden City, NY: A.S. Barnes and Co., 1851), p. 332.

17. Quoted in Barton, *The Myth of Separation*, p. 135. From de Tocqueville, p. 337.

18. Quoted in Barton, *The Myth of Separation*, p. 135.

19. Quoted in Russell Kirk, *The Conservative Mind* (Washington, D.C.: Henry Regnery Company, 1953), p. 37.

20. Charles Hodge, *Systematic Theology*, 3 vols., Volume III (Grand Rapids: Wm. B Eerdmans, 1970), 3:345–46.

# Chapter 7

1. "It is by now well documented that modern science was born in Europe in a theistic culture," so writes scientist Dr. Charles Thaxton in an essay that appears in a book edited by Roy Abraham Varghese, entitled *The Intellectuals Speak About God* (Chicago: Regnery Gateway, Inc.), p. 2. Thaxton has compiled an excellent assembly from a variety of scientists as a footnote to this statement, which is well worth duplicating: "A.N. Whitehead, 1967 originally published 1925). *Science and the Modern World*. New York: The Free Press, chapter 1.; Melvin Calvin, 1969. *Chemical Evolution*. New York: Oxford University Press, p. 258.; M.B. Foster, 1934. Mind 43, 446; R. Hooykaas, 1972. *Religion and the Rise of Modern Science*. Grand Rapids: Wm. B. Eerdmans.; Loren Eisley, 1961. *Darwin's Century: Evolution and the Men Who Discovered It*. Garden City, New York: Doubleday, Anchor, p. 62; C.F. von Weizsacker, 1964. *The Relevance of Physics*. New York: Harper and Row, p. 163.; J. Robert Oppenheimer. *Encounter*, October 1962.; Langdon Gilkey, 1959. *Maker of Heaven and Earth*. Garden City, NY: Doubleday, Anchor, p. 9m 125m 129ff."

2. Francis Schaeffer, *How Should We Then Live?* (Old Tappan, NJ: Fleming H. Revell, 1976), p. 132.

3. Malcom Jeeves, *The Scientific Enterprise and the Christian Faith* (Downers Grove, IL: IVP, 1971), p. 13.

4. Quoted in Henry Morris, *Men of God—Men of Science* (San Diego: Master Books, 1984), p. 35.

5. Schaeffer, *How Should We Then Live?* p. 131.

6. Ibid.

7. Dowley, *A Lion Handbook: The History of Christianity*, p. 48.

8. Ibid.

9. Comenius was also a committed Christian. As you will recall from chapter 4 on education, this bishop in the Moravian Church is often called "the father of modern education."

10. Dowley, *A Lion Handbook: The History of Christianity*, p. 48.

11. Ibid., p. 50.

12. Quoted in Morris, *Men of God—Men of Science*, pp. 34–35.

13. Quoted in Donald DeYoung, *Questions and Answers on Astronomy and the Bible* (Grand Rapids: Baker Book House, 1989), p. 115.

14. Morris, *Men of God—Men of Science*, p. 38.

15. James M. Houston, ed., *The Mind on Fire: An Anthology of the Writings of Blaise Pascal* (Portland, OR: Multnomah Press, 1989), p. 136.

16. Ibid., p. 147.

17. Ibid., p. 149.

18. Although unorthodox in his theology, a seventeenth-century Unitarian was much more Bible-oriented than a Unitarian of today.

19. Ian Taylor, *In the Minds of Men: Darwin and the New World Order* (Toronto: TFE Publishing, 1984), p. 342. However, there appears to be some evidence that he did not accept the biblical miracles. See ibid., p. 343.

20. Quoted in DeYoung, *Questions and Answers on Astronomy and the Bible*, p. 115.

21. Schaeffer, *How Should We Then Live?* p. 35.

22. Quoted in *Heroes of History*, vol. 4 (W. Frankford, IL: Caleb Publishers, 1992), p. 36.

23. Quoted in ibid., p. 34.

24. Morris, *Men of God—Men of Science*, p. 54.

25. Schaeffer, *How Should We Then Live?* p. 138.

26. Morris, *Men of God—Men of Science*, p. 56.

27. Henry Morris, *The Biblical Basis for Modern Science* (Grand Rapids: Baker Book House, 1984), pp. 463–65.

28. From a sermon by Ravi Zacharias delivered at Coral Ridge Presbyterian Church, Ft. Lauderdale, FL on April 26, 1987.

# Chapter 8

1. John Chamberlain, *The Roots of Capitalism* (New York: D. Van Nostrand Company, Inc., 1959/65), p. 47.

2. Larry Burkett, *Your Finances in Changing Times* (Christian Financial Concepts, 1975), p. v.

3. Ibid., p. vii.

4. Chamberlain, *The Roots of Capitalism*, p. 46.

5. Belverd E. Needles, Jr., Henry R. Anderson, James C. Caldwell, *Principles of Accounting* (Boston: Houghton Mifflin Company, 1981), p. 68.

6. Quoted in ibid. From Werner Sombart, *Der Moderne Kapitalismus* (Liepzig: Duncher and Humblot, 1902), p. 119, trans.

7. Richard S. Dunn, *The Age of Religious Wars: 1559–1648* (New York: W. W. Norton and Company, Inc., 1970), p. 117.

8. Max Weber, *The Protestant Ethic and the Spirit of Capitalism*, trans. by Talcott Parsons (New York: Charles Scribner's Sons, 1958), p. 126.

9. Ibid., p. 139.

10. Ibid., p. 109.

11. Ibid., p. 172.

12. Ibid.

13. Chamberlain, *The Roots of Capitalism*, p. 48.

14. John Calvin, Comments on Exodus 22:25; Lev. 25:35; Deut. 23:19. *Calvin's Commentaries*, vol. 1, "The Penteteuch" (Grand Rapids: Associated Publishers and Authors, undated), p. 911.

15. R. H. Tawney, *Religion and the Rise of Capitalism* (New York: A Mentor Book, published by the New American Library, 1922, 1952), p. 95.

16. Quoted in Weber, *The Protestant Ethic and the Spirit of Capitalism*, p. 175.

17. Adam Smith, *The Wealth of Nations*, p. 423.

18. Quoted in Lawrence S. Stepelevich, ed., *The Capitalist Reader* (New Rochelle, NY: Arlington House Publishers, 1977), p. 55.

# Chapter 9

1. Sir Edward G. E. Bulwer-Lytton, *The Last Days of Pompeii* (New York: Dodd, Mead and Company, 1946; first published 1834), p. 26.

2. Pitirim A. Sorokin, *The American Sex Revolution* (Boston: Porter Sargent Publisher, 1956), p. 93.

3. Joseph Free, *Archaeology and Bible History* (Wheaton, IL: Scripture Press, 1969), p. 122.

4. Quoted in Merrill Unger, *Archaeology and the Old Testament* (Grand Rapids: Zondervan, 1979), p. 75.

5. Ibid., p. 173.

6. S. I. McMillen, M.D., and David Stern, *None of These Diseases* (Old Tappan, NJ: Fleming H. Revell Company, 1963; revised 1984), p. 86.

7. Halley, *Halley's Bible Handbook*, p. 529.

8. John Boswell, *Christianity, Social Tolerance, and Homosexuality: Gay People in Western Europe from the Beginning of the Christian Era to the Fourteenth Century* (Chicago: The University of Chicago Press, 1980), p. 27.

9. Durant, *Caesar and Christ*, p. 89.

10. Ibid., p. 134.

11. Ibid.

12. Ibid., p. 369.

13. Latourette, *A History of Christianity*, p. 248.

14. Quoted in Wirt, *The Social Conscience of the Evangelical*, p. 29.

15. Quoted in Dowley, *A Lion Handbook: The History of Christianity*, p. 67.

16. Durant, *Caesar and Christ*, p. 598.

17. Quoted in Dowley, *A Lion Handbook: The History of Christianity*, p. 222.

18. Quoted in Tan, *Encyclopedia of 7700 Illustrations*, p. 793.

19. Ibid.

20. Charles A. Salter and Carlota D. Salter, "Myths About Free Sex," *Signs of the Times*, January 1987, p. 26.

21. Transcript from a CRM TV special, "AIDS: Anatomy of a Crisis" (Ft. Lauderdale: CRM, July 1988), which won the Silver Medal from the 1988 International Film and TV Festival of New York, the highest in its category that year.

22. If you or someone you know needs help in this area, contact Exodus International, a coalition of Christian ministries that are helping gays into freedom from that lifestyle through Jesus Christ. For more information, write: Exodus International, Box 2121, San Rafael, CA 94912.

23. *Miami Herald*, April 1, 1993.

24. Susan Sadd and Carol Tavris, *The Redbook Report on Female Sexuality* (New York: Delacorte, 1977), pp. 97–106.

25. "Focus on the Family: Who We Are and What We Stand For," *Focus on the Family*, Colorado Springs, August 1993, p. 10.

# Chapter 10

1. Roberto Margotta, *The Story of Medicine: Man's Struggle Against Disease—From Ancient Sorcery to Modern Miracles of Vaccines, Drugs, and Surgery*, ed. Paul Lewis (New York: Golden Press, 1968), p. 36.

2. Ibid. See Also S. I. McMillen, M.D., *None of These Diseases*, rev. by David E. Stern (Old Tappen, NJ: Fleming H. Revell Company, 1984), p. 21.

3. See McMillen, *None of These Diseases*, pp. 23–28 as a prime example.

4. Margotta, *The Story of Medicine*, p. 102.

5. Ibid, p. 52–57.

6. John Jefferson Davis, *Your Wealth in God's World*, p. 65.

7. Ibid.

8. Colin Jones, *The Charitable Imperative: Hospitals and Nursing in Ancient Regime and Revolutionary France* (London and New York: Routledge, 1989), p. 12.

9. Quoted in ibid., p. 31.

10. Morris, *Men of God—Men of Science*, p. 89.

11. I. Donald Snook, Jr., *Hospitals: What They Are and How They Work* (Rockville, MD: An Aspen Publication, 1981), p. 3.

12. Ibid., p. 4.

13. George Grant, *Third Time Around*, p. 19.

14. Margotta, *The Story of Medicine*, p. 102.

15. Ibid.

16. Ibid.

17. Ibid.

18. Ibid.

19. Jones, *The Charitable Imperative*, pp. 1–2.

20. Ibid., p. 6.

21. Ibid. Nonetheless, the care of the insane—which prior to the French Revolution had been started by the Church—was converted to medical treatment because of the Revolution (see ibid., p. 21).

22. Ibid., p. 37.

23. Charles E. Rosenberg, *The Care of Strangers: The Rise of America's Hospital System* (New York: Basic Books, Inc., Publishers, 1987), p. 8.

24. Ibid., p. 15.

25. Ibid., p. 23.

26. Quoted in ibid., p. 20.

27. Ibid., p. 35.

28. Quoted in ibid., p. 266.

29. Ibid., p. 8.

30. Jones, *The Charitable Imperative*, p. 7.

31. Quoted in ibid., p. 105.

32. Ibid., p. 15.

33. Ibid.

34. Quoted in ibid., p. 122.

35. Margotta, *The Story of Medicine*, p. 264.

36. Elspeth Huxley, *Florence Nightingale* (New York: G. P. Putnam's Sons, 1975), p. 44.

37. Ibid., p. 72.

38. Rosenberg, *The Care of Strangers*, p. 124.

39. Ibid.

40. Pam Brown, *Henry Durant* (Milwaukee: Gareth Stevens Publicating, 1989), p. 9.

41. Quoted in ibid., pp. 21–22.

42. Quoted in ibid., p. 22.

43. Ibid., p. 23.

44. Morris, *Men of God—Men of Science*, pp. 81, 84.

45. Rene Vallery-Radot, *The Life of Pasteur*, trans. by R. L. Devonshire (Garden City, N.Y.: Doubleday, Page and Company, 1923), p. 462.

46. Ibid., p. 464.

47. Barrett and Johnson, *Our Globe and How to Reach It*, p. 62.

48. D. Martyn Lloyd-Jones, *Healing and the Scriptures* (Nashville: Oliver Nelson, 1988), p. 55.

49. Tucker, *From Jerusalem to Irian Jaya*, p. 327.

50. Ibid., p. 328.

51. McMillen, *None of These Diseases*, p. 48.

52. Mark Hartwig, "For Good Health, Go to Church," *Focus on the Family Citizen*, June 21, 1993, p. 10.

53. Ibid.

54. Quoted in E. A. Rowell, *Prophecy Speaks* (Takoma Park, Washington, D.C.: Review & Herald Pub. Assoc., 1933), p. 115. From *American Magazine*, November 1930, pp. 23ff.

55. Quoted in Rosenberg, *The Care of Strangers*, p. 266.

# Chapter 11

1. "In regard to this great book, I have but to say, it is the best gift God has given to men. All the good the Saviour gave to the world was communicated through this book. But for it we could not know right from wrong." Abraham Lincoln, "Remarks upon the Holy Scriptures, in Receiving the Present of a

Bible from a Negro Delegation," September 7, 1864. Marion Mills Miller, ed., *Life and Works of Abraham Lincoln: Centenary Edition*, In Nine Volumes: Volume V, (New York: The Current Literature Publishing Co., 1907), p. 209.

2. Halley, *Halley's Handbook of the Bible*, p. 160.

3. Merrill F. Unger, *Archaeology and the Old Testament* (Grand Rapids: Zondervan, 1979), p. 174.

4. Durant, *Caesar and Christ,* pp. 276–282.

5. Dowley, *A Lion Handbook: The History of Christianity*, p. 117.

6. Durant, *Caesar and Christ*, p. 667.

7. Ibid., p. 366.

8. Ibid., p. 598.

9. Ibid., p. 599.

10. Brian Tierney and Sidney Painter, *Western Europe in the Middle Ages, 300–1475*, 2nd ed. (New York: Alfred E. Knopf, 1970, 1974), p. 45.

11. H. R. Ellis Davidson, *Gods and Myths of Northern Europe* (New York: Penguin Books, 1964, 1984), p. 55.

12. Quoted in ibid., p. 58. From *History of the Langobards*, p. 41 (Foulke's translation).

13. Tierney and Painter, *Western Europe in the Middle Ages*, p. 80.

14. Henry Charles Lea, *A History of the Inquisition of the Middle Ages*, 3 vol. (New York: Harper & Brothers, 1888), 3:402.

15. Ibid., p. 95.

16. Sverre Steen, *Langsomt ble Landet vaart Eget* [*Slowly the Land Became Ours*], passage translated by Kirsti Saebo Newcombe (Oslo, Norway: J. W. Cappelens Forlag, 1967), pp. 52–53.

17. Reither, *World History at a Glance*, p. 144.

18. For vivid examples of this, see Don Richardson, *Lords of the Earth* (Glendale, CA: G/L Regal Books, G/L Publications, 1977, 1978), pp. 18–89.

19. *Time*, May 25, 1987.

20. A disturbing book that shows the depth of immorality in America is *The Day America Told the Truth: What People Really Believe About Everything That Really Matters,* by James Patterson and Peter Kim (New York: Prentice-Hall, 1991). They conclude: "In effect, we're all making up our own moral codes" (p. 6). Another recommended book on America's immorality points to the correct way back, through Christianity. It's by Harry and Betty Dent and is entitled,

*Right Vs. Wrong: Solutions to the American Nightmare* (Nashville: Thomas Nelson Publishers, 1992).

# Chapter 12

1. Cynthia Pearl Maus, *Christ and the Fine Arts, An Anthology of Pictures, Poetry, Music, and Stories Centering in the Life of Christ*, rev. and enlarged ed. (New York: Harper and Row, Publishers, 1938, 1959), p. 706–7.

2. Dr. Peter Taylor Forsyth, *Christ on Parnassus: Lectures on Art, Ethic, and Theology* (London, New York, Toronto: Hodder and Stroughton, undated), p. 75.

3. Richard Muhlberger, *The Bible in Art: The Old Testament* (New York: Portland House, 1991), p. 6

4. Maus, *Christ and the Fine Arts*, p. 2.

5. H. W. Janson and Joseph Kerman, *A History of Art and Music* (Englewood Cliffs, NJ: Prentice-Hall, Inc. / New York: Harry N. Abrams, undated), p. 41.

6. Ibid., p. 41.

7. When the Muslims conquered the Byzantine Empire in 1453, they converted this church into a mosque.

8. Janson and Kerman, *A History of Art and Music*, p. 58.

9. Ibid., p. 68.

10. Ibid., p. 89.

11. Thomas Howard, "Christianity and the arts." In Dowley, ed., *A Lion Handbook: The History of Christianity*, p. 37.

12. Joseph Nelson Greene, *The Gospel in Literature* (Cincinnati: Jennings and Graham / NY: Eaton and Mains, 1910), p. 5.

13. Ibid.

14. Ibid., p. 10.

15. Quoted in Herbert Lockyer, *The Man Who Changed the World*, vol. 1 (Grand Rapids: Zondervan, 1966), p. 355.

16. Ibid., p. 356.

17. Quoted in ibid., p. 355.

18. Charles Dickens, *The Life of Our Lord* (Philadelphia: Westminster Press, 1986); first published in 1934 by Associated Newspapers Ltd., London), p. 11.

19. Greene, *The Gospel in Literature*, p. 10.

20. Donald Jay Grout, *A History of Western Music*, rev. (New York: W. W. Norton and Company, Inc., 1960, 1973), pp. 21–23.

21. Maxwell Nurnberg and Morris Rosenblum, *How to Build a Better Vocabulary* (New York: Popular Library, 1961), p. 116.

22. Interestingly, with the exception of *It's a Wonderful Life*, every one of these films listed was the Academy Award winning film of the year.

23. Michael Medvid, *Hollywood Vs. America: Popular Culture and the War on Traditional Values* (Grand Rapids: Zondervan, 1992), pp. 63–64, 75–76.

24. Greene, *The Gospel in Literature*, p. 100.

# Chapter 13

1. Tan, *Encyclopedia of 7700 Illustrations*, p. 174.

2. That's why the tax-collectors are consistently viewed as evil in the Gospel accounts.

3. Daniel Boorstin, "History's Hidden Turning Points," *U.S. News & World Report*, April 22, 1991, pp. 52–65.

4. Ibid., p. 54.

5. Recommended reading on great Christians through the ages is the book *Great Leaders of the Christian Church*, edited by John Woodbridge (Chicago: Moody Press, 1988). Also recommended is *What's So Great About the Bible* by James C. Hefley (Elgin, IL: David C. Cook, 1969).

6. Douglas, ed., *The New International Dictionary of the Christian Church*, p. 86.

7. John D. Woodbridge, ed., *Great Leaders of the Christian Church* (Chicago: Moody Press, 1988), p. 85.

8. Augustine, *The Confessions of Saint Augustine*, translated by Edward B. Pusey, D.D. (New York: A Cardinal Edition of Pocket Books, Inc., 1951/1955), p. 20.

9. Woodbridge, *Great Leaders of the Christian Church*, p. 86.

10. Ibid.

11. Ibid.

12. Ibid., p. 234.

13. Ibid., p. 239.

14. Lyle Dorsett, quoted in ibid., p. 356.

15. Lyle Dorsett, "C. S. Lewis: A Profile of His Life," *Christian History*, 4, 3 (1985): 9.

16. *Time*, September 8, 1947.

17. Woodbridge, *Great Leaders in the Christian Church*, p. 360.

18. Douglas, ed., *The New International Dictionary of the Christian Church*, p. 593.

19. See Gordon W. Prange, with Donald M. Goldstein and Katherine V. Dillon, *God's Samurai: Lead Pilot at Pearl Harbor* (Washington, D.C.: Brassey's (US), Inc., 1990).

20. Hefley, *What's So Great About the Bible*, pp. 74–76.

21. Reflecting in 1992 on his involvement in Watergate twenty years earlier, Jeb Stuart Magruder said, "We saw the President as God, not Jesus Christ as God. That's a terrible mistake." (Transcript from a CRM TV interview conducted on location in Lexington, KY [Ft. Lauderdale: CRM, April 29, 1992].)

22. Jeb Stuart Magruder, *An American Life: One Man's Road to Watergate* (New York: Atheneum, 1974), p. 69.

# Chapter 14

1. In fact, the Muslims did succeed in subjugating parts of Spain, until they were ousted in 1492 by the armies of Ferdinand and Isabella.

2. James Harvey Robinson, *An Introduction to the History of Western Europe* (Boston: Ginn and Company, New Edition, 1934), p. 215.

3. Quoted in ibid., p. 223.

4. See John Eidsmoe, *Columbus and Cortez*, pp. 47–78.

5. Dowley, ed., *A Lion Handbook: The History of Christianity*, p. 121.

6. Henry Halley, *Halley's Bible Handbook* (Grand Rapids: Regency Reference Library, 1965), p. 760.

7. The conversion of Clovis to the Roman Catholic Church was extremely important in terms of church history, yet the man's life was seemingly as unregenerate after his alleged conversion as before. His life reflected the barbarity and cruelty typical of that day.

8. Actually it's chic among certain academic circles today to condemn the Founding Fathers on this very point. But the black syndicated columnist Walter Williams writes, "They felt slavery would continue with or without the Constitution. The question was whether there would be a future for liberty. . . . The three-fifths of a vote provisions applied only to slaves, not to free blacks in either the North or South." From Walter E. Williams, *The Framer's Tried* (Los Angeles: Creators Syndicate, May 26, 1993).

9. Armin Robinson, ed., *The Ten Commandments*, p. xii.

10. Count Heinrich Coudenhove-Kalergi, *Anti-Semitism Throughout the Ages*, edited and brought up to date by Count Richard Coudenhove-Kalergi, trans. by Dr. Angelo S. Rappoport (London: Hutchinson & Co., 1935), p. 10.

11. See Psalms 2 and 22; Isaiah 53; Zechariah 12 and 13; and Micah 5:2 for starters.

12. Coudenhove-Kalergi, *Anti-Semitism Throughout the Ages*, p. 223.

13. Reither, p. 178.

14. See Lea, *A History of the Inquisition of the Middle Ages*, vol. 1, chapter 1.

15. Ibid., p. 211.

16. Historians generally list the crusade against heresies in Southern France as part of the history of the Crusades. We deal with it in our discussion of the Inquisition because it was in a sense a part of that as well. It involved the Church taking up arms to suppress what they felt was heresy.

17. Barrett, *Cosmos, Chaos and Gospel*, p. 32.

18. Lockyer, *The Man Who Changed the World*, vol. 1, p. 270.

19. Lea, *A History of the Inquisition of the Middle Ages*, vol. 1, p. 450.

20. Quoted in "The Inquisition," *Encyclopedia Britannica* (Chicago: William Benton, Publishers, 1969 edition), vol. 12, p. 270.

21. Henry Littlefield, *History of Europe, 1500–1848*, 5th ed. (New York: Barnes and Noble, Inc., 1939, 1963), p. 4.

22. Barrett and Johnson, *Our Globe and How to Reach It*, p. 18.

23. Marvin Olasky, "Needed: Testimony of Two Witnesses; Biblical Standards of Justice Would've Prevented Witch Hysteria," *World*, August 15, 1992, p. 10.

24. Ibid.

25. Paul Johnson, "A Historian Looks at Jesus," A Speech Given at Dallas Theological Seminary in 1986 (Washington, D.C.: Wilberforce Forum, 1991), p. 8.

# Chapter 15

1. Winston S. Churchill, *Memoirs of The Second World War*, A One Volume Abridgement of the Six Volumes of *The Second World War* (Boston: Houghton Mifflin Company, 1959/1987), p. 325.

2. Ibid., p. 326, emphasis mine.

3. Andrew Greeley, "Marxists Escape Indictment for Killing Millions," *The Chicago Sun-Times*, July 4, 1993.

4. Barrett, *Cosmos, Chaos, and Gospel*, p. 60.

5. Tan, *Encyclopedia of 7700 Illustrations*, p. 176.

6. Paul Johnson, *Modern Times* (New York: Harper and Row, Publishers, 1983), p. 48.

7. Ibid., p. 1.

8. Ibid., p. 48.

9. Quoted in the Cal Thomas Commentary, Washington, D.C., November 26, 1991.

10. Will Durant, *The Humanist*, February 1977, p. 26. Quoted in Erwin Lutzer, *Exploding the Myths That Could Destroy America* (Chicago: Moody Press, 1986), pp. 47–48.

11. Jean-Paul Sartre, *Being and Nothingness*, trans. Hazel E. Barnes (New York: Washington Square, 1965), p. 627.

12. Ludwig Wittgenstein, "Wittgenstein's Lectures on Ethics," *Philosophical Review* 74 (1965), p. 7.

13. Willimar Thorkelson, RNS Correspondent, April 22, 1987, "Gallup Poll Says U.S. Facing Moral Crisis of First Dimension.'" Reproduced in *The Christian News*, St. Louis, MO, May 4, 1987, pp. 1, 24.

14. William K. Kilpatrick, "School policies are turning out moral illiterates," *Sun-Sentinel* (Ft. Lauderdale), July 25, 1993, p. G1.

15. Ernst Mayr, "Evolution," *Scientific American* 239 (Sept. 1978), p. 47.

16. Quoted in John Whitehead, *The Second American Revolution* (Elgin, IL: David C. Cook, 1982), p. 52.

17. Johnson, *Modern Times*, p. 708.

18. For many of the statistics on how many have been killed in whose or what name, we are heavily indebted to the eminent researcher, writer, and Church statistician, Dr. David Barrett, editor of the massive *World Christian Encyclopedia* (1982). He formerly served on the Southern Baptist Foreign Mission Board. Two of his books were particularly helpful: *Cosmos, Chaos and Gospel: A Chronology of World Evangelization from Creation to New Creation* (1987) and *Our Globe and How to Reach It: Seeing the World Evangelized by AD 2000 and Beyond* (co-authored by Todd Johnson) (1990). Both books are published by New Hope in Birmingham, AL.

19. Lockyer, *The Man Who Changed the World*, vol. 1, p. 270.

20. Newer estimates put the number at 60 million; for our argument here, we'll stick with the traditionally held figure.

21. Barrett, p. 52.

22. Barrett, p. 53.

23. Johnson, *Modern Times*, p. 413.

24. *Information Please Almanac 1993*, p. 112.

25. Barrett, p. 55.

26. Ibid., p. 58.

27. Ibid., p. 60.

28. Barrett, p. 74.

29. We're *not* adding the numbers of those killed in the various wars of Christendom, except for those wars where religion was the key reason for the conflict. So we've added the Crusades, and we've added the number of Christian martyrs who died at the hands of "Christian" perpetrators during the Wars of Religion.

30. Note: one person killed in the name of Christ is one too many.

31. Barrett and Johnson, *Our Globe and How to Reach It*, p. 54.

32. Johnson, *Modern Times*, p. 729.

33. Joseph Sobran, "The Established Irreligion," *The Human Life Review*, Summer 1978, p. 61.

34. Schenck, *Christian Evidences and Ethics*, p. 85.

# Chapter 16

1. Barrett and Johnson, *Our Globe and How to Reach It*, p. 57.

2. D. James Kennedy, Box 40, Ft. Lauderdale, FL 33308.

# INDEX OF PROPER
# NAMES

# ABOUT THE AUTHORS

**D.** James Kennedy, Ph.D., is the Senior Minister of Coral Ridge Presbyterian Church in Ft. Lauderdale, Florida and speaker for the international "Coral Ridge Hour" telecasts.

Dr. Kennedy also serves as President of Evangelism Explosion International and Chancellor of Knox Theological Seminary.

The Kennedys have one daughter.

Jerry Newcombe is an award-winning producer for Coral Ridge Ministries, the television outreach of Coral Ridge Presbyterian Church.

The Newcombes have two children, a daughter and a son.